And Sadly Teach

Jurgen Herbst

And Sadly Teach

Teacher Education and Professionalization
in American Culture

The University of Wisconsin Press

The University of Wisconsin Press
114 North Murray Street
Madison, Wisconsin 53715

The University of Wisconsin Press, Ltd.
1 Gower Street
London WC1E 6HA, England

Printed in the United States of America

Library of Congress Cataloging-in-Publication Data
Herbst, Jurgen.
    And sadly teach: Teacher education and professionalization in
American culture/Jurgen Herbst.
    246 pp.   cm.
    Includes bibliographical references and index.
    1. Teachers—Training of—United States—History. 2. Teachers
colleges—United States—History. 3. Teachers—Training of—
Massachusetts—History. I. Title
LB1715.H395   1989
370'.7'30973—dc19   89-4775
ISBN 0-299-12180-1

FOR ANNEMARIE AND STEPHANIE

Contents

Tables

Preface

With due apologies to Geoffrey Chaucer, whose friar taught gladly, and to
Mortimer Smith, whose teachers taught madly, I write in this book about men
and women who, for a century and a half now, have had cause to do it sadly.
The education of American classroom teachers in elementary and high
schools and the professionalization of American public schools are the subject
of this volume. As I hope will become evident, although the teachers themselves and their commitment and welfare occupy the center of my concerns, it
is the way they have been educated—or miseducated, as James Koerner
would say—that furnishes the subject of my investigation.[1]

If this book has a message beyond the information it seeks to provide and
the understanding it hopes to further it is that American schools will not become what they should and could be until teachers in elementary and secondary
classrooms have attained for themselves true professional status. As professionals, teachers need to be prepared to take responsibility for their own decisions on how and what to teach. Such matters should not be delegated to
various curriculum specialists and administrators. Teachers must take in
hand the on-the-job training of their own apprentices and thus take responsibility for their own and their colleagues' professional development. Again,
this is not a matter to be left entirely to teacher training institutions and educational administrators. Classroom teachers need to have the sure knowledge
that the most highly rewarded positions in their profession are open to them
as teachers. They must not have to accept the practice that these places of
prestige are reserved to those who, after minimal service in the classroom, opt
for an administrative career. They also should be assured that, once having
served as administrators, they ought to have the opportunity to return to the
classroom without loss of benefits or prestige. Only when such careers become possible, not as exception in some highly favored district, but as the rule
in American schools, can we say again that teachers can gladly teach.

The historical literature on teacher education is not very voluminous,
and perhaps we should be grateful for that. The official and quasi-official

reports by government agencies, professional bodies, and individual investi-gators, as well as the dutifully submitted dissertations on teacher education in this or that state or region, rarely go beyond a conscientious listing of develop-ments or a proud parading of accomplishments. They are offset, as it were, by the cannon blasts of critics who find, by now rather predictably, that teacher education in America leaves much to be desired. Thus when it comes to reli-able and comprehensive historical accounts we have only Willard Elsbree's *The American Teacher: Evolution of a Profession in a Democracy,* a volume much out-of-date by now, and Merle Borrowman's two books on the history of teacher education in America.[2] Thoughtful and comprehensive as Borrowman's vol-umes are, they were written from the vantage point of a perceived tension between liberal and technical elements in teacher training. That point of view largely ignores the institutional, social, and political dimensions of profes-sional education that lie at the heart of the present study. A fresh approach to the historical study of teacher education is required today.

For material on teacher education in nineteenth-century Prussia I con-ducted research in the archives of several teacher seminaries in Germany as well as in the Prussian state libraries in Berlin–Dahlem and Merseburg. I gratefully acknowledge the support received from the German Academic Exchange Service, and I want to express my appreciation for the ever helpful archivists at Berlin–Dahlem, Merseburg, Schloss Kalkum near Düsseldorf, Münster, and Koblenz. I also owe much to the advice and help of my friend and colleague Manfred Heinemann at the University of Hannover.

For the American side of the story I want to acknowledge the generous support of the American Philosophical Society in Philadelphia, which per-mitted me to visit normal school archives in Massachusetts, Illinois, Kansas, and Wisconsin. I also thank the Spencer Foundation for research support during the latter stages of the project. Finally, throughout these last few years, I have benefitted from the aid granted by the Research Committee of the Graduate School of the University of Wisconsin–Madison and from the patience, helpfulness, and much appreciated advice of my Madison col-leagues in the Departments of Educational Policy Studies and of History.

Of friends and colleagues I want to single out Michael Apple, Theodore Hamerow, William R. Johnson, Carl Kaestle, Herbert Kliebard, and Michael Olneck, as well as David F. Labaree and John Rury, who read the manuscript for the press. A special word of appreciation is due Richard Baron, Kathleen Cruikshank, Timothy De Vries, Colleen Dickmann, Claus Hagemann, Heidi Harlander, Myrdal Sigurjon, and Meredithe Velie, my students who helped me take this manuscript on its shake-down cruise across the airways of Wisconsin Public Radio. Their spirited debates and piercing critiques helped more than they could have possibly imagined. All of them have kept me from many more egregious errors than would otherwise be found in my manuscript. They have left me, appropriately so and wisely on their part, to shoulder responsibility of all those faults of omission and commission still to be found in the volume. For these the blame is mine alone. As always, there has been Sue, who, year in, year out, has been at my side and supplied the love, encouragement, steadiness, and wisdom without which this book would never have come to be. To her I owe my greatest debt.

I should also tell the reader that I do not claim to present a comprehensive and all-inclusive account of the history of teacher training in the United States. The hundreds of teacher education programs in normal schools and teachers colleges and other institutions of higher education in this country and the bewildering variety of approaches taken in the now 50 states make such a task impossible within the confines of the resources and time that were available to me. My approach has been selective, and all I claim is that my choices have been reasonably representative of the major currents of development. I shall have to beg the indulgence of the partisans of a particular institution or school of thought who do not find their college mentioned or their concern addressed in this book. There are many ways in which to approach a history of my subject, but here I could take only one.

Portions of this book have appeared in different form in previous publications. They are listed here for the convenience of the interested reader: "Towards Compulsory Education: The School Revival Movement in the United States," in *Introduction, Development and Extension of Compulsory Education,* edited by Giovanni Genovesi, Vol. 1 (Parma: Universita di Parma, 1986), pp. 279–302; "M. Cousin's Report in Massachusetts," in *Onderwijs, Opvoeding en maatschappij in de 19de en 20ste Eeuw: Liber Amicorum Prof. Dr. Maurits de Vroede,* edited by M. Depaepe and M. d'Hoker (Leuven: Acco, 1987), pp. 127–132; "Revolution, Reform, and Schooling: The Educational Views of Thomas Jefferson and Wilhelm von Humboldt," *Informationen zur Erziehungs- und Bildungshistorischen Forschung* 24 (1984), 87–97; "Educational Reform: A Transatlantic Faith," in *History of International Relations in Education,* Conference Papers for the 9th Session of the International Standing Conference for the History of Education, Vol. 1 (Pecs, Hungary, 1987), pp. 259–263; "Nineteenth-Century Normal Schools in the United States: A Fresh Look," *History of Education* 9, 3 (1980), 219–227; and "Professionalization in Public Education, 1890–1920: The American High School Teacher," in *Industrielle Welt: Bildungsbürgertum im 19. Jahrhundert,* Part I, *Bildungssystem und Professionalisierung in internationalen Vergleichen,* edited by Werner Conze and Jürgen Kocka (Stuttgart: Klett-Cotta, 1985), pp. 495–528. A summary of the argument is to appear in a volume on the "History of Teachers, Teaching, and Teacher Education in the United States," sponsored by the American Educational Research Association.

And Sadly Teach

Introduction

Teachers, the Public Schools, and Teacher Education

Teachers have not fared well in the United States. Throughout most of our history, teachers in the elementary schools have been regarded as little more than hired help who would perform their duties until marriage or other employment beckoned. In secondary education only the college-educated masters of the colonial Latin grammar schools, of private boarding schools, and of public preparatory schools enjoyed public recognition and rewards. The large majority of the country's high school teachers were seen as little different from their colleagues in the elementary schools. Their education in normal schools and teacher colleges and their conditions of employment did not differentiate them sufficiently to justify a claim to separate consideration.

This low esteem in which teachers have been held bears directly on the issue of a teacher's self-concept or self-image. Public school teachers have always been at the beck and call of the public. That has been their greatest asset and their greatest liability. Society has always needed teachers for its young, but it has not always—in fact, rarely—been willing to reward them generously. Society wants teachers to be present when needed, but it does not appreciate hearing them remonstrate about conditions in their schools. Like their students, teachers are to be seen in school, but they are not to raise their voices.

During the early 1980s the place of school teachers in American life and society came under intensive public scrutiny. A variety of reports, books, magazine articles, newspaper stories and editorials reviewed the accomplishments and failings of America's public schools.[1] Concerns were expressed about the low quality of the education teachers have received, the meagre awards they have been able to reap, and the discouraging outlook for their development as professionals. A public debate began that sought to understand why it has been that men and women to whom people entrust those who

3

are dearest to them have nonetheless been granted scant respect and rewards for their labors.

I set out to write this book with the intent to clarify these questions for myself. It has been my assumption that by looking at the history of the institutions and practices of teacher education I might come to understand better the linkage of teacher education, teacher performance, and attitudes held by the public toward their schools. Thus I went back to the origins of modern public education and teacher education in the United States during the common school revival of the 1830s and 1840s.

My discussion there focusses on what I have called a Whig attitude characteristic of political and educational leaders on both sides of the Atlantic, an attitude that was reflected in their pronouncements and policies. It takes us to Europe where in Prussia an agitation for public elementary schooling had begun in earnest. In that country the French philosopher and government official Victor Cousin and many American school reformers claimed to have found their inspiration, and they conveyed their impressions to the American public. I investigate in particular the accuracy and the relevance of what Cousin had to say. I try to show how his influential report on schooling in Prussia was permeated by conceptions of social class that to most of his American readers were unknown and which were therefore overlooked and ignored. I discuss how Americans adopted the Prussian ideas and institutions and adapted them to conditions in the United States which, in themselves, differed among various parts of the country.

I begin my survey with a brief glance at public education and the training of teachers in private academies and colleges and then take a somewhat detailed look at the first two American state normal schools and their students in Massachusetts. It became obvious to me from the very start that, different from the European seminarists who regarded schoolteaching as a desirable lifetime career, American normalites used the normal schools as gateways to occupational or professional advancement beyond the narrow circle offered by the public schools. Whereas Prussian seminary students were mainly males, the Massachusetts normalites were predominantly women. Most of them were girls or young women who sought temporary employment as teachers; others were older single women or widows who had no other opportunities to support themselves.

Massachusetts normal school educators soon became disappointed with the low academic preparation of the normalites and their continuing refusal—particularly among the male students—to commit themselves to lifetime careers in school teaching. The educators therefore tended to assign the preparation of elementary teachers to short-term city training schools. Most of the educators preferred to use their state normal schools for the training of secondary school teachers and administrators as well as educational specialists. Only the disciples of Colonel Tillinghast, in what came to be known as the

Bridgewater tradition, continued to emphasize the necessity of training in the state normal schools the teachers of elementary schools as well as the teachers, administrators, and specialists for secondary schools.

Once the normal schools arrived in the Midwest by midcentury and later, little was left of conscious memories of Prussian examples. The issues that concerned the normal school educators here related to an emerging conflict among three possible courses. The first was to persist with and finally satisfy the original demand for the training of qualified teachers for the rural elementary schools. Those in the Midwest who wanted to pursue this avenue followed one of two paths. Some—primarily those at the Illinois State Normal University and elsewhere who followed the Illinois example—wanted to keep alive the Bridgewater tradition of combining the training of elementary teachers with advanced professional studies for administrators and high school teachers. Others, particularly in Wisconsin, wanted to divide these tasks between county and state normal schools. They preferred to have the usually female teachers for rural elementary schools prepared in county training schools close to the students' homes and to reserve the state normal schools for what they considered more demanding and more prestigious educational tasks.

The second course was followed by those who gave up on the training of elementary school teachers as hopeless and beneath their dignity. This happened in Kansas after 1870, in Missouri, and in several other states as well. These normal educators sought instead to turn the state normal schools into professional institutions through research and advanced training of high school teachers and various educational specialists. Their ambitions would sooner or later bring them into conflict with education professors and administrators in the universities who had always prepared teachers for the secondary schools and who, toward the end of the century, also began to pursue research in education and in-service training of administrators and other education professionals.

The third direction, finally, arose from the desire of normal educators to respond to the demands of a frontier population for easily accessible higher education for both general and vocational purposes. When the state normal schools came to be located across the length and breadth of their states, they offered at first secondary and eventually higher education at many locations. In that process they encountered the American public's aversion to vocational training that was restrictive rather than enabling in its scope. Midwesterners resented a school that expected its graduates to become and remain teachers. Instead of pedagogical vocational schools they wanted "people's colleges," which would allow their graduates easy transfer into liberal arts colleges and universities and which would open the door for them to any occupation or profession.

This course sharpened the battle between the spokesmen of the educational establishment on the one hand, and students, parents, and legislators on the other. The educational establishment sought to keep in sharp focus the training of teachers and education professionals as the exclusive task of the normal schools. The students, parents, and legislators saw the normal schools and later the teachers colleges as true community colleges or people's colleges. These institutions carried the torch of democracy into the hinterland. The normal schools and teachers colleges, far more so than the centrally located state universities, took higher education to where the people lived and worked. With the eventual transformation of the teacher training schools and colleges into state colleges and universities the American democratic revolution in higher education accomplished one of its greatest triumphs. It also meant that, from the point of view of the age-old battle between vocational specialists and liberal arts generalists, the generalists carried the day.

Teacher Professionalism

In writing this book I have come to the conviction that the questions debated by the public—How well do we educate our teachers? Are their qualifications sufficient? Do we grant teachers the recognition and rewards they deserve?—are inseparably linked to the issue of teacher professionalism. But what is teacher professionalism? As my inquiries proceeded I began to redefine it for myself as the recognition and practice of a teacher's right and obligation to determine his or her own professional tasks in the classroom. All else—how well teachers are prepared for the classroom, how they acquit themselves there, and how well the results of their labor show in the achievements of their students—is secondary in importance because it awaits, depends on, or is derived from the teacher's professionalism in action.

Teacher professionalism takes its cues from the traditional professions trained in the faculties of our universities. Ministers, lawyers, doctors, and university professors—the original professions—derive their status from the education they receive and the individual and collective autonomy they claim and enjoy in the exercise of their professional duties. Within the confines of a given task, professionals decide for themselves how to proceed. They work without supervision and carry full personal responsibility for the results. They are guided by a code of ethics and are accountable for observing its commands to their professional colleagues. Society, in turn, holds them collectively responsible for faithful performance of the profession's assigned duties.

As a right, teacher professionalism derives from the education and training teachers receive. As an obligation, it is the natural result of that education applied in daily practice. Professionalism thus shows in the competence and confidence teachers display in their classrooms with their students. It is manifest in their relationships with the taxpayers who employ them, with the administrators who facilitate their work, and with the parents whose children they teach. But most of all, because most crucially tested there, teachers demonstrate their professionalism in their collegial relations among themselves. When competence and confidence alone matter, then teachers recognize each other as professionals without regard to their racial, national, or ethnic origin, their age, sex, religion, school, or grade. Their relationships among each other will rest on the certainty of shared aims and mutual respect.

In looking at the history of public education I asked whether our ways of educating teachers have been conducive to the growth of such professional attitudes. How have we gone about or failed to go about introducing our teachers to their professional responsibilities? Have we in our institutions of teacher education been willing to encourage and make possible the assumption of professional responsibilities by classroom teachers, or have we, wittingly or unwittingly, conspired to subvert such aim? What do we find when we listen to teachers and to those who work with them or are affected by them? Have our institutions and programs given us professionals, or must we always be content with teachers as temporary workers, transients, and birds of passage, as one nineteenth-century commentator once said?

Although there are encouraging signs today that we are on the move towards greater professionalism among teachers, still the picture in the United States is not encouraging. Teacher professionalism as defined above does not exist everywhere in our public schools. Teacher unions, despite their long and ardent struggle for improvement in working conditions and financial compensation, have been slow to address the status of teachers as autonomous professionals. Neither have the criteria of professionalism usually cited by sociologists ever been applied to teachers.[2] Classroom teachers do not receive their professional training in a graduate school of education as lawyers do in law school or physicians in a medical school. Bureaucratic commands and guidelines compromise the teacher's autonomy in the classroom. There is no code of ethics to define professional probity and, despite the often heard complaints about unfair administrative practices, few teacher unions have demanded or endorsed peer evaluation. A teacher's responsibilities toward students are diluted with obligations toward the students' parents, toward administrative supervisors, and toward an employing school board. And, what in my view is the most discouraging aspect of all, outstanding classroom teachers cannot reach positions of highest prestige, responsibility, and reward in the classroom. To advance professionally they must leave the classroom for the administrator's or specialist's office.

Professionalization in Public Education

Although teachers have not made significant advances toward their professionalism in the classroom, a process of professionalization has indeed been taking place in public education. Judged by the sociologists' criteria—professional or graduate training comparable to that of lawyers or physicians; professional autonomy in the workplace; professional guidance through a code of ethics; performance evaluation by peers; immediate responsibility toward clients and ultimate accountability to society—administrators and specialists, not the teachers, are seen as the professionals in public education. Professionalization thus is held out to teachers if they are willing to leave the classroom. It is synonymous with specialization and diversification of "education personnel" and the patent exclusion of the classroom teacher from the ranks of professionals.

I find it distressing and discouraging to have to report that the professionalization of American public education that ignored and shut out the teacher began in the early centers of teacher education. During the post–Civil War decades of the nineteenth century in the state normal schools in Massachusetts and elsewhere, teacher educators began to shift the emphasis from training teachers for elementary and secondary classrooms to the preparation of specialized subject-matter teachers, school administrators, and journalists. They were eager to supply faculty members for normal schools and research specialists in the new disciplines of educational psychology and administration. Professionalization was encouraged during the same period also in the newly founded education departments of public and private colleges and universities.

In that development the usually female elementary classroom teachers received the short end of the stick. Their training was left to the less prestigious county normal and city training schools. The schools of education of the universities relegated the education of secondary school teachers—if they continued it at all—to their undergraduate departments. They reserved their graduate-degree work to entice the largely male candidates into programs in educational administration, educational psychology, educational journalism, and college or normal school teaching. Professionalization became a nearly uniformly male preserve.

Inevitably, professionalization led to a growing differentiation among education personnel. The use of that phrase itself characterizes well what happened to American teachers who in the nineteenth century used to recognize only the distinction between assistant and principal teachers. By the end of the century supervisory personnel, predominantly male, came to be regarded with unease and suspicion by the overwhelmingly female classroom teachers. In large urban school systems women teachers spearheaded the reaction and, to a significant degree, shaped the early teacher union movement as a response to male professionalization.[3] Their efforts help us to see more clearly the historical roots of the tensions and differences between a teacher professionalism that has eluded American classrooms and the professionalization of public education that came to distinguish its modern period.

The Current Proposals

Today the time is opportune to rethink and reshape teacher education in America and, if we are willing and have the stamina to battle the forces of entrenched professionalization, to aid teachers in their battle for professionalism in the classroom. Two of the recent reports on teachers and teaching in America speak in eloquent terms of the need for teachers to become and be accepted as true professionals. The Holmes Group's *Tomorrow's Teachers* asks that teacher education be made more solid intellectually; that distinctions among teachers in training and experience, commitment and skill be recognized; that standards of entry and performance be made more professionally relevant and intellectually defensible; that teacher training institutions and public schools be more meaningfully linked; and that we strive for less bureaucracy and more professional autonomy. *A Nation Prepared* of the Carnegie Task Force advocates a national board for professional teaching standards, a professional environment in classrooms, a restructured teaching force similar to the distinctions called for by the Holmes Group, more liberal arts undergraduate work and more professional graduate studies for teachers, a greater determination to recruit minority teachers, increased financial support to schools, and career and salary incentives for teachers "competitive with those in other professions."[4]

There are proposals here, then, that appear to bring together forcefully and succinctly the major demands that have been made and can be made for true professional status for classroom teachers. In fact, some of the most eloquent passages of the reports speak directly to the issue of teacher professionalism.[5] And yet, as one glances over the list of signatories to the reports, one cannot help but wonder whether what is called for here is not the further professionalization of public education rather than a determined attempt toward teacher professionalism.

I draw this conclusion from the list of appended names because there is not a single active classroom teacher among the signers of either the Holmes or the Carnegie report. Deans and professors make up the list of the former; the latter presents scientists, industrialists, businessmen, teacher union presidents, a state superintendent, a commissioner of education, a writer, an attorney, several public officials, and an education dean. It is as if teachers have no place in the discussion of American schools and education. Once more they have been confirmed in their role as objects rather than subjects.

The proposal supported by both reports to phase out the undergraduate major in education likewise should make readers of this book uneasy. The call to exchange a teacher education curriculum and degree for one in the liberal arts is certainly fashionable today, but rests on very little solid study or thought. There can be no question that a strong liberal arts degree is preferable to a weak teacher education program. But it is not as easy to see why a strong teacher education program that takes seriously and conscientiously the task of preparing classroom teachers could not be in every way as academic and pedagogically sound as a strong liberal arts program. This book will show that, with few exceptions, our normal schools, teachers colleges, and universities have forsaken the task of devoting themselves single-mindedly to the education of classroom teachers for the elementary schools. Deficient performance in the past, however, need not preclude change and improvement in the future.

The argument for an undergraduate program and degree in teacher education begins with the proposition that young people need assistance in finding out for themselves whether they will be and can be the teachers they would like to be. That takes time and constant practice and experimentation. If I plead for any particular way of teacher education, I call for more and earlier exposure of the student to classroom teaching and internships than is common now; I urge a closer collaboration of university and public school and far more intensive participation of the latter in that process.[6] Practice, to be sure, needs to be grounded on theory; but theory and methods are never successfully taught to students who have never faced a class and stood in the teacher's place.

The case for an undergraduate program and degree in teacher education rests most heavily on the students' need to be attuned from the beginning to a process of learning that points toward future teaching. Students who want to become teachers learn in order to learn how to teach. Everything they encounter in class—whether English or chemistry or music—is grist for their own mill and waits to be taught again. Such students need and have the right to be taught by instructors who understand precisely that motivation and challenge. A history class that recognizes its subject matter as a future teaching assignment need in no way be academically inferior to a class that is "strictly academic." In fact, the case can be made more easily in reverse: a class that affirms the pedagogical implications of history as a subject matter will be a better class than its academic counterpart that remains just that. We know that the motivation to learn is decisive for success in learning. We learn through teaching, said the Romans. We still do.

The recommendation of both the Holmes and Carnegie reports for the student of teaching to follow up an undergraduate liberal arts education with a graduate course in teacher education needs to be stood upon its head. For classroom teachers setting out on their teaching careers with an undergraduate degree in education, there is ample time in future years to earn a master's degree in an academic subject. If we keep in mind here that, unless they intend to leave the classroom for a more lucrative administrative position, professional teachers have no need for technical administrative training, then the demand for a master's degree in an academic subject will be appropriate in itself and desirable for the candidate. Additional professional skills and information will, as now, be available to the practicing teacher who desires them in the in-service programs and workshops offered by graduate schools of education.

One final remark with regard to the veritable flood of reports on education that have deluged the nation in the last few years. They have left the American people bewildered and uncertain. Just what have all the recommendations and suggestions accomplished? What have been the results of all the discussions and debates? If we are serious in our many proclamations that we face a national crisis in our public schools, then an annual comprehensive survey of what we have learned is very much in order. A national clearinghouse should make it its business to keep close watch on all the recommendations. It should challenge school districts across the nation to put into practice for five-year experimental periods some of the many suggestions laid before us. If possible, it should support these experiments financially and keep the nation advised of the costs and benefits. Once the results accumulate, we shall have a basis for comparative analysis, and school districts across the country will be in a far better position to arrive at decisions for their future.

If the members of such a clearinghouse were to ask what help or guidance they might obtain for their task from a historical account such as this, I would point them to the central thesis of this book: When beginning in the late nineteenth century teacher educators in the normal schools followed the siren song of the professionalizers and handed over the education of elementary school teachers to city and county training schools, when by the third decade of the twentieth century in the graduate departments of education they exchanged their original purpose of educating classroom teachers for the more prestigious tasks of training specialists and administrators, then the outlook for creating a genuine teacher professionalism grew dim. Classroom teaching became the least rewarded post in public education.

This history of teacher education says that to reverse the slide of America's public schools into mediocrity we must train and allow our teachers to function as genuine professionals, autonomous in their own sphere of classroom responsibility and accountable to their professional conscience, the students they teach, and the people they serve. The biggest mistake we have made was to pursue professionalization in public education while failing to foster the professionalism of our classroom teachers. It is time now to redress the balance and enable our teachers to function as true professionals.

1
Public Schools and
Teacher Education
The Beginnings

The Public School Revival

The origins of our public schools as we know them today and the traditions of our ways of teacher education go back to the public school revival of the pre–Civil War decades. The record of accomplishments and the problems of America's public schools and their teachers have emerged over a century and a half. To understand them and to shape educational policies today requires not simply a grasp of current problems and future challenges but also a sense of direction that is rooted in an appreciation of the course pursued in the past. That appreciation cannot rest on a reading of the educational record alone. It must include a sense for the complexities of the social, political, and economic climate in which the schools developed, struggled, flourished, or suffered. A study of educational policies thus must include history in its social and political dimensions.

To turn our attention to the origins of our public schools means to look toward antebellum New England where the appointments in 1837 of Horace Mann as secretary of the Massachusetts Board of Education and of Henry Barnard to the same post in Connecticut marked the beginning of a determined effort to strengthen and increase the common schools. In New England the movement was called a revival, because when the Massachusetts legislature acted in 1837, it breathed new life into an old idea. Already in colonial days the people of Massachusetts had believed that the public bore responsibility for the common schooling of all its children. Accordingly, the General Court had ordered the towns to provide and support schoolmasters.[1] To be sure, the enforcement of that legislation proved problematic, but the idea of public responsibility for common schooling never disappeared in the state and in 1837 received a new lease on life. From Massachusetts it spread to neighboring states, was carried west by New England emigrants, and, by the end of the century, could be found in all of the states of the Union.

The concern with common schooling for all children of elementary school age had arisen not only among the settlers of New England but also among the long-established and economically well-to-do residents of the large eastern cities outside of that region. In these urban areas a growing number of youthful vagrants, petty criminals, orphaned and homeless children, many of them of immigrant parents, had caused consternation and fear among the settled families. Undisciplined, illiterate, without family ties and church affiliation, frequently unable to speak or understand the English language, these children threatened an orderly civic life and proved to be inefficient and unreliable as employees in shops, stores, or factories. The very diversity of ethnic background and religious tradition, the variety of languages and dialects spoken, and the apparent crudity or simplicity of life-styles prompted many of the older residents to demand that these newcomers and their children be converted to the ways of the established citizenry.

The public school movement thus took the New England tradition of common schooling as a model and extended it to both the settlers of the agricultural hinterland and the newcomers in the large cities. Everywhere the public schools were to introduce children to American civilization. It was the firm belief of the school reformers that such an introduction would also present to the newcomers and their children opportunities for economic and social advance. It would enable them to learn of and follow the advice of Benjamin Franklin to "a rising people." It would bring them success in business or trade.[2] The public, or common, schools were to become gateways through which all competent Americans would pass on their way from poverty to riches. They provided the least expensive and most effective way of removing the threat of internal strife and chaos.

The American Whigs as Educational Reformers

The message of social stability and economic progress through public schooling appealed particularly to Americans who through their professional and entrepreneurial pursuits saw their present and future prosperity directly tied to manufacturing and trade. By the 1830s many of them had found their political base in the Whig party. The Whigs were deeply distrustful of the Jacksonian Democrats, whom they accused of plundering the country and mismanaging its government. Though like the Democrats the Whigs, too, believed in laissez-faire economics, they were nonetheless committed to economic planning. Many of them supported Henry Clay and his neomercantilist "American System" of central banking, a high tariff, and internal improvements. They loathed Jackson for his war on the national bank, and they preferred to see the economy in the hands of conservative, respectable, sound businessmen like themselves.

Whigs, in short, viewed themselves as the proper element in a business society. Many of them belonged to Protestant families of long-established lineage in the United States. The advocacy of public education came to them naturally. They saw it as a perfect antidote to Jacksonian coarseness and rudeness. Schooling would guarantee that only the deserving ambitious poor would rise to fame and wealth and that those less well trained would keep their place in the supporting, lower ranks of the economic hierarchy. To the Whigs public schools would secure a stable society by permitting the greatest benefits and profits to go to those on the top. To those on the bottom the schools would bring a level of comfort sufficient to have them be content with their lot.

This did not mean that public education became exclusively the cause of the economically successful Whig businessman or professional. The gospel of the rising people appealed as much—if not more—to the small entrepreneur, the artisan, and the tradesman in the middle ranks. They, too, supported the public school movement. In Philadelphia even workingmen proclaimed in 1830 that common schooling was a right to be enjoyed by every American. They resented private schools as "irresponsible institutions established by individuals from mere motives of private speculation and gain." In them, they said, "ignorance, inattention, and even immorality prevail. . . ." They accused the colleges of holding on to a knowledge monopoly which "should be rendered, by legal provision, the common property of all classes." They maintained that a republic needed all of its citizens "alike instructed in the nature and character of their equal rights and duties. . . ."[3] The workingmen wanted the public schools to educate their children and thus to open doors for them to all the opportunities the country had to offer.

Although Whigs and workingmen both endorsed the public school movement, they did so for different reasons. For the children of workingmen, tradesmen, artisans, and small businessmen the availability of public schools promised a better chance in their own battles for economic survival in the marketplace. For Whigs public schooling improved the general prosperity of business by providing a more disciplined workforce and a more supportive business climate. Whigs therefore sought to persuade taxpayers—and primarily the owners of prosperous business establishments and factories—to support the common schools even if they had no school-age children of their own or were unwilling to entrust their sons and daughters to the public schools.

Horace Mann himself provides a case in point. When he addressed himself to Massachusetts manufacturers he relied on the argument that the nation's welfare and prosperity rose and fell with the people's willingness to support the common schools. "An educated people," Mann wrote in 1846, "is a more industrious and productive people. Knowledge and abundance sustain to each other the relation of cause and effect. Intelligence is a primary ingredient in the Wealth of Nations." By the same token, vice and crime flowering in the absence of education "are not only prodigals and spendthrifts of their own, but defrauders and plunderers of the means of others. . . ."[4] It was good business, if nothing else, for the industrialists and owners of property to invest their surplus in public education. Their tax dollars would help create an educated working force and accustom citizens of all walks of life to good order, moral discipline, regularity, punctuality, and reliability. Only a short-sighted or willful misunderstanding of their own advantage could tempt securely established property owners to vote against public education.

Whig Stewardship: In the Public Interest

How should the public's schools be organized? As the Whigs watched the squalor of the eastern cities and the spectacle of hordes of settlers pouring across the Appalachians, squatting on or preempting western lands and setting in motion President Jackson's Indian removal on the "trail of tears," they were determined to protect the common schools from the greed and corruption of private selfishness. Undisciplined and unregulated laissez-faire meant not only degradation and poverty in eastern cities but also the brutal subjugation of the Indians, a dog-eat-dog existence on the frontier with vigilantes and lynch law, and an unscrupulous exploitation of natural resources. For the Whigs this "release of energy" was unconscionable, not because they objected to individual initiative but because that initiative showed no regard for the opinions and directives of the older established elites they themselves represented.[5] They could not understand a labor spokesman like Stephen Simpson, who in 1831 rejected their insistence on law and regulation with the remark that "to substitute LAW for the distribution of labor is to introduce the chief features of the feudal systems of Europe into the free, self-formed, and equitable republic of this country. . . ."[6] To the Whigs such sentiment sounded like a wish for national self-destruction.

Whigs were not alone in their belief that something needed to be done to stem the tide of lawlessness. Reformers of many persuasions criss-crossed the American landscape, urging their countrymen to change their ways and to adopt this or that policy as a corrective. Ralph Waldo Emerson satirized them well:

> What a fertility of projects for the salvation of the world! One apostle thought all men should go to farming, and another that no man should buy or sell, that the use of money was the cardinal evil; another that the mischief was in our diet, that we eat and drink damnation. . . .[7]

Reformers ranged from the advocates of homeopathy and mesmerism and phrenology to the fighters for the improvement of prisons and mental hospitals and to the leaders in the greatest reform cause of them all: abolition of slavery. The reform mentality demanded unconditional, unreserved allegiance to whatever cause was being promoted.

Disconcerted by such uncompromising vehemence, the Whigs remained distrustful. They saw in these reform causes a manifestation of that same individualism which, in their thinking, lay at the root of all the evils they deplored. In so many cases they saw reformers act at cross-purposes, producing no lasting visible results. This, the Whigs felt, was particularly true in private education. Here charity had been the preferred means of reformers who pledged contributions to colleges or financed church or privately sponsored schools such as those of the Free School Society in New York.[8] The Whigs came to reject such efforts on the level of elementary schooling. In the Pennsylvania Assembly in 1835 Thaddeus Stevens spoke for them with his plea for the establishment of a public school system in the state. In charity schools and pauper legislation, he said, "the names of those who have the misfortune to be poor men's children shall be forever preserved, as a distinct class, in the archives of the country! . . . Hereditary distinctions," he continued, "are sufficiently odious; but that which is founded on poverty is infinitely more so."[9] With that Stevens dissociated the Whigs from private efforts in the common schools and ruled out charity as an acceptable policy.

Horace Mann and Henry Barnard had additional reasons to reject charity and private schools. They considered private schools divisive and un-American. Said Mann in 1837:

> The tendency of the private school system is to assimilate our modes of education to those of England, where churchmen and dissenters, each sect according to its own creed, maintain separate schools . . . where the gospel, instead of being a temple of peace, is converted into an armory of deadly weapons for social, interminable warfare.[10]

Henry Barnard seconded Mann in Connecticut. Private schooling, he complained,

> classifies society at the root, by assorting children according to the wealth, education, and outward circumstances of their parents into different schools; and educates children of the same neighborhood differently and unequally. These differences of culture as to manners, morals, and intellectual tastes and habits . . . open a real chasm between members of the same society, broad and deep, which equal laws and political theories cannot close.[11]

Mann and Barnard saw private schools as instruments for social and sectarian separation. On both counts they found them antithetical to the perceived needs for harmony and agreement among the American people. Once again they thus came to an affirmation of the public schools as the most promising agencies for nationalization and socialization of the country's young.

Although the Whigs thus rejected private and charity schools, they also remained distrustful toward self-help. This had once been pioneered by Benjamin Franklin in his Philadelphia junto and was practiced during the nineteenth century in Boston by workingmen who had founded in 1820 the Apprentice Library and in 1826 the Mechanics Institute. Other groups supported Josiah Holbrook's American Lyceum, an organization intended to come to the aid of school boards "by introducing uniformity and improvements in common schools."[12] A similar undertaking began in 1829 as the Society for the Distribution of Useful Knowledge. For many advocates of common schools these projects were at best inefficient in that they did not pressure legislatures to create public schools. At worst they were seen as harmful because they generated a false sense of accomplishment. New York workingmen insisted in 1830 that, though they were sympathetic to self-help efforts, they could not prefer them to the public schools.

> Unless this safeguard of liberty is secured, [they insisted] and by the enlightenment of the mass, the axe of knowledge is laid at the root of aristocracy, there is effected, as it were, nothing. The best labours are lost, and the success of the present is ever hazarded in the future.[13]

Although differing in their reasons from those of labor, the Whigs could not but agree with the conclusion.

Should public schools be chartered directly by state legislatures and placed under the government of their own trustees, such as was done with colleges, academies, and business corporations? The public school–minded Whigs shrank back from this suggestion also, because it appeared to them to be afflicted with the cancer of self-serving acquisitiveness which beset the nation's economic life. Once chartered, how could an educational corporation be controlled by the public? John W. Vethake expressed the Whigs' disgust with the Jacksonians' abdication of responsibility for chartered corporations:

> It has happened [he said in 1835] that . . . when . . . all the cardinal interests of society were utterly forgotten in a mere money-making mania, the tacit and thoughtless assent of the people to some one exclusive privilege or the establishment of a monopoly . . . was greedily seized upon . . . until special grants and charters have come to constitute the whole mass of legislative enactments. . . .[14]

Common schools, the Whigs felt, were far too important to be handed over to boards of private trustees.

What the Whigs preferred instead were school systems organized as public service corporations under the guidance of the best minds and warmest hearts of a community. The directors of such systems should constitute an elite of well-established, generous, and compassionate community leaders, incorruptible and capable of effective administration, without harboring the slightest expectations of private gain. Such corporations would protect and serve the public interest. They would unite rather than divide the community. They would derive their funds from public taxes and thus neither deplete nor deflect private capital needed for investments. Government by a community's disinterested, capable, and public-spirited elite would insure Whig leadership and confer on school board members as governors of the public schools the halo of public trust. This, then, was the Whigs' answer to the question of how the common schools were to be organized and governed. It would prove to be quite a different matter whether local school boards or committees could ever live up to the Whigs' expectations of disinterestedness, particularly in small rural communities.

A Common Language, Faith, and Discipline

Once a public school system was in place, what did the Whigs consider to be its mission, and how was it to be accomplished? What concerns were foremost in the minds of school reformers like Horace Mann and Henry Barnard? There was near unanimity that the schools had to try to unify the people through a common education of all youngsters. They had to instill in and convert Americans to a shared endorsement of what were essentially Whig values—a middle-class morality centering on a sense of human decency and on what has become known as the Protestant work ethic, a bourgeois conception of economic security based on a commitment to hard work and the ownership of private property. Civil order, security of property, decency and gentility in interpersonal relationships among the members of a white, middle-class, and overwhelmingly Protestant citizenry—these were the antidotes to anarchy and dissension. They were to be held up as values to be protected or, for those who did not fit the white, middle-class, Protestant ideal, to be accepted as given and normative. The schools were to implant them firmly throughout all classes of American society.

How to accomplish this? The Whigs took their cue from Noah Webster and acknowledged the English language as the chosen means for imparting a sense of national consciousness and culture. Educators were supported in this concern by poets and philosophers, political observers and ministers. Writers like James Fennimore Cooper and Ralph Waldo Emerson, a foreign commentator like Alexis de Tocqueville, and a Boston Unitarian clergyman like William Ellery Channing all joined in stressing the teaching of a common national language as the primary responsibility of the public schools. Without such a language America could not hope to contribute to the world's culture and science, let alone create a national life of its own. Horace Mann warned that

> language is not only a necessary instrument of civilization, past or prospective, but it is an indispensable condition of our existence as rational beings. . . . Science itself can never advance far beyond a scientific language in which to record its laws and principles.[15]

Noah Webster's spellers thus became the ubiquitous primers of America's young. They reigned supreme in the common schools.

Next to the creation of a common language, the propagation of a common faith was the common schools' greatest challenge. Mann saw the public schools as secular temples of a common-core or nonsectarian Protestant Christianity. In the *Annual Report* of 1848 he stated that he regarded as "eternal and immutable" the proposition "that no community will ever be religious without a Religious Education." The public schools were to be Christian schools, but they had to eschew denominational doctrines.

> Our system [Mann declared] earnestly inculcates all Christian morals; it founds its morals on the basis of religion; it welcomes the religion of the Bible; and, in receiving the Bible, it allows it to do what it is allowed to do in no other system, —*to speak for itself.* But here it stops, not because it claims to have compassed all truth; but because it disclaims to act as an umpire between hostile religious opinions.[16]

Mann obviously believed that it was possible to teach Biblical religion in a nondenominational fashion. That, in fact, was the cornerstone of his contention. He endorsed this view all the more easily because it corresponded to the belief held by New England Unitarians that people of goodwill could avoid sectarian and denominational controversy. It was a belief which many Protestants found acceptable. It did not recommend itself to Catholics and non-Christians.

In 1844 Mann had received support for his defense of nonsectarian Christianity from the Supreme Court of the United States. Stephen Girard, founder of a college for orphans in Philadelphia, had included in the college charter a provision that barred ministers and missionaries "of any sect whatsoever" from holding office in or being admitted to the college. The Court had found "nothing in the charter which is inconsistent with the Christian religion." Girard had explained his policies against men of the cloth in phrases that could easily have been seconded by Mann and applied to religious instruction in the schools:

> I do not mean to cast any reflection upon any sect or person whatsoever; but as there is such a multitude of sects, and such a diversity of opinion

amongst them, I desire to keep the tender minds of the orphans, who are to derive advantage from this bequest, free from the excitement which clashing doctrines and sectarian controversy are so apt to produce; my desire is, that all the instructors and teachers in the College, shall take pains to instill into the minds of the scholars, *the purest principles of morality,* so that, on their entrance into active life, they may *from inclination and habit,* evince *benevolence toward their fellow creatures,* and *a love of truth, sobriety, and industry,* adopting at the same time, such religious tenets as their *matured reason* may enable them to prefer.[17]

In a will such as this we can find expressed to perfection the sentiments that motivated Whigs to act as stewards of a common faith assumed to pervade and unite all classes of society.

A common language and a common faith, however, were not enough. Discipline to enforce, if need be, adherence to common values and standards of behavior was required as well. Public education was to be promoted not only as opportunity and right but as obligation and duty as well. This was particularly true when Whigs considered the children of Irish immigrants, who, they felt, had to be coerced to attend school. If left to the direction of their parents, a writer in *The Massachusetts Teacher* stated in 1851, they

will be brought up in idle, dissolute, vagrant habits. . . . Instead of filling our public schools, they will find their way into our prisons, houses of correction and almshouses. Nothing can operate effectually here but stringent legislation, thoroughly carried out by an efficient police;—the children must be gathered up and forced into school, and those who resist or impede this plan, whether parents or *priests,* must be held accountable and punished.[18]

The fear of disorder, chaos, or anarchy prompted such sentiments and called for the truant officer and policeman to stand behind the classroom teacher.[19]

Henry Barnard expressed the final link between the duty to attend school and the right to enjoy the benefits of American citizenship. Only the schooled American was to be a full-fledged citizen, because, Barnard proclaimed,

the law of self-preservation imperiously demands that political institutions which are embodied in written constitutions and laws, should not pass into the keeping of juries, witnesses, and electors who cannot write the verdict they may render or read the vote they may cast into the ballot box. The right of suffrage should be withheld from such as cannot give the lowest evidence of school attendance and proficiency.[20]

In the last analysis, then, for the Whigs, schooling for all in a common language, a common faith, and common values was a requirement of citizenship. Without a common school they doubted whether there could be a common country and a united people. They fervently hoped that the school revival of the antebellum years would insure the stability and permanence of the nation.

The Place of the Teacher

Central to Whig thought about schooling was the place of the teacher. American Whigs loved to quote a saying that, presumably, had been coined by the French philosopher Victor Cousin when he visited the schools of Prussia in 1831: "As is the teacher, so is the school." The phrase was subsequently to become the Whigs' battle cry in their crusade for common schools in antebellum Massachusetts. Whigs and school reformers generally needed little convincing that the quality of the teacher would largely determine the quality of the classroom, but that message did not appear to make much of an impression on the people of rural Massachusetts. To them, teachers were cheap, easily and quickly replaced when necessary, and not expected to possess extraordinary capabilities or devotion. In the view of the ordinary school committee member, anyone could teach in a pinch. The school reformers thus had to persuade a doubting people that teachers needed to be trained and that such training would indeed pay for itself in the benefits communities could derive from their common schools.

Late in the summer of 1834 one of these reformers, the 39-year-old Charles Brooks, a Unitarian clergyman of Hingham, Massachusetts, happened to be on his way back from Liverpool to the United States. On his steamer he shared a cabin with a Dr. Heinrich Julius of Hamburg, Germany. Julius was then travelling on commission from the king of Prussia to prepare a report on prisons, hospitals, schools, and other institutions in the United States. During their Atlantic passage he talked to Brooks about the necessity for an adequate supply of competent, dedicated, and well-trained teachers if the United States were ever to enjoy flourishing common schools.

Brooks took his cue from that conversation. Beginning with a Thanksgiving sermon in his parish on December 3, 1835, he embarked on a series of speeches and addresses before conventions and legislatures in Massachusetts, New Hampshire, Vermont, Connecticut, New Jersey, Pennsylvania, and Rhode Island. His theme was everywhere the same: "Town schools are the people's colleges and their teachers should be able professors. . . ." To bring this about, Massachusetts and her sister states should follow the example of Prussia and train teachers in specially designed seminaries or normal schools. As he said in retrospect in 1864, "The Prussian system is my client."[21]

Brooks had not been the first New Englander to sound the trumpet for teacher education. In 1823 Samuel Read Hall, Congregational clergyman, later to become famous for his 1829 *Lectures on Schoolkeeping,* had opened a three-year course of teacher training in his Concord, Vermont, home. Seven years later he moved his operation to the Phillips Academy in Andover, Massachusetts, where it became the academy's normal department. Until its dissolution in 1842 the department graduated about 100 students.[22] A similar venture had begun in 1827 in Lancaster, Massachusetts. James G. Carter, who with his 1824 and 1825 "Essays on Popular Education" in the *Boston Patriot* had called for public normal schools, started a private teacher seminary. Other projects and proposals followed. Another Congregational clergyman, William Channing Woodbridge, published in 1831 a report on Prussian teacher seminaries in the *American Annals of Education and Instruction,* a journal of which he was the editor. Four years later Victor Cousin's *Rapport sur l'état de l'instruction publique en Prusse* appeared in New York in an English translation. In August of the same year a summary of Cousin's remarks on Prussian teacher training was read before a meeting of the American Institute of Instruction in Boston.[23] When later that same year Brooks gave his Thanksgiving sermon the ground had been well prepared for a concerted effort to train teachers for service in the common schools.

In the colonial period the New England teacher had been a clergyman charged with the education of adults in matters of creed and faith. It was the schoolmaster—and in the South the tutor—who was specifically employed for the education of children. Schoolmasters and tutors were men, the one teaching children in elementary and grammar schools, the other instructing them in private homes or neighborhood schools. Women often assisted them and, in their homes or in so-called dame schools, instructed boys and girls in the rudiments of reading and writing. And though the fame of some New England schoolmasters—a man like Ezekiel Cheever, for example—has been enshrined in literature and history,[24] young men who taught school in the seventeenth and eighteenth centuries usually did so while preparing themselves for more rewarding careers in the ministry, in public service, medicine, or business. The schoolmaster of colonial times rarely, if ever, basked in the sunshine of popular acclaim.[25]

By the first few decades of the nineteenth century things had not changed much. Massachusetts common school teachers were an odd group. They did not count among themselves ambitious and aggressive men out to forge their careers, make their fortunes, or otherwise set the world afire. For many of them teaching was neither vocation nor profession but simply a job, seasonal and temporary for the most part, and as in the past often taken up to permit an impecunious college student to finance his studies for the ministry, the law, or medical practice. David Allmendinger tells us that "in the first half of the nineteenth century, at least one-third of all the New England students took leaves of absence each year after the winter vacation in order to teach." Most

New England students supported by the American Education Society taught three months during three of the four winters they attended college. They spent their schoolkeeping stints in isolated rural locations where they had to board around with the parents of their pupils. The practice became so common that several New England colleges arranged their winter vacations so that students could take advantage of them to keep school.[26]

Not all the men keeping school in antebellum Massachusetts were college students. Drifters shunning hard physical labor and handicapped fellows unable to perform it sought out the schoolhouse as a place to sustain themselves for a season. Consequently, whether deservedly or not, common school teachers often ranked low in the opinions of their countrymen who were used to a hard and frugal life on the farm. Typical of this sentiment are the words of a Connecticut school board member:

> He—the young man out of work—thinks of turning peddler, or of working at shoemaking. But the one will expose him to storms, the other he fears will injure his chest. . . . He will nevertheless teach school for a meager compensation.[27]

And who does not remember Ichabod Crane, the village schoolmaster in Washington Irving's charming story "The Legend of Sleepy Hollow"? Crane presented a slightly ridiculous appearance with his "hands that dangled a mile out of his sleeves" and "feet that might have served for shovels."[28] Crane, too, was a bird of passage as a schoolteacher, and he was said eventually to have studied law and become a politician.

Along with the men, both older and younger women could be found keeping school. Many of the older women were widows, whereas the younger women usually had barely finished their own schooling. Women ordinarily taught during the summer when the older school boys and girls and the more rambunctious teenagers stayed on the farm or at home, working with their parents or hiring out as seasonal laborers. The older women kept school to sustain themselves economically and be independent; the younger ones usually because they had shown themselves good in school at academic work and were asked to stay on. In general people thought it fitting that, while men and boys worked in the fields, women took care of the children at home and in school.[29]

How effective were these men and women who kept school in the days before the common school revival? The answer, of course, must vary from place to place and from teacher to teacher. But whatever encouraging reports we might receive could be attributed neither to any uniform insistence on teacher qualifications nor to any consistent policy of teacher preparation. Given the absence of such standards and policies the frequent complaints about unqualified, ill-tempered, and incompetent teachers should surprise no one. James G. Carter remonstrated in 1826 that the teachers of the primary summer schools have rarely had any education beyond what they have acquired in the very schools where they begin to teach. Their attainments, therefore, to say the least, are usually *very moderate*. But this is not the worst of it. They are often very young, they are constantly changing their employment, and consequently can have but little experience; and what is worse than all, they never have any direct preparation for their profession.

The particular target of Carter's anger was the practice of qualifying individuals to keep school. A visit of the applicant to the local minister was sufficient. It was left to the clergyman's discretion to examine and certify. Carter called this "a perfect farce" that amounted "to no efficient check upon the obtrusions of ignorance and inexperience." Which minister, Carter asked, could refuse to approve a candidate who was "sustained by his own influence in the parish, and that of a respectable father and perhaps a large family of friends. . . ?"[30]

Equally discouraging to the school reformer was the rapid turnover of teachers in the district schools. After his first year as secretary of the Connecticut Board of Commissioners of Common Schools, Henry Barnard reported that

most of the teachers employed the past winter, have not taught the same schools two successive seasons. Out of 1,292 teachers returned, but 341 have taught the same school before. Omitting those who are engaged for the whole year as permanent teachers, the number is less than 240. And these were not engaged in the summer, but only for the winter. . . . This practice [Barnard concluded] excludes from our common schools nearly all those who have decided to make teaching a profession and drives them, almost as a matter of course, into private schools or academies.[31]

Keeping school, it appears from this, did not rank high in the concerns and interests of most Americans. There were more important things to be done. Those who valued education put their efforts into private academies and colleges. It was this obvious neglect of the common schools that the school reformers set out to remedy.

Women in the Classroom

Our best estimates of just how many of the teachers in Massachusetts were men and how many were women come from Maris Vinovskis and Richard Bernard. Their figures show that in the three years before 1837 women teachers already outnumbered their male colleagues in the common and private day schools of Massachusetts. As the percentage of women teachers began to rise from its 56.3 mark in 1834, the percentage of men teachers fell and reached 42.2 two years later. By 1850 only one out of three teachers was a man, and in 1860 nearly four out of every five teachers in Massachusetts (77.8 percent) were women. A similar picture emerges when we ask how many residents of Massachusetts kept school at any one time. In 1834/1835, 1.3 percent of Massachusetts' white males and 1.6 percent of the state's white females aged 15–29 were teachers; by 1850/1851 these percentages stood at 0.8 and 1.7, respectively. If we ask how many white Massachusetts residents ever kept school during their lives, the same increase in the proportion of women over men is evident. In 1834/1835, 13.2 percent of the men and 18.3 percent of the women and in 1850/1851 8.7 percent of the men and 21.8 percent of the women were schoolkeepers at one time or another.[32]

What accounts for the growing proportion of women teachers throughout this period? As Table 1.1 shows, during the 1820s at a time of expanding economic opportunities in the West, Massachusetts experienced a sudden steep rise in its population. That rise, caused in the main by immigration from Europe, continued until it reached its peak with a growth rate of 34.8 percent during the 1840s and then slowed somewhat to 23.8 percent in the 1850s. As noted in Table 1.2, in the same two decades the rate of growth for the number of teachers of the state's public and private schools was only 9.6 and 6.8 percent, respectively. It thus becomes evident that the increase in Massachusetts' population far outpaced the supply of teachers for the common schools. Certainly, holding fast to past employment practices and patterns would not have assured the required supply of teachers. New sources had to be tapped.

What stands out in these figures, however, is the contrast between the decline in the number and percentage of male teachers and the rapid growth in the number and percentage of female teachers. Women not only overtook

Table 1.1. Massachusetts Population, 1810–1860

	Population	Rate of Growth during Preceding Decade (%)
1810	472,040	—
1820	523,287	10.9
1830	610,408	16.6
1840	737,699	20.9
1850	994,514	34.8
1860	1,231,066	23.8
Rate of growth from 1841 to 1860:		66.9

Source: Based on U.S. Bureau of the Census, *Historical Statistics of the United States* (Washington, DC, 1960), series 127, p. 13.

Table 1.2. Gender Distribution of Teachers in Massachusetts in the Mid-1800s

	Men	Women	Total
	NUMBER		
1839/40	2,586	4,256	6,842
1849/50	2,469	5,031	7,500
1859/60	1,782	6,229	8,011
	PERCENTAGE OF CHANGE		
1840s	−4.5	18.2	9.6
1850s	−27.8	23.8	6.8
1840–60	−31.1	46.4	17.1

Sources: Massachusetts Board of Education, *Annual Reports* for 1839–1860; and U.S. censuses, as cited in Table A7.12 by Carl F. Kaestle and Maris A. Vinovskis in their *Education and Social Change in Nineteenth-Century Massachusetts* (Cambridge, England: Cambridge University Press, 1980).

men in the classrooms, they also displaced and replaced them at an ever-increasing pace. Apparently, when an expanding country siphoned off young men, tempting them with economic opportunities that were not open to women, the common school classrooms attracted women with surprising ease.

But if the figures cited thus far tell us about the 1840s and 1850s, what about the preceding decade when Charles Brooks began his crusade for state normal schools? Here we are on less certain ground, since the available statistics presented in Table 1.3 do not begin until 1834. Yet the picture they give us is, in its rough outlines, identical with the one of later years. In 1835, when Brooks opened his campaign at Thanksgiving, and two years later when the legislature chose Horace Mann as the Massachusetts Education Board's first secretary, Brooks might not have discovered convincing evidence that male teachers were about to leave the schools. He could, however, have noted the beginning of the trend toward the employment of women in the common schools. By 1837 their number had risen by nearly 27 percent over the past three years, while men had increased by barely 8 percent over the same period. In retrospect we know that the feminization of the American common school classroom had begun.

As men were drawn off to other regions and found more challenging and rewarding tasks than schoolkeeping, salaries began to rise in the district schools. But school boards, dependent on local resources alone, were unable or unwilling to sustain the rise. In 1837 Massachusetts men teachers received, on the average, monthly wages of $23.13. By 1842/1843 that amount had risen to $41.17, only to decrease again to a low of $35.69 in 1845/1846 and to reach a second high of $43.62 in 1848/1849. Though school board members were not oblivious to the need for improved compensation for teachers, they

Table 1.3. Gender Distribution of Teachers in Massachusetts Schools, 1834–1840

	Men		Women		Total	
	Number	Percent Change since Previous Year	Number	Percent Change since Previous Year	Number	Percent Change since Previous Year
1834	2,358	—	3,035	—	5,393	—
1835	2,405	2.0	3,077	1.4	5,482	1.7
1836	2,411	0.2	3,306	7.4	5,717	4.3
1837	2,536	5.2	3,842	16.2	6,378	11.6
1838/39	2,584	1.8	4,043	5.2	6,627	3.9
1839/40	2,586	0.1	4,256	5.3	6,842	3.2
Percent change from 1834 to 1837		7.5		26.6		18.3
Percent change from 1834 to 1840		9.7		40.2		26.9

Sources: Massachusetts Board of Education, *Annual Reports* for 1839–1860; and U.S. censuses, as cited in Table A7.12 by Carl F. Kaestle and Maris A. Vinovskis in their *Education and Social Change in Nineteenth-Century Massachusetts* (Cambridge, England: Cambridge University Press, 1980).

nonetheless failed to support it after 1849. As a result the state's male teachers improved their economic situation for about a decade. Thereafter their economic fortunes dwindled.[33]

Though the pattern of fluctuating salaries was similar for women, they suffered from two significant exceptions. Their salaries generally equalled only 40 percent of the amount paid to their male colleagues, and the increases they received between 1837 and 1842/1843 and between 1837 and 1848/-1849, when compared with those paid to their male colleagues, fell short by 19 percent in 1843 and by 12.6 percent in 1849. In addition, women did less well in urban than in rural areas, where working conditions were more strenuous and fewer women applied. Thus, in the country it was often possible for them to earn as much as 60 percent of a male teacher's pay. However, because the rural pay scale for both men and women was lower than that in the cities, the gain for rural women teachers was more apparent than real.[34]

How, then, do we explain the apparent attractiveness of teaching for young women at the beginning of the school revival? There was, first of all, the barrage of arguments by school reformers like Brooks who preferred well-bred young women to the male drifters, incompetents, and disabled as teachers of the state's children. Teaching children, it was said, was a female occupation par excellence. It enhanced the motherly and nurturing qualities presumed to be inherent in women. Not only would school children benefit from women teachers, but also the women themselves—and through them their own children and their husbands—would derive advantages. The temporariness of a woman's teaching, her decision to forgo teaching for marriage, was a blessing in disguise. Said one contemporary observer: No evil consequences would follow

> for it is believed that in all cases the school room is the truest avenue to domestic happiness. Every such departure can be made good by new recruits, who will find their best friends and firmest supporters in their predecessors, settled around them as the wives and mothers of the most influential members of society.[35]

School and home belonged together in what was called the woman's sphere of domesticity. For female teachers as much as for female students, school was preparation and the home was fulfillment.

Horace Mann was to sum it up grandiloquently:

> Is not woman destined to conduct the rising generation, of both sexes, at least through all the primary stages of education? Has not the Author of nature preadapted her, by constitution, and faculty, and temperament, for this noble work? . . . In the great system of society, what other part can she act, so intimately connected with the refinement and purification of the race?[36]

In the school reformers' minds, to be a woman was to be a teacher.

As the years went by, school reformers succeeded in persuading women that their teaching was not so much a service they rendered to society as an opportunity society graciously offered them. Women, the reformers said, could continue their own education and receive pedagogical training that would prepare them for their later duties as mothers. In their role as continuing students the women teachers thus were at best junior members of a school faculty, at worst underpaid and subordinate assistants. Principal teachers, invariably men, saw them as apprentices or daughters. They wanted them to do well in that role, but they did not care to accept them as colleagues who would one day challenge them as equals and competitors. The classroom with its children, not the principal's office, was the woman's sphere.[37] In it began the relegation of education to the realm of domesticity and gentility, a realm sharply different from the male world of enterprise, industry, and government.

Middle- and upper-class women, the wives of professionals, encouraged the feminization of the classroom and the notion of the woman's sphere. They felt it to be in their interest to place young women of farm and urban working-class background in the classrooms. They saw them as allies in their efforts to entrench the values of domesticity and gentility among the nation's young. They could then all the more easily pursue their own cause of softening the harsh realities of the nation's work-a-day life by influencing and persuading their husbands to tone down the often brutal struggle for economic survival. Wives in well-off homes and teachers from less well situated families in the common schools could make "domesticating" the nation a common cause.

In that cause American middle-class women struck a strategic alliance with Protestant clergymen, who in many states were soon to hold positions as promoters and superintendents of the common schools.[38] Ministers and missionaries together with middle-class women became the staunchest supporters of the schools.[39] As these women offered themselves and the nation's daughters as helpmates in the battle for a Protestant civilization, they strengthened the appeal of teaching as a mission for young women of humble origins. The ministers' preaching then served to complement the women's teaching.

Young women of farm or working-class families listened sympathetically to the pleas and exhortations of the reformers and the ministers. Being suspended, as it were, between their own common school days and their hoped-for marriages, they were ready to make themselves useful, to introduce the immigrant children of the eastern cities to American ways of life, and to "civilize" America's young in the rural settlements of the interior. They happily returned as teachers to the classrooms they had just left as students.

In Massachusetts the near simultaneous arrival of industrialization and the common school revival offered women a choice between employment in the mills or in the schools. Of these alternatives, the schools gradually emerged as more attractive. Though employment there was often seasonal and in the most subordinate positions, it offered reasonably pleasant working environments and, beginning in the 1840s, better pay as well. The prospect of steadier employment in the mills and the likelihood that there one's status as a common school graduate would lead to a supervisory position soon ceased to be persuasive. During the 1840s women's weekly wages in Massachusetts public schools averaged $0.39 higher than in several of the cotton mills.[40] Thus, common school graduates tended toward the schools, even though, as one school board member candidly admitted, boards "paid a woman about one half what we should under the circumstances have paid a man." The truth was, the social and economic position of women gave them no leverage to protest. Their better-off sisters, whose voices might have carried more weight, saw no reason to raise them, and wage scales in other available employment were even lower.

Common school teachers, whether male or female, did not fare well in antebellum Massachusetts.[41] The esteem in which they were held by their fellow citizens, the financial rewards they were allowed, and the expectations they were asked to meet were minimal. When Charles Brooks began to insist that schools could be only as good as the teachers in them, he told his neighbors what they already knew: The common schools of Massachusetts did not impress anyone. If that were to be changed, the reformers thought, the point to begin would be with an effort to educate the state's common school teachers. Perhaps that would persuade parents and voters that the common schools of their children deserved their support.

Teacher Education: The Agitation Begins

The first stirrings of school reform in Massachusetts had appeared in the 1820s. James G. Carter's newspaper publications, "Essays on Popular Education," were written at a time when, according to recent estimates, enrollment in the state's public and private schools had reached approximately 60 percent of the state's children between the ages of 5 and 19, and when the proliferation of district schools increased the demand for teachers.[42] Though financially supported by the 300 townships, these schools were under the control of separate district committees. Often consisting of but one man, such committees hired the teacher, selected the books, and generally kept an eye on things in the school. Although by and large the farming population of Massachusetts was happy with its more than 2,000 district schools, the decentralized and quite amateurish nature of school supervision prompted some parents to send their children to private rather than common schools. This persuaded the school reformers and their supporters that there was a growing need for consolidation. District schools should be brought under a stronger and more centralized administrative control by town or state authorities.[43]

It is with this latent dissatisfaction with the decentralized district system in mind that we must read Carter's call for the legislature's creation of a public institution for the training of common school teachers. Carter said that, though such a school could not be another college or university seeking to advance literature and science, it would have to develop a literature and science of its own dealing directly with teaching. He called this literature "the science of the development of the infant mind and . . . of communicating knowledge from one mind to another while in a different stage of maturity." Districts, townships, and private persons would not be capable of sponsoring and supporting such a school. The state would have to take over that task. Only if it did so could Massachusetts "secure, at once, a uniform, intelligent, and independent tribunal for decisions on the qualifications of teachers." Carter made clear that, in his view, the road to improvement of the common schools led through a uniform system of teacher training and qualification. Right from the start he asked for what later generations would call professionalization.[44]

As to the school's main subjects of instruction, Carter felt they should be anatomy, physiology, and physical education, child and adult psychology, and the philosophy of language. Carter's own terms, to be sure, were different. Child and adult psychology he called the philosophy of the infant mind and of the passions and affections of the human heart. By his philosophy of language he did not mean the study of Greek, Latin, or English, but the arts of human communication. These fields were to be taught by instructors who were able to translate principles into practice that their students might "become artists in the profession." To aid in that process, a school for children would have to be part of the training institution. In it, the teachers-to-be could put their own learning into teaching practice and be guided and corrected by their instructors. Finally, Carter provided for a board of trustees to regulate the general government and set the objectives of the school. The essential ingredients that Carter proposed in his call to action were centralized administrative supervision at state level over the professionalization of the state's common school teachers in a separate institution with a specialized curriculum.

Carter was not the only one calling for professionalization through teacher training. Thomas H. Gallaudet, principal of the Hartford school of the deaf, published a virtually identical appeal at about the same time in the *Connecticut Observer*. Training and experience were necessary for teaching as for any other occupation, he wrote. They were to be offered in a state institution "for the express purpose of training up young men for the profession of instructors of youth in the common branches of an English education." The institution was to have a staff of professors, a library, a practice school, and, if possible, an endowment of two or three fellowships. Because the public was to finance the undertaking, opportunities would be created for poor young men to devote their lives to public benefit. Properly trained teachers, Gallaudet thought, could shorten an English common school education for Connecticut's children from eight to five years. Teacher training at public expense would thus be a most profitable investment for the community as well as for individuals.[45]

By the end of the 1820s the ground was prepared in Massachusetts to propose reform of the common schools as a matter of state initiative. Whigs were ready to assume the leadership of this cause and to advance it as a public trust. They believed that the new nation, born in revolution and formed by the steady accretion and amalgamation of older settlers and immigrant newcomers of diverse national, ethnic, and religious origins, needed a common language, a uniting civic commitment, and a discipline of work. To instill this in the young and thereby to turn them into Americans was to be the task of the public schools. To do this well a concerted statewide effort had to do away with the haphazard nature of school organization and the virtual absence of teacher education. Thus, high on the Massachusetts reformers' agenda for the 1830s stood legislation for the creation of a state board of education and for the opening of state schools for teacher education.

2
The Atlantic Community of Whigs

First News from Prussia

The Massachusetts Whigs found support abroad as well as at home for their reliance on state initiative in matters of public schooling. Charles Brooks's 1834 Atlantic encounter with Dr. Julius had been preceded by travellers' reports and newspaper accounts of Prussia's public schools. In 1829 Henry Edwin Dwight had published his *Travels in the North of Germany.* In it he praised the Protestant countries of northern Europe for having excited a thirst for knowledge among their citizens. In Prussia the government had taken up that task among its peasants and supervised more than 20,000 common schools, of which 17,000 were to be found in rural areas. Only trained and certified teachers were permitted to teach. In order to have a sufficient number of such teachers available, the government had created special teacher seminaries in which applicants for teaching were instructed for two or three years in "the best methods of educating and of governing children as well as [in] the subjects they are to teach."[1]

Dwight was quite taken with the insistence of foreign educators on going beyond the transmission of facts to the excitement of curiosity which, he wrote, "will prompt him [a student] to make subsequent inquiries for himself. . . . He should be made a thinking, reflecting being. . . ." Dwight felt that if such a pedagogy could find a home in the United States through the establishment of teacher seminaries on the Prussian model, then the twin enemies of teacher professionalism—better opportunities in the West for male teachers and marriage for female teachers—could be overcome. Teaching then would "soon become a distinct profession."[2]

A second report from Prussia appeared in June of 1831 in the *American Annals of Education and Instruction.* The journal's editor, William Channing Woodbridge, a Congregational clergyman and ardent promoter of Pestalozzian pedagogy, took advantage of a resolution passed at the May meeting of the American Lyceum and published in the *Annals*. The members of the Lyceum, a society formed for the purpose of aiding common schools, resolved to "consider the establishment of Seminaries for the education of teachers a most important part of every system of public instruction."[3] Woodbridge apparently intended to strike while the iron was hot, and in the same issue published a translated report on teacher seminaries in Prussia.

Woodbridge's comments highlighted what he considered the most significant aspect of the Prussian approach to teacher training: that teaching was viewed as a profession. Woodbridge summed up his observations thus:

> School-keeping in Germany appears to be a very healthy employment. The teachers pursue the business for life and, like clergymen, are settled in particular places from which they rarely remove. The average of the time which they are usually able to devote to their professions [*sic*] is about *thirty-three* years; and they are generally about twenty-four years old when they engage as instructors.

Quite obviously, the Prussian public school teacher as portrayed in this description could hardly find his counterpart in New England.

According to Woodbridge, the teacher seminaries of Prussia were boarding schools in each of which about 55 young men lived and studied together for two or three years. They were supervised and taught by a director who in most cases was a clergyman. The seminaries were quite independent of local school boards, secondary schools, and the universities. Their curricula covered basic instruction in religion, German, arithmetic, geometry, natural philosophy and natural history, history, geography, pedagogics and didactics, drawing, writing, the theory of music, and singing. All these subjects, wrote Woodbridge, "are taught in the most practical manner; technical terms and subtle niceties, divisions and arrangements, are avoided as much as possible." There were plans underfoot soon to add gardening and the planting and pruning of fruit trees. All of the seminaries had model schools attached to them in which the would-be teachers could try their hands at actual classroom teaching. Practical instruction for teaching in a rural school and preparation for life in the country, not academic instruction and introduction into the lifestyle of the educated bourgeoisie, were the obvious tasks of these seminaries.[4]

Almost all of the reports from abroad concerned schooling for boys and the training of male teachers for boys schools in areas of rural poverty. Yet in August of 1831 Woodbridge carried in his columns an essay on the professional training of women teachers. He translated and printed an article by Sophia Frommichen, a Prussian woman who for 39 years had taught in girls schools in Germany and Russia. Frommichen maintained that knowledgeable persons agreed that schools for girls taught by women were in better condition than those taught by men. This, she concluded, should persuade educators to open seminaries for female teachers. Their graduates would surely improve the quality of schools. Besides, Frommichen wrote, female teachers would be more economical to employ because they were without families to support. Most important, however, seminaries for female teachers would be a godsend for

> poor females [who] frequently, after the death of a father or guardian or husband [are] left to a life of affliction, without shelter or support, and consider themselves happy, if they can eat the bread of tears and dependence, at the table of some prosperous relation; or serve as domestics, while they are young, and look forward to a helpless age.[5]

Schoolteaching by women was a winning proposition for everyone involved—the teacher, the children, the community.

Frommichen's case for teacher seminaries for women was strong. The seminaries would attract a previously untapped reservoir of good teacher prospects; they would lessen the financial burden of the taxpayers supporting the common schools and, by reducing poverty and dependence among single women, would relieve the demands on private charity and public welfare. For women to be schoolteachers was preferable to being seamstresses or milliners. Teachers of the common schools, Frommichen wrote, need not be learned. Their job was "to render others dutiful, and to communicate instruction."[6] That task required skills equally necessary for marriage and motherhood, skills the women would learn from the example of the seminary's superintending housemother, from their instructors, and in practice school.

Reflecting a thoroughly middle-class outlook on the duties and status of women, Frommichen advised would-be teachers to draw on and improve their knowledge of a housewife's duty in the kitchen, the nursery, and the garden while they were studying the elementary school curriculum. It would be preferable, Frommichen thought, if future teachers were to come "from the middle ranks of life."[7] Lower-class girls, she wrote, were too often awkward and ignorant and, besides, they were far better able than their middle-class sisters to take care of themselves with physical labor. Middle-class girls should remember that it was not degrading to teach children in a common school: "It is more honorable to be the independent teacher of a village school than to be the housekeeper in a nobleman's mansion, or the domestic or humble companion of an elevated, and often sickly, proud and peevish woman."[8] Teaching the children of the poor and degraded brought gratitude and honor to any woman who devoted her life to that task.

Woodbridge introduced and commented on the article with enthusiasm. While he thought the references to the class position of women teachers needed to be modified to fit American conditions, he emphasized the importance of the common school teacher to Church and state, the necessity of parents to respect and support teachers, and the particular fitness of women for teaching. He was persuaded, he wrote, that "there is something in the *maternal spirit,* the *untiring patience,* which are characteristic of the sex, that qualifies them peculiarly for the instruction of children." Teaching, he added,

> presents one means of providing a respectable and useful occupation for the great number of females who, even in our country, are dragging out a wretched existence, or [are] driven to the practice of crime by the want of adequate compensation, and often for want of employment.[9]

The time seemed ripe for the idea that women might take on honorably and cheaply and with great benefit to the community a function carried out in the past with little distinction by men.

M. Cousin's Report

The most comprehensive and, judging by its separate publication in book form in New York in 1835, the most widely read account of teacher education abroad was Victor Cousin's report on Prussia's public schools.[10] In 1831 Cousin, then a professor of philosophy at the University of Paris, had been commissioned by the count of Montalivet, France's minister of Public Instruction and Ecclesiastical Affairs, to study the schools of Prussia and other German states. For nearly two weeks Cousin travelled from Paris to Berlin via Frankfurt, Weimar, and Leipzig. On the way he briefly visited elementary and secondary schools, the teacher seminary in Weimar, and the University of Jena. Once in the Prussian capital he stayed four weeks. He was well received by Baron von Altenstein, Montalivet's Prussian counterpart, and spent most of his time reading ordinances, reports, and correspondence in the baron's ministry as well as visiting schools in Berlin and Potsdam. On his return he travelled through Halle, Bonn, Cologne, and Aachen.[11]

As becomes apparent when one follows Cousin's route and his activities in Berlin, his personal acquaintance with conditions in Prussia's schools was heavily influenced by a view from the top of the administrative hierarchy and by his visits to several universities and large city schools. This is of some moment for a better understanding of his report, in which, as will soon become apparent, he went to great lengths to praise the preparation of teachers for the rural schools. He learned about these schools primarily from studying office files; his direct acquaintance with a seminary appears to have been limited to those in Weimar and Potsdam. The latter, however, was a relatively large and prominent establishment which trained teachers mainly for city schools.[12] It is doubtful that he could have learned much from it about the preparation of Prussian country schoolmasters.

Reading Cousin's report, one is struck by the evident approval with which he describes the paternally protective spirit that pervaded the administration of Prussia's teacher seminaries. He wrote glowingly of the requirements that schoolmasters be pious and discreet and unshakably loyal to the state. Given the European system of established churches, Prussia's teacher seminaries were under the sponsorship of either the Protestant or Catholic church, or they were jointly administered. They were located in towns of moderate size "to preserve the pupils from dissipation, allurements, and habits of a kind of life which does not accord with their future condition." They were usually placed in close vicinity to schools for paupers and orphans to insure a ready supply of candidates.[13]

Future elementary teachers were evidently not expected to come from well-to-do and middle-class homes. "Any man of mature age, of irreproachable morals and sincere piety," Cousin quoted a Prussian law of 1819, "who understands the duties of the office he aspires to fill, and gives satisfactory proofs that he does, is fit for the post of public teacher."[14] To be a foreigner or a woman was not an obstacle, although in 1825 schoolmistresses made up only 3.1 percent of Prussia's elementary school teachers.[15] Cousin did not tell us how many schoolteachers of foreign citizenship kept school in Prussia. All through the report his references to women teachers are perfunctory at best and indicate that schoolmistresses did not play any significant role in Prussian thinking on education.

Cousin was much taken with what he had read in Berlin about the seminaries in small, rural towns. Though he gave us no evidence of direct personal acquaintance with them, he let us know that in these small establishments academic requirements were of little moment for teachers and students alike. Religion was the subject of primary importance, outranking the other fields of German, arithmetic and geometry, drawing, natural philosophy and history, geography, and history. Cousin quoted with obvious approval this excerpt from the director's report of a Catholic seminary: "Religious instruction is placed at the head of all other parts of education; its object is to implant in the seminaries such a moral and religious spirit as ought to pervade the popular schools."[16]

In Protestant seminaries things were not different. The director of the Potsdam seminary, a Protestant clergyman himself, was instructed by the government ministry to be for his school "all that a rational and pious father of a family is to his household, . . . the kind friend and colleague of all the pupils and masters who are animated with a true feeling of their duties; . . . the severe and inflexible ruler of those who refuse to listen to the voice of reason and of religion."[17] The director reported in 1826 that his students must "be able to explain the articles of faith and the most important duties as laid down in the catechism," and must know by heart Bible chapters and hymns.[18]

Farm boys confined to a school required, it seems, a good deal of corrective physical exercise. The Prussian education ministry, however, strongly opposed any systematic study of physical education. Remembering only too well that physical exercise and gymnastics had been a favorite pastime of revolutionary student clubs during the era of the Wars of Liberation, the ministry drew back. Such exercise, it stated in a circular of 1826, was "wholly contrary . . . to the destination of the students, to the station and character of the masters and teachers. . . ." Yet, the pronouncement continued, physical training *was* necessary for the teachers' health, their deportment and good carriage, and their professional expertise. Because teachers of youths were to set an example "of a masculine and sustained activity," they had to avoid "an air of retirement and grandeur incompatible with the position of a country schoolmaster. . . ."[19] His health and the example he was to set for his students and his village should make the teacher determined to overcome the temptations of inactivity.

It seems strange that in reviewing the plans and curricula of these seminaries Cousin found relatively little to report on instruction in pedagogy proper. There are references to methods and didactics and the practice schools. Yet over and over again, the discussion reverts to discipline and moral instruction as the heart of a sound pedagogy. Thus, as Cousin pointed out without comment, the encouragement of singing and music in the seminaries was coupled with strictures against the profane use of this art. Music was not to be regarded "as a course of mere amusement" or to be displayed "in public concerts, which, though innocent, are of a light character." It was to be performed publicly "in church-music alone."[20]

Just how important the concern with physical and moral discipline was for the Prussian authorities and Cousin can be seen from Cousin's quoting with evident approval this statement of one of the Prussian seminary directors:

> We have abundant proof that the well-being of an individual, like that of a people, is nowise secured by extraordinary intellectual power or very refined civilization. The true happiness of an individual, as of a people, is founded on strict morality, self-government, humility, and moderation; on the willing performance of all duties to God, his superiors, and his neighbors. A religious and moral education is consequently the first want of a people.[21]

The first requirements for a candidate for a teaching position were not superior upbringing, intellect, or bodily agility, but a pure heart and an upright character.

It becomes evident, too, that as the bulk of Cousin's report on elementary teaching concerns schools and teachers in farming villages and small towns, Cousin found the religious-moral heart of the entire Prussian approach to teacher education embodied in the directions issued by the Berlin ministry for these small seminaries for rural schools. He called the discipline enforced in the smaller schools "somewhat monastic and military," but he found it appropriate and necessary for "young men taken from the lowest classes and not yet divested of a certain coarseness. . . ."[22] "Never," he wrote,

> can there be veneration enough for these humble labourers in the field of public instruction who . . . seek obscurity rather than fame; who devote themselves to the service of poverty . . . and who impose restraints on every personal desire and feeling, while others are excited by all the stimulants of competition.[23]

The small, rural seminary, substandard by anyone's definition of academic and institutional adequacy, but above all competition in its moral and spiritual tone, was Cousin's prime exhibit for the superiority of the German system of teacher education.

Cousin was so taken by these paragons of moral excellence that he included the entire set of regulations for two of these seminaries in his report. Part of one of them reads:

1. This school is specially designed for poor young men who intend to become country schoolmasters, and who may, in case of need, gain a part of their subsistence by the labour of their hands.
2. Nothing is taught here but those things necessary for small and poor country parishes, which require schoolmasters who are Christians and useful men, and can afford them but a very slender recompense for their toils.
3. This school is intended to be a *Christian school,* founded in the spirit of the Gospel. It aspires only to resemble a village household of the simplest kind, and to unite all its members into one family. To this end, all the pupils inhabit the same house, and eat at the same table with the masters.
4. The young men who will be admitted in preference, are such as are born and bred in the country; who know the elements of what ought to be taught in a good country school; who have a sound straightforward understanding, and a kindly cheerful temper. If, withal, they know any handicraft, or understand gardening, they will find opportunities for practice and improvement in it in odd hours.[24]

In other sections of the document it was reiterated that to teach "the humblest peasant . . . to think . . . does not mean to make him learned. . . . The grossness of mind and the obstinate prejudices to which uneducated husbandmen are prone" could be combatted in other ways. Singing and horticulture served that purpose, the one "by ennobling and animating the public worship of God and the general course of country life," the other "by providing the pupils with an agreeable recreation, and, at the same time, a useful occupation. . . ."[25] Although Cousin recognized that the larger seminaries looked beyond the boundaries of village life, he did not hide his sympathy and admiration for the smaller ones which, to him, symbolized the spirit of Prussian common school education.

The Ambiguities of Prussian Reforms

By the mid-1830s the Massachusetts Whigs had had several opportunities to learn about German schools and teachers through occasional reports of German teachers, American visitors, and Victor Cousin's lengthy account. They believed themselves to be well informed about the schools and teacher seminaries of Prussia. They tended to think that the similarities of the decentralized rural district schools of Massachusetts to the small village schools of Prussia recommended the small seminaries of Prussia as likely solutions to the lack of competent teachers in Massachusetts. Cities like Boston might get along reasonably well with their more differentiated systems of primary, grammar, and high schools, and their distinctions between masters of grammar and high schools and teachers of the primary schools. But the Massachusetts Whigs were concerned with the rural schools. In his Thanksgiving sermon of 1835 Charles Brooks spoke to the lack of teachers in the rural areas. That was the problem that cried most urgently for reform, and here Victor Cousin seemed to have something to contribute.

But how well informed were the Massachusetts Whigs about the public schools of Prussia? Did they really understand the Prussian system in its historical and social setting? Did they have any idea how trustworthy their reporters were? Had those who had come from abroad been immersed long enough in Prussian homes and schools, villages and cities, offices and workplaces to appreciate the wider social context of their foreign experience? Was a report such as Cousin's, written for his superiors in the French government, an adequate means of communication with an American audience? And, the most perplexing question of them all: Did it ever occur to the Massachusetts Whigs to wonder whether it was at all plausible that the school system of one of Europe's traditional monarchies could provide a model for a democratic people who prided themselves on their republican constitution?

Cousin's book certainly was the most substantial, the most widely read, and the most influential account of Prussia's schools available in Europe as well as in the United States. But was it reliable? How well did it describe the actual situation of Prussia's schools and teachers during the early years of the Vormärz, the period that stretched from the onset of Metternich's restoration in 1819 to the March revolution of 1848? Cousin himself was aware that people might question the wisdom of trying to adopt the policies of other countries and thus be skeptical of his report. Yet he affirmed the legitimacy of learning from foreign examples and assured the Count de Montalivet that "the true greatness of a people does not consist in borrowing nothing from others, but in borrowing from all whatever is good, and in perfecting whatever it appropriates."[26] But would Americans be able to select wisely and discard those aspects that would not fit their conditions?

The question that needs to be raised first, however, is whether Cousin had in fact been in a position to interpret circumspectly what he was shown. Had he perceived the full complexity of the Prussian situation, or had he accepted too eagerly all those manifestations of a progressive and modern educational system that corresponded to his own liberal predilections? Had he reported accurately on the Prussian schools and their provisions for teacher training? Had he understood the conflicting currents in political and educational thought that beset the Altenstein ministry responsible for the administration of Prussia's educational, cultural, and religious affairs? Had he realized, as Thomas Nipperdey expressed it so well, that the relationship of school and state in Prussia was characterized by ambivalence, a simultaneity of development and restriction, and a slowing-down of educational reconstruction through administrative, ecclesiastical, and pedagogical resistance?[27]

In 1831, the year of Cousin's visit to Berlin, the light of Prussia's great educational reforms following the liberation from Napoleonic occupation had already grown dim. Karl von Altenstein, the official responsible for education in the cabinet of Friedrich Wilhelm III, had informed his monarch in July that to his great joy and relief Cousin had told him that France had begun to combat threats to her internal security by strengthening churches and schools. Thus, Altenstein continued, he had felt justified in his conversations with Cousin to tell him at length of the great importance he placed on bringing Prussia's Catholic schools into closer harmony with her Protestant schools and, above all, of the attention he paid to the election of bishops. By giving these Church dignitaries free hand in confessional matters, Altenstein had confided in Cousin, he obliged them all the more to support governmental policies.[28] The tone and message of Altenstein's letter, with its self-congratulatory pleasure in having co-opted the bishops into carrying out the government's wishes, make clear that Altenstein wanted to let his monarch know that Prussia's policy of co-optation of and cooperation with the churches under government direction had found the applause of his foreign visitor.

Still, the original impetus for Altenstein's policies had come from the neo-humanism of Wilhelm von Humboldt and the nationalism of Johann Gottlieb Fichte. Appointed by the king in 1809 to initiate Prussia's recovery from French occupation by a restructuring of the country's schools, Humboldt had sketched out a three-tiered system of elementary schools (*Volks-*

schulen), city schools (*Bürgerschulen*) and higher Latin schools (*Gymnasia*), and universities.[29] These institutions were to be common schools, that is—similar to what Thomas Jefferson had proposed for Virginia—they were to be open to all students who possessed the academic qualifications to succeed in them. Humboldt's insistence on offering the same general education for all, regardless of the students' later occupations, was echoed by Fichte. Fichte called for the country's elementary schools to create among their students a national consciousness and to replace drill and memorization with the humane and progressive methods of the Swiss educator Johann Heinrich Pestalozzi.

In the early days of the reforms it looked as though a liberal education for all children of Prussia and a progressive, humane spirit in its schools were about to become reality. The country's reformers and educators sent several young teachers to Ifferten, Pestalozzi's school, instructing them to look beyond methods, doctrines, and skills to the spirit that lay behind the outward appearances of Pestalozzi's pedagogy. They hoped that teaching in all grades of schools—but particularly so in the elementary schools—could be transformed from a routine drudgery carried out by retired noncommissioned soldiers and ignorant, handicapped, and ill-tempered incompetents, to a professional, life-long commitment of well-educated pedagogues.[30]

It is easy, particularly in retrospect, to see that the plans of the Prussian reformers were plagued with internal contradictions. How were they to harmonize their goals for the free development of each individual's gifts and abilities with their demands that all children were to grow up as loyal citizens of Prussia committed to the ideals of German nationalism? How were they to succeed in educating an entire new generation of schoolteachers in the principles and practices of Pestalozzian pedagogy and humanistic philosophy when they continued to insist that, despite their belief in a common general education for all, they should train the teachers of elementary and city schools in special seminaries separate from the universities in which the teachers of the *Gymnasia* received their education?

One will not understand these contradictions until one realizes the combination of a pedagogical progressivism with a social conservatism and the place of religion in their social and political philosophy that characterized the Prussian ruling elite. Prussia's reformers liked to portray their progressivism as a manifestation of Christian love. In their endorsement of Pestalozzian pedagogy it appeared as the love of a father for his children. It was, thus, a benevolent paternalism that never questioned the basic rightness and justice of social and economic arrangements. Social inequalities as well as injustice and poverty were to be borne patiently as part of God's order. People should rest in the assurance that government existed to minimize the effect of injustice. But protest and rebellion were never justified. In Prussia the established state religion of evangelical Protestantism was to provide the spiritual legitimation of the government and its conservative administrators. The public schools, then, in close alliance with the established Church existed to maintain order and protect the state against subversion.

Altenstein's remarks of 1831 already had shown to what degree the government relied on the support of the churches and how it would insist on religious instruction in the schools to preserve that support. Altenstein and his colleagues in the ministry insisted on the teaching of religion and the practice of daily prayer and worship in school. For Protestants they recommended joint communion services for teachers and students, and they asked the Catholic bishops to provide for similar common services for their communicants. They implored teachers to remember their position as exemplars and to accept faithfully the performance of religious duties as part of their responsibilities. Religion, wrote Johann Wilhelm Süvern, one of the more liberal members of Altenstein's office, was an important means to teach discipline. Character education had as its object not only the strengthening of a moral sense in children but also the implanting of loyalty to king and state, of unswerving obedience to law and respect for order, and of a growing spirit of love of country.[31]

Altenstein was convinced that for religion to perform its stabilizing function in the schools, it had to be taught confessionally. Thus he recommended to his king early in 1820 that there should be no further authorizations for confessionally mixed schools. Whenever Jewish, Catholic, and Protestant children were given joint religious instruction, the resulting compromises led to a rational religion of the mind, a form of Deism that left no room for the emotions or for revealed religion. Parents and teachers alike would become distrustful, and religion would not be taken with becoming seriousness. Suspicions, strife, and disunity would be the result.[32] Several years later Süvern recommended to the theological faculty of the University of Berlin that it send its best students for a period of years as instructors into the teacher training seminaries. Having had such exposure to pedagogy, the future country ministers would be in an excellent position to serve as superintendents and inspectors of the rural schools.[33]

Reform Encounters Reaction

As conservative in their social views and committed to organized religion as Prussia's educational statesmen had been at the outset of the reform era, they were far more progressive then than they came to be in the wake of the reaction of 1819. In that year in which, with the Carlsbad decrees, the reactionary policies of Metternich began to hold sway over most of continental Europe, Johann Wilhelm Süvern had drafted a comprehensive education bill. In its insistence on general education for all citizens of the nation in elementary and city schools and in the *Gymnasia,* the bill breathed the spirit of Humboldt's

neo-humanism. None of the three schools was to offer vocationally specialized training or to take account of regional differences in its general orientation. Separate schools were recommended only for girls, though in them, too,
the general liberal education should prevail. Differences, however, were permitted on religious grounds. Schools could be either Protestant or Catholic,
yet all of them were required to make provision for the religious instruction of
the minority faith. None was allowed to seek the conversion of children of the
other confession, and all of them were asked to share the spirit appropriate to
a Christian state, "piety and the true fear of God."[34]

Conservative as this document may appear to modern eyes, it provoked
objections to the idea of a general education for all students. One of Süvern's
colleagues, Ludolf von Beckedorff, argued that the bill presupposed a gov-
ernment-imposed demand for a uniform education of all citizens that was
intended to bring about a sameness of outlook and abilities among Prussia's
citizens. Yet, Beckedorff insisted, men are by nature unequal, and their inequality and consequent need for mutual assistance makes for the bonds that
hold society together. Given the impossibility of everyone experiencing the
same desires and becoming alike, a general and common education, designed
toward that end, could only make for discontent, mutual blame, and inces-
sant restlessness and disquietude.

> Educate people to become Christians [wrote Beckedorff] and you will
> introduce true equality on earth; not the equality of claims, of limitless
> striving, of selfish wants and of arbitrariness, but the equality of love, of
> mutual care, of devotion and of unshakable confidence in the all-com-
> pensating justice of God.[35]

Natural inequality versus artificial equality—these were the terms in which
conservatives like Beckedorff phrased the issue. His words also illustrate how
the precepts of a state religion could be put to use to choke off progressive
reforms.

Beckedorff could claim that his views only continued the educational
traditions of pietistic Protestantism which had governed Prussian school
practice since the seventeenth century. Friedrich Wilhelm III had decreed in
1799 that teachers should be taught to convey to youths the *prima principia
Christianismi* and to keep science out of the elementary curriculum.[36] Beckedorff agreed with this because he thought that neither elementary teachers
nor students could possibly be expected to handle as many fields as Süvern
thought made up a general education. The attempt would result in a village
population half educated and superficially knowledgeable. Members of the
lower classes would be arrogant and demanding, unwilling to carry out any
longer the necessary menial work of society, and, as a result, thoroughly dis-
satisfied with their lot.[37]

Regarding school practice Beckedorff complained of the failure of many educators to distinguish clearly between rural and city schools. According to Beckedorff, the rural schools were elementary schools designed to teach only the basics of literacy and numeracy without encouraging their students to leave their communities or their occupations. The city schools were intended, in Humboldt's words, to teach students not only to learn but also to learn how to learn.[38] Because Beckedorff believed that the education of teachers for the country schools was the seminaries' primary task, he protested the frequent attempts of some seminary directors to offer advanced subjects like algebra, geometry, surveying, physics, psychology, and mineralogy. These should be left, Beckedorff held, to the few seminaries training teachers for city schools.

Above all, wrote Beckedorff, teachers and teacher educators should forswear the principles of Pestalozzian pedagogy. That pedagogy was designed only to stimulate the mental powers to lively activity.

> It did not intend to communicate knowledge but to develop it out of the human soul itself. It insisted that the student was to discover and invent all truths for himself. It was unwilling to accept authority, and, instead, elevated the individual judgment as the touchstone for the correctness of each doctrine. Such pedagogy [Beckedorff concluded] will educate only sophists and doubters and, while it maintains that it fosters independence, will create undisciplined views and arbitrariness of character.[39]

The specter of an overeducated peasantry, made rebellious and unmindful of their "proper place in life" by a radical Pestalozzianism, haunted officials like Beckedorff. His great antagonist, Süvern, however, saw things differently. When in 1814 Süvern visited a teacher training course in Düsseldorf—a course, we can be sure, not taught by a Pestalozzian—he commented: "It's nothing but mechanical memory and recitation work."[40]

By 1822 Beckedorff's views appear to have gained the upper hand. A royal edict of June 15 confirms that elementary school teachers were sufficiently trained if they were able to teach reading, writing, arithmetic, and religion. Subjects like grammar, geography—at least insofar as they concerned foreign countries—political and natural history, science, and drawing were unnecessary, wrote Friedrich Wilhelm III.[41] Altenstein in turn notified all provincial school offices, urging them to stress "not many and diverse subjects, but thorough knowledge of what is necessary and indispensable," and, of course, the basis of all true education: piety, fear of God, and Christian humility.[42]

Yet Beckedorff's victory was not complete. Although Altenstein, Beckedorff's superior, felt it necessary to assure the king of his agreement with the royal views, he went on to specify the knowledge and abilities he thought it necessary for peasant children to acquire. In what sounds like the language of Pestalozzi he wrote of the skills to express "their thoughts and judgment correctly, clearly, and without reservations; to read fluently, understandably and thoughtfully; to write legibly and according to all the rules; to carry out in their minds the calculations necessary in their households, and to sing hymns well." Altenstein also thought the future peasant should know enough science to keep him from error and superstition and enough history and geography to be well informed about his own country, provided, of course, "that he receive this knowledge not as useless information feeding his conceit, but with constant reference to his station and work. . . ."[43] The unease and ambivalence of the conscientious pedagogue serving as loyal official of his king is only too apparent.

Yet the conflict between those who wanted to train elementary teachers at a minimum level and those who aspired to educate them in the spirit of Humboldt and Pestalozzi would not die. The 1826 regulations of the Protestant seminary Neuwied in Prussia's Rhine Province admonished the instructors not to teach their students as they expected their students to teach their own pupils later on, but in a way commensurate with their adult capabilities and maturity. There should be no rote learning and training, but plenty of stimulating, thoughtful discussion. This would enable the would-be teachers on their own to adapt their teaching to the level of their future pupils.[44] Not long thereafter the Altenstein ministry received a pained message from the director of the seminary in Königsberg, in Prussia's eastern province. His students, the director wrote, were to be examined in from 20 to 24 subjects. The result was that those who passed emerged as insufferably vain and conceited. This was not what was wanted for future village schoolmasters! Could not something be done about that?[45]

By 1829 we encounter a complaint of a different nature. It came from Adolph Diesterweg, a known progressive, then director of the Rhine Province seminary at Moers. He had attended examinations at the Catholic teacher seminary at Trier and had been appalled by the students' ignorance of basics, by the awkwardness and listlessness of their expressions, and, above all, by the examiner's ignorance of current pedagogy and his attitude that it was superfluous and harmful. The examiner, wrote Diesterweg, made demands of the students that only the worst pupils of an old-fashioned Latin school would have been able to satisfy. He was probably an expert in his field, Diesterweg added, but in the wrong spot as educator in a teacher seminary.[46] Examples of such divergent initiatives and reactions concerning pedagogy could be multiplied easily. There was no unanimity among the leaders of Prussian teacher education.

Yet on questions of the social and political significance and function of the elementary schools and their teachers the leading officials in the Altenstein ministry found it easier to agree. Partly this was due to their ingrained Whiggish attitude of combining educational progressivism with a social conservatism of noblesse oblige and to the conciliatory approach of Altenstein himself. It also stemmed partly from their determination to continue pursuing an educational renaissance during an era of political reaction.[47] Throughout it all, these German officials remained ardent nationalists. They argued, for example, that the elementary schools in Prussia's border areas were to be used as means for Prussianizing or Germanizing an ethnically different population. Thus we learn from official instructions sent from Berlin to Cologne that teacher seminaries were to be used along the Belgian border to propagate German language and culture among the Walloons. Authorities in Aachen advised school officials in Koblenz that the seminaries must "consecrate" Walloon teacher candidates for the "holy sanctum of German pedagogy."[48] There was, unfortunately, no indication whether this sanctum included the views of Pestalozzi.

There was agreement, too, on the banning of gymnastics in the schools and seminaries. In the eyes of Prussian conservatives this activity had been tainted because of its association with the Turners, who had been charged with the promotion of liberal-radical attacks against constituted authority, first as patriots against the French occupiers and now as subversives against the Prussian government. In May of 1820 Altenstein received a memorandum which charged the Turners with promoting freedom and republican equality through a mixing of all social classes in their exercises and through the use of identical costumes by all participants. They were held to be arrogant because they claimed to be more effective than the government in working for the future welfare of Prussia and in being contemptuous toward non-Turners. They also were attacked for promoting travel as a means toward fostering German unity, and they were held to be dangerous because of their romanticism, their discontent with the existing order, and their youthful conceits. Therefore, the author concluded, gymnastics was "incompatible with the principles of our state." The memorandum bears an annotation by Süvern, who remarked dryly that it was "a pleasant habit of some to blame what the government had already blamed and rejected and to propose as a vast improvement what it had ordered long ago."[49]

Nonetheless, the issue remained troublesome for many years because it was difficult to distinguish between gymnastics as a subversive activity and as useful, healthy, and even necessary physical exercise. Altenstein's ministry felt continually constrained to walk a narrow path, defending itself against the charge of tolerating subversion and responding to accusations that it contributed to ill physical and mental health of its teacher candidates. Thus we find the ministry advising the provincial authorities in Koblenz in 1827 to shun any *turnen* in schools and yet to be mindful of students "who, for the most part, come from the country, . . . are used to fresh air" and, "unused to mental exertion," will soon be disadvantaged if they are forced to accustom themselves to an almost completely sedentary way of life."[50] As Cousin had correctly observed, the seminaries were therefore urged somehow to provide for physical activity without, however, succumbing to the lure of *turnen.*

The clearest examples of governmental unanimity in prescribing curricular concerns stem from incidents of direct political involvement of teachers. The best way to avoid conflict with governmental authority, therefore, was for the schools to shun the topic altogether. This becomes particularly clear in the city schools and *Gymnasia* where more of the older and more advanced students were being taught. Let the students delve into classical antiquity, the authorities said, where honorable and "safe" examples of virtuous political conduct can be found in great profusion. This was the reply to a *Gymnasium* teacher in Minden, Westphalia, who in 1830 asked for permission to print a speech he had given publicly at a school festival. The request was denied because, the provincial school authorities in Münster wrote, the teacher had ignored "the beautiful privilege of schools to be relatively free of the happy or sorrowful events in the lives of states and people, where . . . teachers and students may wander without prejudice on the becalmed heights of classical antiquity." A teacher should know that the thoughts of young people were not to be turned to an area "in which only men of education, experience, and power" were supposed to move. The teacher's obvious ignorance of such a precept showed his pedagogical ineptitude in endangering his students' youthful innocence and freshness. Altenstein in Berlin subsequently used this occasion to remind all Prussian school authorities to prevent the teaching of current events.[51]

Victor Cousin: A Second Look

While in his book Cousin quite faithfully reflected the cautious attitude of the Prussian educational administrators, he failed to look beneath the surface of what was shown to him and to probe critically into the reasons and motivations behind the policies he described. We do not know whether on his German visit Cousin had not recognized the full complexity and ambiguity of the Prussian situation or, whether, for reasons of his own, he decided not to report it fully. He had accepted all too eagerly those manifestations of a progressive and modern educational system that corresponded to his own Pestalozzian predilections. There is in his pages no mention of the battle that was being waged by conservative critics like Beckedorff with the supporters of the neo-humanist legacy of Wilhelm von Humboldt and of the progressive pedagogy in the tradition of Pestalozzi.

There can be little doubt, however, that Cousin felt sympathy and admiration for Karl von Altenstein and was willing, even eager, to overlook the Prussian official's shortcomings. Cousin agreed fully with Altenstein's cautious and benevolent endorsement of pedagogical progressivism, and he approved of Altenstein's reliance on the authority of the established Church as a stabilizing factor in public education. But if he realized it, he never acknowledged that Altenstein had to pursue a precarious balancing act between his own liberal sympathies and the reactionary policies promoted by the Crown.

Cousin never made plain for his readers that the basic problem for Prussia's educational policy planners had been to bring about the country's modernization through education without at the same time weakening the existing state and social order. He also reported nothing of the social and professional dissatisfaction and plain poverty that beset the German schoolmasters. One is left to ask whether his own enthusiasm for liberal pedagogical philosophies as he discovered them in Süvern's bill blinded him toward the reactionary tendencies of the Prussian state that never permitted the bill to become law.

Cousin's report was less an objective account of Prussian schools and education than the projection of a French philosopher's ideal version of a school system intended to wed progress and stability. And it was this ideal combination of a nation's progress under responsible conservative guidance that appealed to the American educational reformers and assured the enthusiastic reception Cousin's report received in the United States.

The American reformers failed to note just how Cousin had adopted his philosophy of the *"juste milieu"*—the golden mean—to the school situation in Prussia and in France. Cousin had sought to reconcile the principles of the French Revolution with the traditional norms of the ancient regime. He had rejected the empiricism and materialism of the enlightenment as an evil philosophy and had sought to replace them with a belief in the existence of God, free will, and objective standards of good and evil.[52] These principles, he thought, would insure a stable and orderly society while yet permitting individual enterprise and initiative.

Although the Massachusetts Whigs approved all that, their own brand of New World Whiggery with its faith in the manifest destiny of an expansionist public school made it difficult for them to perceive the restrictive and discriminatory aspects of Cousin's views. Whether in France or in Prussia, for Cousin the stability of society and state in the hand of constituted authority was always a chief aim. He solved the apparent contradictions between the demands for economic development and preservation of the social status quo, between individual mobility and social stability, by drawing a clear distinction between schools for city dwellers and schools for a rural population. For Cousin the dividing line between city and country became a line dividing progress and tradition as well as social classes.

Cousin had noticed and endorsed this distinction in Prussia. There the difference between the extreme paternalistic attitude taken by the authorities toward the rural population and their quite ambitious academic programs for the urban common and normal schools had made the greatest impression on Cousin. It encouraged him after his return to France to advocate a new advanced primary school, a school type that was in fact introduced in the so-called Guizot law of 1833. The law distinguished between regular primary schools for the children of the poor and of semiskilled and unskilled workers and advanced primary schools for the children of artisans, clerks, and small shop owners.[53] It was no accident that the advanced primary schools were located in the cities.

For Cousin the great attractiveness of the advanced primary schools was twofold. These schools opened avenues of advancement for gifted children of the *petite bourgeoisie*, a class too advanced and potentially productive to have their children restrained to attend the rural and pauper elementary schools for the proletariat and peasantry, yet not prosperous and cultivated enough to encourage their young people to apply for entrance to the Latin secondary schools. But even more important, the advanced elementary schools would prevent an overcrowding of the *collèges*, or municipal high schools, with large numbers of children of the *petite bourgeoisie*.[54]

What held true for the advanced primary school students held true in like manner for their teachers. The instructors for the advanced primary schools were to be more highly trained than their colleagues in the regular primary schools. From them could be drawn a corps of elementary school administrators and inspectors as well as normal school instructors and directors. At the same time, these better-trained teachers were to remain firmly in the world of elementary schooling. They lacked the university training and certification necessary for teaching in the secondary schools. Thus the structure of France's elementary education could draw more precisely and build more firmly the dividing wall between the *petite* and the *haute bourgeoisie*.[55]

In his promotion of these innovations Cousin not only demonstrated his approval of Altenstein's efforts to modernize Prussian education while keeping to a minimum any disturbance of the inherited social stratification. He also reflected the conventional views of the European bourgeois middle class, which felt threatened above all by large numbers of people educated beyond society's ability to employ them according to their educational attainments. Unrealistic aspirations and unmet expectations, so it was said, created nothing but social dissatisfaction and unrest. The advanced primary schools would provide a near-perfect solution. They would reward the ambitions of the gifted poor, whether as students or as teachers, while they protected the new bourgeoisie of property and intellect from being crowded from below.

Here, then, we get at the heart of the matter: Altenstein and Cousin both had wrestled with the problem of how to provide education for an intermediate population—the *Kleinbürgertum* of Prussia and the *petite bourgeoisie* of France. The Prussian answer had been the urban *Bürgerschule;* the French were to devise the *école élémentaire supérieure,* which Cousin helped to introduce with the Guizot law of 1833. Cousin's report reflected his enthusiasm for the conservative educational philosophies that stressed the training of rural children in the basic skills of literacy and numeracy and emphasized a spirit of God-fearing acceptance of and satisfaction with the status quo. But his report also conveyed his admiration for the quite exacting and demanding curricular requirements of the *Bürgerschulen,* the Prussian city schools, and the seminaries that trained their teachers.

Cousin's enthusiasm, in short, approved and promoted distinctly different educational approaches. One approach was intended by his German mentors for their rural elementary schools, where all that mattered were moral education and basic skills which could safely be assumed to be present in the instruction of schoolmasters trained in rural normal schools. The other approach was designed for the children of an urban lower middle class. Here the Prussian administrators relied on a corps of teachers well trained in city normal schools, skilled in conveying literacy and practical skills, but kept sharply apart from the university-educated secondary school instructors.

An Enlightenment Heritage: Jefferson and Humboldt

The American readers of Cousin's report may be forgiven if their unfamiliarity with European class structure prevented them from seeing the Frenchman's subtle distinctions. Their commitment to a fluid, classless society encouraged them to deny the existence of an intermediate population. Massachusetts Whigs did not recognize a lower middle class. Thus for them Altenstein's and Cousin's two separate approaches were bound to merge, and they saw a picture of efficiently trained teachers bringing educational progress to rural and urban schools alike. Their own faith in the inevitability of the progress of republicanism made it difficult for them to perceive the incongruities inherent in the attempt to develop a system of public schooling and teacher education for a democratic people from models and inspirations that reflected a bourgeois society deeply split among social classes and between country and city.

When American Whigs appreciated Cousin's philosophy of the *"juste milieu,"* they saw in it not much more than what they themselves desired—an accommodation of Jacksonian America's farmers, working people, and immigrants to the leadership of an educated and moral elite. An educational policy that took well-trained teachers into rural and city schools alike would accomplish just that. Their appreciation rested in part on their unfamiliarity with European affairs, but also to a large extent on their own commitment to republicanism. This, they felt, immunized them against any possible corruption by traces of Old World feudalism and monarchism. Their crusade for the common schools, after all, was derived from the public school philosophy of Thomas Jefferson first set forth six decades earlier.[56] In much the same way that Humboldt was to sketch out plans for a national system of education in Prussia, the sage of Monticello had done so for Virginia.[57] Enlightenment philosophers both, Jefferson and Humboldt had combined their optimistic estimates of human potential with a cautious regard for inherited customs and social stability.

For the Massachusetts Whigs, then, their borrowing from Europe was not meant to be a wholesale importation, but an addition to a heritage that was native to the United States. They had begun with the utilitarian liberalism of a Thomas Jefferson and had then added the pedagogical humanitarianism of a Pestalozzi and the neo-humanist philosophy of a Humboldt and a Süvern. The result was an ethical philosophy that, as Daniel Walker Howe wrote of the Harvard Unitarian moral philosophers, enabled the educational theory of Horace Mann and his friends

> to be humanistic, even democratic, and still conservative. . . . Such an education [wrote Howe] offered the ultimate solution to the problems of society: train good men and they would freely make a good society. In this hopeful vision of human destiny, there would be no conflict between individual self-realization and the need for order.[58]

The thought of Jefferson and Humboldt would surface, in much diluted form, to be sure, in the educational ideology of the Massachusetts school reformers.

As one would expect, Jefferson's and Humboldt's plans differed from each other in many details. The distance in the social and political circumstances of Virginia and Prussia and the passage of time between the publication of Jefferson's "Bill for the More General Diffusion of Knowledge" in 1779 and of Humboldt's "Königsberger and Litauischer Schulplan" in 1808 account for that. Jefferson had been an active participant in his country's revolution, conscious of the historical mission taken up by his fellow Virginians in replacing monarchical rule with government by the people. Humboldt was concerned with reform of the Prussian monarchy that had been overwhelmed by the armies of Napoleon and incapacitated for revival by the rigidity of its structures of class and caste. The one, author of the Declaration of Independence, was a true revolutionary; the other, scholar and diplomat, an aristocratic reformer.[59]

The heart of Jefferson's revolutionary ideas for education lay in his insistence on the people as "the only safe depositories" of a country's government. Therefore, he had written, the elementary schools—or ward schools as they were called in Jefferson's Virginia—deserved his countrymen's special attention. In them the people were to receive their whole education, and there they were to be taught chiefly through historical reading. Properly apprised of the past, they would be qualified, wrote Jefferson, "as judges of the actions and designs of men."[60] By contrast, the people's rulers, lawyers in the main, were to be trained as professionals to execute the people's directives. They had to be watched to abide by their written orders, just as judges were not to be allowed to stray from the text of the law into questions of equity. Lawyers and judges, Jefferson emphasized, were not lawgivers, but only the executors of the will of the people.[61] Jefferson's revolution required education for the people and training for the professionals, a turnabout of traditional priorities when the rulers had been educated to govern and the people trained to obey.

Humboldt's reform proposals, though remarkably similar to those of Jefferson, were not spurred by the same revolutionary ideology. Humboldt's concern for the common people sprang from his neo-humanist conviction that all human beings deserved the opportunity to develop their moral sensibilities and intellectual abilities. Nothing but their own strength and means should be permitted to interfere with that aim. Those whose material and intellectual resources gave out along the way would still have received during their school days the same balanced development of their moral and intellectual powers as those who were able to continue.

American Whigs familiar in diluted form with the Enlightenment heritage of Jefferson and the neo-humanist views of Humboldt were nonetheless sure to recognize and respond to ideas that embodied the liberal sentiments espoused earlier by these two men. They would also acknowledge and endorse the socially conservative features contained in their educational proposals. Neither Jefferson nor Humboldt was a social egalitarian. Not only did Jefferson restrict his plan for public education to free whites and exclude slaves, but he also proposed it as a means by which "twenty of the best geniuses will be raked from the rubbish annually. . . ."[62] While he saw to it that the gifted and talented were favored and supported by the state, he showed little consideration for youngsters who lacked academic ability beyond their elementary capacity to read, write, calculate, and participate productively in debates on public issues. He never mentioned the children of slaves.

Humboldt, too, took it for granted that human beings were born into different circumstances of poverty or wealth and showed different abilities. Unlike Jefferson he refused to use public funds to overcome the barriers set to genius by poverty and class. Rather than permit the state to interfere in education, Humboldt was willing to accept the limits set by private means to an individual's schooling.[63] The poor would send their children to free charity schools; those of few means would patronize the less expensive pay schools, and those who could afford it would send their boys to grammar schools.[64] Because, as he proposed, all schools at every level sought the fullest general individual development of their youngsters and shunned specialized training, all students, no matter when they terminated their schooling, would receive a liberal education.

Both men also agreed that great care had to be taken not to permit religious instruction to interfere with the schools' aim of serving the common good. Jefferson, ever suspicious of sectarian interests, wanted to replace the Bible as elementary school text with instruction in history. Because children were not mature enough to understand religious controversies, he demanded the exclusion of any "religious reading, instruction, or exercise . . . inconsistent with the tenets of any religious sect or denomination." Once, however, students had grown up and attained the full use of their reason, they were to subject any view or opinion to its scrutiny. "Your own reason is the only oracle given you by heaven," Jefferson told his nephew Peter Carr, "and you are answerable, not for the rightness, but uprightness of the decision."[65] Religion in the common schools, then, was to be a religion of reason.

Though Humboldt shared Jefferson's distaste for sectarian religion, he nonetheless believed that in the grammar schools confessional religion should be taught to stimulate the pupils' moral sensibilities. As he rejected state interference in education and religion, he wanted to leave the choice of confession to the local schools and their constituents. Their choice could only be for one of the country's accepted confessions. The significance of this confessional instruction lay in its being given to all the students in common. Each and every one, the poorest day-laborer and the most exquisitely educated scholar, wrote Humboldt, will have to be morally attuned in the same manner. Only then can a nation avoid rudeness in the former and sentimentality and awkwardness in the latter.[66]

It is easy to see in the institutional structures projected by Jefferson and Humboldt the basic outlines of the school system described by Cousin and contemplated by the Massachusetts school reformers. Both Jefferson and Humboldt thought of a three-tiered system of elementary and secondary schools and a university. Both envisaged a pyramid with access for everyone at the bottom and a common curriculum until students reached the university.

In the elementary schools considerations for the future occupations of their pupils were unimportant. What mattered was the need to teach basic skills and instill a consciousness of common citizenship and humanity. When Jefferson wrote that the laboring people of Virginia needed the same elementary schools as the learned—the laborers "to qualify them for their pursuits and duties," and the learned "as a foundation for further acquirements"—Humboldt would have agreed. Elementary education, he said, prepares all for future instruction as it enables them "to learn things and to follow a teacher."[67]

However greatly the similarities of the two plans may have impressed the Massachusetts reformers, they would have had to notice also the differences in basic political philosophy. Jefferson spoke to them as a republican committed to the preservation of the republic and its revolution. He saw pupils as future citizens in whose hands the fate of the republic would ultimately rest. His proposed law, he wrote to John Adams in 1813, "would have raised the mass of the people to the high degree of moral respectability necessary to their own safety and to orderly government." Thus educated, he continued, they would have been qualified "to select the veritable aristoi for the trusts of government. . . ."[68] Those who believed like Jefferson would hardly find it possible to accept the class-conscious and class-maintaining features of the educational system described by Cousin.

The progressive features that Humboldt built into his system had nothing or little to do with political knowledge or social mobility, but touched rather on what in America came to be known as character, or moral, education. Humboldt never assumed that the primary task of elementary schooling was the training of students in the exercise of government. Rather, it was to deepen and strengthen knowledge, skills, and qualities of character. Thus educated, he taught, men and women could improve their lives wherever circumstances of birth and ability would place them. Thus, he suggested, it might be possible "to form all peasants and tradesmen into *artists,* i.e. people who love their trade for the sake of their trade, improved it through their own ability and inventiveness, and thereby cultivated their intellectual powers, ennobled their character, and increased their enjoyments."[69] Humboldt took as given and fixed the social positions into which men and women were born. His plan had little room for social mobility. He would find agreement among all those who in Massachusetts distrusted a laboring population of immigrants.

But despite these differences the two men agreed on their insistence that all students, as long as they attended publicly sponsored and regulated schools, should receive their education in common. For Jefferson the need for a common education derived from the nature of democracy: All future citizens were legislators responsible for the commonweal. For Humboldt it stemmed from the common humanity of all and from the nation's need to compensate for, though not overcome, the differences of class, religion, and region. This, he felt, could be achieved best through a general, liberal education shared by all as long as each attended school.

The Meaning of Whiggism

Whether German educational officials like Karl von Altenstein and Johann Wilhelm Süvern and their French interpreter Victor Cousin were faithful to the humanism of Wilhelm von Humboldt, and whether American reformers like Horace Mann and Henry Barnard were committed to the republicanism of Thomas Jefferson, they all held in common what we may call certain Whig principles. While they were firm believers in the necessity and eventual inevitability of progress, they also believed in an established order of society where individual advance was possible only within a set framework of established classes and orders. As "old liberals" they admired revolutions provided they had occurred in the past and could be praised for the political and economic improvements they had brought to the people, but in the "real" world of politics they feared revolutions as harbingers of anarchy.

In their respective societies these men were intellectuals of rank and stature, whose sense of moral elitism and noblesse oblige prompted them to promote the common education of their people. Afraid as they were of revolution and anarchy they sought the support of religion in that enterprise. In Prussia and France the establishment of Church and state required the cooperation of the public schools with the churches and the inclusion of confessional religion in the schools' curriculum; in the United States, where churches had been disestablished, Mann appealed to a nonsectarian Protestantism as a common religious philosophy and urged that the Bible be read in the common schools.

Their promotion of a common education in public schools for all constituted a nineteenth-century equality-of-opportunity doctrine that was meant to permit the sifting out of the gifted and deserving. Whigs did not claim that everyone needed or should be educated in the same way for the same length of time. A common education for all in elementary schools was to be followed for a cultivated elite by an uncommon, selective further education in secondary schools. A philosophy of common schooling could and did go hand in hand with a conservative social philosophy. It did not matter whether the country was Prussia, France, or the United States.

There runs, then, a common Whig sentiment through the writings and utterances of these men. Certainly, they did not agree in every one of their conceptions and beliefs, but their shared attitudes toward education help to make us understand why American Whigs adopted Cousin's report so enthusiastically and without reservations. They did not ask themselves whether Cousin, who wrote as a supporter of Louis Philippe and saw in the bourgeois constitutionalism of that monarch "the signal for a general improvement in opinion and in morals," set a proper example for republican America.[70] Horace Mann approved of Cousin's endorsement of the constitutional monarchy in France as the equivalent of his preference for government by talented gentlemen. He did not wince at Cousin's endorsement of the conservative trend of European restoration policies that saw in an alliance of throne and altar the best guarantee for social stability and political order. In Cousin's substitution of a national secular educational philosophy for the official

Catholicism of the ancient regime, Mann saw a French version of what he so vigorously hailed as the nonsectarianism of the American common school.

American Whigs, and Horace Mann in particular, heard in Cousin only the voice of the progressive reformer, the Pestalozzian, the admirer of Süvern and Humboldt. They admired him as the French philosopher and statesman whose lectures held out hope that a genuine people's system of elementary schools could be established, and who promised that the new normal schools and teacher seminaries would turn schoolkeeping into a respectable profession. For the American Whigs that was promise enough.

3

The Massachusetts Normal School

Academies, Normal Schools, and the Citizen–Teacher

Soon after New Year's Day in 1837 the Massachusetts Whigs began in earnest their campaign for state-supported normal schools. Until then many had felt that it was hopeless to seek their establishment. As long as teachers earned less than mechanics or planned to teach only in the winter, when there was no work available on the farm, their expenses of attending normal school full-time would be prohibitive. Under such circumstances it appeared preferable to follow the example of New York and offer or expand teacher training courses in existing academies. These institutions had always sought to combine academic and practical instruction and had done reasonably well in that task.

As already mentioned in Chapter 1, the Phillip's Academy in Andover, Massachusetts, had added a teacher's seminary as a department in September of 1830. Its assignments were varied: it offered instruction in civil engineering and agriculture besides its three-year course of teacher training. Under the direction of their first principal, the Reverend Samuel R. Hall, the future teachers were introduced to collegiate studies and, with the aid of a preparatory department for boys as a training school, to what was called the theory and practice of teaching.

But even though Hall had come to Andover well prepared—in 1823 he had established his own teacher training school at Concord, Vermont, and, six years later, had attracted considerable attention with the publication of his *Lectures on Schoolkeeping*[1]—his Andover seminary failed five years after Hall had given up the principalship in 1837. The reason given was distressingly familiar: insufficient financing. The reference was to lacking scholarships for the students, but low salaries for graduating schoolmasters played their part as well. In any case, fewer than 100 boys had completed the course in the seminary's existence of 12 years. By 1842 the seminary was merged with the academy's classical department.[2]

Though that failure could not have been foreknown in 1837, there had nonetheless always been room for doubt that teachers could be trained in sufficient numbers in the state's private academies. Others, therefore, had urged that state teacher seminaries or normal schools be opened after the model of Prussia or France. As mentioned earlier, Charles Brooks, who described himself as an advocate for "the Prussian system," had begun a series of public lectures in 1835.[3] He repeated over and over again that there was

> one provision preparatory to a full instruction of our youth, which I deem of vast moment; I mean *a seminary for preparing teachers*. After this is established all other improvements may be easily carried forward; and until it is done we shall I fear advance but in very slow and broken steps.

Brooks appealed for support of his contentions directly to the two European countries most deeply involved in the development of institutions for teacher training.

> In Prussia there are 42 such seminaries, and they are there found to be the very life blood of their school system; a system vastly superior to ours. . . . Victor Cousin, a Peer of France, and the most distinguished scholar in the realm, was sent by Louis Philip [*sic*] to Germany and Prussia purposely to learn the topics of study and the modes of pursuing them in those countries. On his return he published an octavo volume which has been the means of introducing through France the improvements he recommended. If our clergymen will read this volume, and make it the subject of their next Thanksgiving Day's Sermon they will do a positive good to the republic and the church.[4]

The crusade began to gather momentum.

In the meantime in Boston the American Institute of Instruction had taken up the cause.[5] Founded in 1830 by Samuel Hall and others, the institute managed to gather among its members "nearly all major American figures interested in educational reform from 1820 to 1860." During its first seven years from 1830 to 1837, however, it mainly represented the learned and affluent Boston intellectual establishment. Its annual meetings, attended usually by several hundred teachers, were devoted to lectures on educational issues. Through them the institute hoped to inform and sway the public to support educational reforms. By 1837 it concentrated its efforts on two campaigns: to establish a state board of education and to create a number of state normal schools for the education of elementary school teachers.[6]

In January of 1837 the institute complained to the Massachusetts legislature about the lack of competent teachers for the district elementary schools. In their memorial the members repeated the familiar litany. Teachers were "exceedingly incompetent in *many* respects." Young men taught to support

themselves during their studies or because they were waiting for more lucrative employment or because they had failed in everything else. They experi-
mented and learned on the job, disappointed their employers, and failed to be
rehired for the next term. "The time, capacities, and opportunities of thou-
sands of the children are now sacrificed winter after winter to the preparation of
teachers, who, after this enormous sacrifice, are, notwithstanding, often very
wretchedly prepared." The only workable response to that situation, asserted
the institute, was for the state to provide for the education of teachers.[7]

The institute came to that conclusion because even when, as they stated,
"the highest salaries have been offered," teachers could not be found. Men who
had graduated from colleges and academies had not pursued their academic
interests to spend the rest of their lives watching over unruly little boys and
girls. They did not relish the thought that the great majority of available positions were to be found in small, out-of-the-way rural district schools. By 1837
only 400 of the roughly 6,000 Massachusetts teachers taught in city schools.[8]
They were thus understandably wary of the often seasonal nature of employment and of the capriciousness of supervision inherent in the district school
system. College and academy graduates, we are left to infer, sought respect and
deference from their fellow citizens for their educational attainments. Respectable employment in prestigious careers was their goal. That was not to be had
in elementary school teaching, particularly not in rural areas.

The members of the institute recognized their predicament. They might
have preferred college- or academy-educated men as teachers in the common
schools. But they were unavailable. They might have wished that seminaries
or normal schools on the Prussian or French model could begin to train a
corps of full-time professional teachers. But under the circumstances in Massachusetts they knew they had to reach out to those young men who actually
spent time in the classroom, even though that happened only during the
winter, when the lack of farm work made it possible. The problem was how to
improve the preparation of the temporary teachers of the district schools and
perhaps entice these men to remain in the classroom the year round.

To achieve this, the members of the institute not only called for a new
institution—the state-supported normal school—but also challenged their
fellow Massachusetts citizens to acknowledge as unchangeable and accept the
fact that for the present, at least, elementary school teachers were temporary
workers. The institute therefore called for what they termed the citizen-
teacher. This person, they proposed, was a male who, accepting gladly, even
proudly, his seasonal employment as schoolteacher, had learned to make a
virtue out of a necessity:

As in the early history of Rome, the generous husbandman left his plow
to fight the battles of the state, so, in Massachusetts, the free and intel-

ligent citizen will, for a time, quit his business, his workshop, or his farm, to fight, for the sake of his children and the state, a more vital battle against immorality and ignorance.

This was all to the good, the institute's memorial continued. School and society would happily support each other:

So shall the hearts of the fathers be in the schools of their children; so shall the teachers have that knowledge of the world, that acquaintance with men and things, so often wanting in the mere schoolmaster, and yet not among the least essential of his qualifications.

State-supported normal schools would usher in a new age in which the school would find its place at the center of society's concerns and in which the old-fashioned, inadequate schoolmaster would give way to the well-trained citizen-teacher.[9]

Realistic as the members of the institute believed themselves to be in their acceptance of the temporary teacher, they remained oblivious to the by then clearly apparent trend toward increasing numbers of women teachers. By 1837 in Massachusetts women already accounted for more than 60 percent of common school teachers. Their ranks were going to swell until by 1870 the percentage would have increased to 88 (Table 3.1). At the very least, the institute members should have acknowledged the female as well as the male citizen-teacher in their temporary roles. More to the point, they should have recognized—as they eventually did—that women, unlike the only seasonably available men teachers, could teach in summer as well as in winter and thus would increase in some measure the stability of the state's district schools.[10]

The Legislature Acts

As it was, by 1838 the Massachusetts legislature decided to embark on another course when it proceeded to establish the first state normal schools. In response to a private donation of $10,000 by Edmund Dwight for the purpose of "qualifying teachers of the common schools," the legislators appropriated an additional equal sum and placed the total at the disposal of the Massachusetts State Board of Education. The board preferred to open three normal schools in different parts of the state, and called upon localities to shoulder the building and maintenance costs of such institutions for three years. Eventually, the schools were located in Lexington, Barre, and Bridgewater.[11]

The board of education had deliberately placed the normal schools in different parts of the state. These schools were to serve local towns and school districts where they would do the most good. And that meant above all in the

Table 3.1. Percentage of Women Teachers in Massachusetts, 1837–1870

	Number of Women	Total Number of Teachers	Women as Percent of Total
1837	3,591	5,961	60.2
1838	3,825	6,236	61.3
1840	3,928	6,306	62.3
1841	4,112	6,603	62.3
1842	4,281	6,781	63.1
1843	4,301	6,715	64.1
1844	4,581	7,110	64.4
1845	4,700	7,295	64.4
1846	4,997	7,582	65.9
1847	5,238	7,675	68.2
1848	5,510	7,934	69.4
1849	5,737	8,163	70.3
1850	5,985	8,427	71.0
1851	6,262	8,693	72.0
1852	6,456	8,910	72.5
1853	6,838	9,201	74.3
1854	7,063	9,277	76.1
1855	7,333	9,447	77.6
1856	7,602	9,671	78.6
1857	7,925	9,904	80.0
1858	7,992	9,973	80.1
1859	8,009	10,203	78.5
1860	8,403	10,311	81.5
1861	8,638	10,565	81.8
1862	8,742	10,722	81.5
1863	9,071	10,753	84.4
1864	9,340	10,884	85.8
1865	9,625	11,002	87.5
1866	9,885	11,262	87.8
1867	10,158	11,533	88.1
1868	10,513	11,870	88.6
1869	10,621	12,077	87.9
1870	10,793	12,236	88.2

Source: Based on David A. Gould, "Policy and Pedagogues: School Reform and Teacher Professionalization in Massachusetts, 1840–1920," Ph.D. dissertation, Brandeis University, 1977, p. 29.

rural areas, where the need for teachers was greatest. There school enrollments were high—higher than in the cities—and resources low. The smaller towns and rural districts excelled in school enrollments and average daily attendance. But because of the seasonal nature of farm work, they could not hold their schools open for as long a period during the year as was done in the cities. If school reformers wanted to increase the length of the rural school year, they had to persuade parents to allow their sons to attend and they had to find teachers prepared and willing to serve the year round. For the winter sessions in particular they preferred men capable of coping with the discipline problems created by the older male students.[12]

The Lexington school for the northeastern part of the state opened on July 3, 1839, under Cyrus Pierce as principal. It was for women only. At Barre in central Massachusetts, instruction for both men and women began in September with the Reverend Samuel P. Newman as principal. A year later Colonel Nicholas Tillinghast took command over students of both sexes in the state's southeastern corner at Bridgewater. A fourth school was eventually opened at Salem in 1854 with Richard Edwards as principal. Like that in Lexington it accepted women only. The schools' daily affairs were to be administered by a principal who in turn was to be supervised by a board of visitors chosen for each school from among members of the board of education.[13]

In its wisdom the legislature had left the determination of the students' gender to the discretion of the members of the board of education and to local community leaders. At both Lexington and Barre the women applicants were to be at least 16 years of age at entry, but the men at Barre and Salem were to be a year older. To enter, applicants had to pass an examination in the common school subjects and prove their intellectual capability and high moral character. They had to be in good health and were asked to declare their intention to teach in the common schools after they finished their course. Those who committed themselves to do this were exempted from paying tuition.[14] Their course of study was to extend over one year, yet at Barre and Bridgewater students were admitted also for shorter periods of study to enable them to earn their expenses by keeping school.

How were these state normal schools to improve the common schools of rural Massachusetts? Would their directors keep in mind the modest goals outlined by the American Institute of Instruction, or would they strive to equal the fame of the Prussian seminaries and French normal schools? Would they heed the warning of one of their strongest supporters, the Reverend Charles Brooks, who, after having spent several years in recommending the European institutions as models, pointedly asked them to make sure that the monarchy, that is, Prussia, not "bear off the palm from the republic?"[15]

The Massachusetts normal schools were charged with making sure that teachers in the district schools knew well what they were going to teach. They were to review thoroughly the common school subjects of spelling, reading, writing, grammar, geography, and arithmetic. If there was time, they might add more advanced studies such as rhetoric, logic, geometry, bookkeeping, navigation, surveying, history, physiology, mental and natural philosophy, and "the principles of piety and morality common to all sects of Christians."

But normal school professors should stay away from the ancient languages. They should convey to their students some appreciation of child development and the principles and methods of elementary school teaching and classroom management. Practical experience should be provided through a model or experimental school.[16]

It is clear from this list that academic requirements were intentionally kept low. The planners did not take it for granted that graduates of the common schools had fully absorbed the elementary curriculum. At the same time, they were afraid that, unless told to the contrary, the normal school professors would strive to imitate their colleagues in the colleges and try to teach Latin and Greek. As the future would show, that was no idle fear. The desire to become like academy and college teachers, to seek to rid themselves of the elementary classes, and to introduce advanced academic subjects would come to be a constant theme of normal school instructors.

Because it was the duty of Massachusetts teachers to obey the laws of the state, namely to impress upon their students

> the principles of piety, justice, and a sacred regard to truth, love to their country, humanity, and universal benevolence, sobriety, industry and frugality, chastity, moderation and temperance, and those other virtues which are the ornament of human society, and the basis upon which a republican constitution is founded,

the board of education prescribed the Bible as a daily text for normal school students. The Bible, the board emphasized, gave students "the whole scheme of Christianity,—the rule of life and the means of salvation," not some particular tenets of sectarian religion. "The Normal Schools are not Theological Seminaries," the board emphasized, "and disputed questions of polemical or dogmatical theology will find no place in their exercises or instructions." Obviously, the board took it for granted that Protestant Christianity was the common creed of Massachusetts' citizens.[17]

The Battle over School Reform

By the winter of 1839/1840 storm clouds appeared to threaten the Massachusetts Board of Education and the normal schools it had created. In the context of the state's politics the largely urban Whigs appeared as forward-looking reformers who were assaulted by Democrats from the state's western rural districts. The professed reasons for the assault on the board were the board's powers, which, according to some legislators, either constituted a threat to the legislature's authority or were superfluous. The opponents also were not pleased by the board's commitment to nonsectarianism. It, they felt, would only encourage doubt and skepticism.

But it was the tendency toward administrative centralization and the board's usurpation of the authority of local school committees—characteristics which to many observers suggested the baneful influence of foreign ideas—that bothered the critics most. Thus they warned: "The establishment of the Board of Education seems to be the commencement of a system of centralization and of monopoly of power in a few hands, contrary, in every respect, to the true spirit of our democratical institutions."[18] How could the common schools continue to fulfill their task, the critics asked, if in their newly devised administration and with the normal schools they showed themselves to be un-American in derivation and inspiration? Had not the schools' promoters openly advocated distrust of local school superintendence and had they not announced their intent to impose on local school committees "one plan, as uniform and exact as the discipline of an army"? When the Whigs relied on M. Cousin's laudatory reports on Prussia's schools, their enemies cited Cousin's fellow Frenchman Alexis de Tocqueville and his celebration of the American spirit of local self-government. As far as the normal schools were concerned, the critics asserted, they did not appear to offer "any peculiar or distinguishing advantages" over existing academies and high schools.[19]

The Massachusetts House Committee on Education picked up the theme and moved bravely into the waters of educational theory. It appeared to them, they wrote, "that every person, who has himself undergone a process of instruction, must acquire, by that very process, the art of instructing others." Certainly, they added, this was true if such a person possessed intelligence; if he or she did not, then no amount of instruction would help anyway. From this it followed that normal schools were superfluous. Besides, to keep a district school open for three or four months in the year one did not need specially trained professionals. In any case, there was no guarantee that teachers trained at state expense would stay in Massachusetts.[20]

The real cause for badly performing teachers, the committee added, was not to be found in their insufficient preparation, but in their lack of adequate compensation. And that was a local matter which, as the teachers of Worcester County had stated earlier in the year, was traceable to "a deficiency of interest on the part of the people." That lack of interest and support manifested itself also in the local school committees' failure to provide suitable school buildings and text books and their reluctance to visit the schools and watch the progress of the pupils. It showed when parents kept their children away from school "for trifling causes" and failed to cooperate with teachers in upholding discipline.[21] A state board of education and normal schools were not likely, the committee implied, to remedy these matters.

Much has been made of the opposition to Mann and the board by the orthodox foes of Unitarianism.[22] Yet a roll-call analysis of the 1840 vote in the Massachusetts legislature to abolish the board and the normal schools has shown that religion, though an important factor in the deliberations, was not the major one. If there was a major determinant of the outcome, it was the political affiliation of the legislators. By and large, Whigs supported the board and Democrats opposed it. But even here, a recent study concludes, "the influence of party loyalty, though paramount, was substantially modified by the socioeconomic characteristics of the legislators and their towns."[23] A preference for established ways and a strong attachment to the battle cry of local control and independence of school boards and committees emerged at the very beginning of organized efforts to establish uniform standards and state systems of teacher education.

In the United States, public support for teacher education as a means for school reform has been problematical from the very beginning. No matter how conservative the Whigs were in their social views and how progressive in their approach to education, they were intruders from afar in the eyes of their opponents. They faced antagonists who habitually identified themselves as defenders of school-district autonomy, democracy, the American way of life, and religious liberty. The Whigs' adversaries glossed over their xenophobia and unwillingness to pay for improved public schools with patriotic pretensions, and decried calls for uniform standards of schooling and for meaningful statewide criteria for teacher qualification as foreign impositions. They sought to declare their own particular religious sentiments a majority consensus, and they dismissed the calls for nonsectarian instruction as godless. They feared teachers who were unfamiliar with local conditions, preferences, and prejudices and who were likely to introduce alien mores as disturbers of the local peace. In contest with their adversaries, the Whigs, as conservative as they were in their own social philosophy, appeared as radical reformers and foreign intruders.

Father Peirce's School for Young Women

The first Massachusetts normal school, opened in July of 1839 in Lexington, did not stay in that town very long. It was transferred to West Newton and opened there in November of 1844. A second move took it farther west to Framingham where it continued in 1853.[24] At all three locations the students were expected to attend for one year. In Lexington and in West Newton new classes continued to enroll three times a year, in September, January, and May. In Framingham, however, a new schedule was adopted with semesters beginning in September and March.

For young women in northeastern Massachusetts the school in Lexington offered one of the few opportunities for advanced public education. Though students had to provide their own expenses for board, books, and incidentals, they found the arrangement to be attractive financially, because it promised release from tuition fees for those who committed themselves to a period of teaching in the common schools. In 1839 the alternatives available to Massachusetts women for formal education beyond elementary and grammar schools were high schools and academies. But the high schools were usually located in cities and not all of them would admit women. As Horace Mann stated in his 1837 report, only 14 towns provided such schools for all students.[25] Of the academies about 75 existed in Massachusetts by 1840. They were usually organized as boarding schools and entailed expenses for room, board, and tuition.[26]

When the Lexington school opened in 1839 its principal was Cyrus Peirce. Father Peirce, as he was called by his students, was then 49 years old. He was a graduate of Harvard College and the Harvard Divinity School. For eight years he had served as pastor of the North Reading Unitarian Church, but it was apparent that his real love lay not in preaching but in teaching. His career reveals just what opportunities and what roadblocks awaited the gifted and committed teacher in antebellum America. During his days at college and divinity school, term teaching in district and private schools provided him with the necessary income to continue his studies. Again schoolteaching filled the interval between graduation and his ordination. When he gave up his pastorate, he returned to full-time teaching at various schools in North Andover and Nantucket.

Peirce came to Lexington from his duties as town school principal in Nantucket. By September he had 12 students under his charge. In October he opened a model school for about 30 children of the neighborhood. It functioned as a practice field for the normal school students. While the normal school students were expected to serve as model school instructors, Peirce himself carried responsibility for both the normal and model schools and their students. He was to remain at the helm of the nation's first public normal school until overwork forced him to resign in 1842. Yet he came back to his post to oversee the school's move from Lexington to West Newton and to preside there for another seven years.[27]

Given the age range of the Framingham normalites—as the students of such normal schools were often called—the school must have impressed the contemporary visitor as being similar to a woman's college. The average entrance age for the first 30 years of the school's existence remained a little below 18.5 (see Table 3.2). Although there were older students present— almost every year there were women in the mid- and late 20s, the 24- and 28-year-olds representing the highest numbers among this group—the appearance of the group as a whole was dominated by the younger women. In its first decade the school's 16-year-olds—the youngest students officially permitted to enter—and by 1850 the 17-year-olds usually constituted the largest share. Occasionally, however, an even younger girl would be admitted. Still, even at

Table 3.2. Average Age of Students at Entrance into Framingham State
Normal School in the Mid-1800s

BY LOCATION	
Lexington (1839–44)	18.27
West Newton (1845–52)	18.35
Framingham	18.61

BY DECADE	
1840s	18.32
1850s	19.07
1860s	18.16

Average age from 1839 to 1869:	18.46

Source: These and subsequent data on the ages and parental occupations of 1,649 Framingham students are taken from the manuscript entrance and graduation register of the Framingham State Normal School,
1839–1869, subsequently referred to as the Framingham entrance register.

16 the youngest members were older than the pupils of the female seminaries
and academies.

This meant, too, that the Framingham women were similar in age to the
male students of nearby Harvard College, though they were younger than the
male students at the colleges in the interior. These newer and less expensive
schools like Williams and Amherst in Massachusetts, Bowdoin and Water-
ville in Maine, or Middlebury in Vermont attracted men from the rural areas
of New England. By the 1850s their share of students older than 21 was to
increase more rapidly than that of the Framingham normalites (Table 3.3).

For the largest single group of the Framingham students, farming was
their parents' occupation. Daughters of farmers were followed by almost the
same number of women who were the daughters of nonfarming blue-collar
fathers. Daughters of fathers employed in nonprofessional white-collar occupations furnished the third largest contingent. These three groups were fairly

Table 3.3. Average Age of Students at Entrance into Framingham, Harvard, and the Newer
Colleges in the 1840s and 1850s

	1840s	1850s
Framingham (women)	18.32	19.07
Harvard (men)	18.76	18.34
Harvard and Yale combined (men)	18.64	18.90
Newer colleges (men)	19.90	19.99

Source: The data on students from Harvard and the newer colleges in the interior are taken
from Colin B. Burke, *American Collegiate Populations: A Test of the Traditional View* (New York: New
York University Press, 1982), p. 102.

Table 3.4. Distribution of Framingham State Normal School Students by Parental Occupation, 1848–1869

	Number of Students	Percent of Total	Percent of Total[a]
Blue collar			
Farm	356	29.8	32.3
Nonfarm	341	28.6	30.9
White collar			
Nonprofessional	304	25.5	27.6
Professional	102	8.5	9.2
Unlisted	90	7.5	—
Total	1,193	100.0	100.0

Source: Framingham entrance register.

Note: Columns may not add to totals shown because of rounding.

[a]The percentages in this column exclude the unlisted parents.

evenly balanced. At the bottom of the list, then, ranked the daughters of professionals such as ministers, missionaries, physicians, lawyers, and teachers (Table 3.4).[28]

When we consider that many of the students whose parental occupations are not listed on the school's records were also likely to have come from one of the three major groups, the blue-collar and nonprofessional character of the Framingham students stands out even more clearly. And we should note also the roughly 9 percent of the students who came from professional families. Of these, half were the daughters of ministers, followed by daughters of physicians, lawyers, and, last of all, teachers (see Table 3.5). Cyrus Peirce's students reflected the school's proximity to the more urban sections of the state during its years at Lexington and West Newton.

When the school first opened its doors at Lexington, offering an education beyond the common school level at public expense, women students hesitated to seize the opportunity. Their small numbers greatly disappointed Mann and Peirce. Unlike young men planning to go to college, the young women who applied to Lexington had not received preparatory training either in academies or privately from a local minister or tutor. Except for a few

Table 3.5. Distribution of Framingham State Normal School Students from Professional Families, by Occupation, 1848–1869

Clergymen	52
Physicians	21
Lawyers	16
Teachers	13
Total	102

Source: Framingham entrance register.

who had been able to attend a grammar or other private school, none of them had been exposed to formal educational influences after their graduation from common school. Instead they had spent from four to five years at home or at work. They needed a great deal of encouragement to pursue their studies, and "Father" Peirce struggled valiantly to supply it.

Cyrus Peirce was disappointed also in his students' prior training and capabilities. He found their academic knowledge and skills discouragingly defective. He complained that "some of them seem to have been out of school until they have grown rusty." This was true, he felt, not only of the graduates of the common schools but of grammar and private schools as well.[29] They were "generally very backward," and lacked "the power of generalization and of communication." He felt that they definitely needed at least one year of instruction, even though it would take three to prepare them fully for their tasks. The school's role thus had to be primarily remedial.

It was clear to Peirce that a liberal arts training such as academies and colleges offered was out of place in the normal school. This was not because Peirce felt the liberal arts to be inappropriate for a future elementary school teacher, but because there were more immediate needs for the graduates of the common schools who applied to Lexington. "They have come to learn the Common Branches rather than to learn to *teach* them," he confided to his diary on June 22, 1840.[30] A review of the common school curriculum and a first introduction to classroom teaching was all that could be accomplished in the time at hand.

Then, too, there were never as many students in attendance as Peirce would have liked. In his view, their small numbers and their low level of preparation testified to the public's lack of concern for the common schools. "Schools are all running into Sectarian Institutions," he confided to his diary in May 1840, "and what stands on common ground no body cares about."[31]

Peirce's frustrations increased as time went on. He was particularly chagrinned to find that some of his students did not even want to become teachers, and others did not have the necessary ability. He concluded that the normal school students at Lexington were less talented than his high school students at Nantucket had been: "What miserably clumsy work some of these girls make in Arithmetic, Grammar, Philosophy and Algebra! And they manifest very little Curiosity. . . ."[32]

Peirce's reflections contrast strangely with the enthusiastic reports printed in the *Common School Journal* by friends and supporters of the enterprise. These letters stressed the excellence of the instruction given by Mr. Peirce and the alertness and enthusiasm with which it was received by the students.[33] There can be little doubt that Peirce's reflections on his own effectiveness and abilities do not necessarily contradict the impression he created for his visitors. While Peirce may have pleased the visitors, even swept them off their feet, he could not please himself. And if his students fared better in the eyes of outsiders than in his own, who could not imagine that their stellar performances when on parade outshone their everyday behavior in their master's class?

Peirce had other reasons to be exasperated. Vituperation and insinuations followed the school's progress because of religious antipathies. The long battle in Massachusetts between orthodox Congregationalists and Unitarians affected the normal schools as well. It did not help that Mann was a Unitarian layman and Peirce had been ordained as a Unitarian minister. These two schoolmen were marked from the beginning as targets by orthodox opponents, and charges that the Lexington school was a "real engine of Unitarianism" were easily repeated.[34]

The tentative nature of the school's establishment and the uncertainty over its continued financing did not help either. Money for equipment and apparatus was not included in the budget. Peirce himself had to serve as principal, normal school and model school teacher, supervisor of practice teaching, and janitor. These difficulties were lessened only in March of 1845, when the legislature accepted the school as one of the new Massachusetts state normal schools and thus officially recognized its existence as a state institution. Still, Peirce's assignment had been no bed of roses; the Lexington students, by anyone's reckoning, had not been prodigies. Could other schools do better?

"Earnest Men and Women" in a Country Normal

The second normal school began its work on September 4, 1839, at Barre in the central, rural part of the state. Twelve women and eight men enrolled. Samuel P. Newman, who had been a professor of rhetoric and political economy and acting president of Bowdoin College, was its first principal. Though students were expected to attend a full-year course of three terms, by the summer of 1840 many enrolled for only one term. This policy was suggested by the seasonal nature of farm work. The men students wanted to take advantage of the teaching opportunities open to them in the winter and enrolled primarily in the term beginning in August. Few of them were present at the normal school during the December term. The women students, on the other hand, signed up least frequently for the April term, when they preferred to teach in the common schools. Winter, by contrast, was a good time for them to be at the normal school. As Horace Mann observed: "In very few instances, if in any, would it be prudent to employ a young female, for her first term, in a winter school." Her first teaching should take place in the summer when the more obstreperous boys and young men were working on the farm.[35]

A sudden fatal illness of Principal Newman led to a closing of the school in November of 1841. At that time difficulties of access and a shortage of accommodations experienced by students led to a search for a more suitable location. Thus when the school reopened in September of 1844 the town of Westfield in Hampden County was its new home. The Reverend Emerson Davis, a local clergyman and former member of the Massachusetts State Board of Education, became its interim principal. Attendance increased so rapidly that two years after the school had opened in the town's academy it moved into a building of its own and was now officially called a state normal school. At the same time, David S. Rowe, a graduate of Bowdoin College, began his duties as the new principal.

The Westfield school differed from the one in Framingham most obviously in its coeducational student body. The young women and men came from farming families and from a country-town population of small tradesmen and merchants. Of the more than 2,000 students attending between 1844 and 1876 and included in my survey of parental occupations, a little over three-quarters were women (Table 3.6). Over time their representation varied, gradually increasing from a low of a little over 50 percent in the mid-1840s to about 70 percent after 1850, when students were again required to attend for at least three terms. During the Civil War and in the late 1860s the women's share reached 90 percent. Quite obviously the school proved to be far more attractive to women than to men.

From the Westfield enrollment records it is also evident that women, on the whole, entered the school at an earlier age than men (Table 3.7). During the 11 years from 1844 to 1855 the women's age at entrance averaged a little over 19. It rose from 18.73 before 1850 to nearly 19.5 thereafter. Just as in Framingham, the youth of the Westfield women was accentuated by the contingent of 16- and 17-year-olds, which in every year was by far the largest in each entering class. Again as in Framingham, a few women in their mid- and late 20s could be found in almost every year.

Westfield men, by contrast, waited to enter the school until they were on the average at least 20.5 years old. They showed fewer young students and a more even spread among the ages from 18 to 23. Their difference in age with the Westfield women becomes even more striking when we look at the mini-

Table 3.6. Gender Distribution of Students at Westfield State Normal School in the Mid-1800s

	Women		Men		Total	
	Number	Percent	Number	Percent	Number	Percent
1844–55	1,259	71.21	509	28.79	1,768	100
1868–76	606	90.04	67	9.96	673	100
Total for years counted	1,865	76.40	576	23.60	2,441	100

Source: Typescript of Early Enrollment Records of the Westfield State Normal School.

Table 3.7. Average Age at Entrance into Westfield State Normal School in the Mid-1800s, by Gender

	Women	Men	Difference for Women
1844–49	18.73	20.57	−1.84
1850–55	19.47	20.73	−1.26
1867–70	18.31	20.48	−2.17

Source: Typescript of Early Enrollment Records of the Westfield State Normal School.

mum of the annual average entrance age. For women at Westfield it stood at 16, the legal minimum. But for men it reached almost 19. Women, in other words, entered at the first opportunity given to them, whereas men took that step a few years later. The same pattern also characterized the largest age group in each class. For the Westfield men it was usually found among the older students.

When we compare the entrance ages of Westfield students with those of their contemporaries at the newer colleges in the interior, we note that not only are the men at Westfield older than the women there, they are also older than their fellow male students at the other colleges (Table 3.8).[36] Economic and social conditions, we can assume, forced the relatively few men who wanted to avail themselves of the chance to be trained as a teacher to wait until their early 20s.

Farming stands out as the occupation listed for most of the parents of men and women students at Westfield (Table 3.9). For men the percentage was considerably higher during the 1840s and 1850s than in the late 1860s and early 1870s, and it was followed in the earlier period by other blue-collar and by white-collar families in even proportions. In the later period, however, white-collar workers, particularly professionals, showed a marked increase among the men's parents and outranked or equalled the blue-collar families. For women students, the pattern differed. In the 1840s and 1850s the percentage of nonfarm blue-collar parents was slightly higher than that of white-collar parents, and in the late 1860s and 1870s the two groups were nearly equal.

Table 3.8. Average Entrance Ages of Students at Westfield and Other Colleges in the 1840s and 1850s

	Other Colleges (Men)	Westfield		Difference for Westfield	
		Men	Women	Men	Women
1840s	19.90	20.57	18.73	+0.67	−1.17
1850s	19.99	20.73	19.47	+0.74	−0.52

Sources: Typescript of Early Enrollment Records of the Westfield State Normal School; and Burke, *American Collegiate Populations*.

Table 3.9. Distribution of Westfield State Normal School Students by Parental Occupation in the Mid-1800s

| | 1844–1855 | | | | 1868–1876 | | | |
| | Men | | Women | | Men | | Women | |
	Number	Percent	Number	Percent	Number	Percent	Number	Percent
Blue collar								
Farm	372	73.1	597	47.4	27	40.3	276	45.5
Nonfarm	34	6.7	182	14.5	12	17.9	125	20.6
White collar								
All (including professional)	34	6.7	144	11.4	20	29.9	120	19.8
Professional only	21	4.1	61	4.9	12	17.9	38	6.3
Total[a]	509	100.0	1,259	100.0	67	100.0	606	100.0

Source: Typescript of Early Enrollment Records of Westfield State Normal School.
[a]Includes students whose parental occupations are unknown or fall into other categories.

It appears, then, that in this western hinterland the normal school proved especially attractive to men past high school age. They flocked to Westfield to an even higher degree than they sought out the New England colleges. With almost 7 out of 10 men students from 1844 to 1855 coming from a farm background, the appeal of normal schooling was the prospect of being able to leave farming behind. Because many of the farm men entered the school at a somewhat older age than the women, it also appears that the decision was not taken lightly. Family bonds and obligations kept men on the farm longer than women. After the Civil War, then, the decline of agriculture is reflected in the growing percentages of children from nonfarm families and, among the men, of professional and other white-collar fathers.

The Westfield school also attracted a large share of both younger and older women. Between 1844 and 1855, 7 (71.2 percent) out of 10 and, between 1868 and 1876, 9 (90.0 percent) out of 10 Westfield students were women. The young women came, we can assume, for many of the same reasons their sisters near Framingham did. They found in the normal school an inexpensive and convenient way to resume their formal education and to prepare themselves for desirable gainful employment. The older women very often had taught school already. About half of them had listed on their entrance records that they had been employed for from one to five terms.

The Westfield State Normal School thus was better suited for young women and men than the high schools in Westfield and nearby Springfield. The Springfield high school had been opened in 1841, and admitted students who had just finished the common schools.[37] In Westfield a high school was in operation by 1843. But little is known about its history, and there is some question whether it ever functioned as an advanced school before 1855.[38]

These early high schools, then, did not seem very attractive to men and women who had been out of school for several years. This was particularly true for the older male normalites who had been working on farms, in trade, or business, and for the women who had already been teaching in the common schools. They chose the Westfield normal school as their avenue to occupational advance.

James Greenough knew the Westfield normalites from first-hand experience. He had served as assistant to Principal Dickinson from 1856 to 1871 and, after a 16-year term as principal of the Rhode Island State Normal School, had returned to preside at Westfield. He characterized the Westfield students as "diverse in age, in ability, and in acquisitions." They were a motley gathering, he wrote, whom many on the outside thought to be nondescript, queer, and funny folk. Greenough himself felt that one could not but admire their devotion, and "even if they were somewhat narrow in their mental vision, one could see that it gained in intensity what it lost in breadth." He compared them with Loyola and his companions at the University of Paris. They were "earnest men and women" who, through their intensity, transformed that earnestness into enthusiasm.[39] Perhaps he could also have said that it was through their devotion to their vocation that they tried to make up for the shortcomings of their academic preparation and the narrowness of their vision.

A Profile of Massachusetts Normalites

Gender and Parental Occupation

What, then, can we say of the normal students of Framingham and Westfield? What manner of women and men were attracted to the new state normal schools, presumably to prepare themselves for assignments as teachers in the common schools? Two things are very clear: Given the location of the normal schools and the population they drew from and appealed to, the majority of the students were women, and most of them came from farm families.

As we know, Framingham was a women's school only. At Westfield over three-quarters of the students were women (Tables 3.6 and 3.10). What is more revealing, by 1849 the women's share among the Westfield students alone was larger than among all Massachusetts teachers (Table 3.11). That bode ill for the dream cherished by the members of the American Institute of Instruction, who had hoped that many more male teachers would follow their call and assume the duties of citizen-teachers. The normal schools that some had hoped would train the state's elite teachers obviously had failed to persuade men to regard teaching as a citizen's duty. Women, rather than men,

Table 3.10. Proportion of Women Students at Framingham and Westfield State Normal Schools in the Mid-1800s

	Total Number of Students	Women Students	
		Number	Percent
Framingham (1848–69)	1,193	1,193	100.0
Westfield (1844–55 and 1868–76)	2,441	1,865	76.4
Total	3,634	3,058	84.1

Sources: Manuscript Entrance and Graduation Register, Framingham State Normal School; typescript of Early Enrollment Records; manuscript General Record Book 1864–1876, Westfield State Normal School.

appeared ready to devote a period of their lives to teaching children in the common schools.

Mann and the Massachusetts Board of Education, however, applauded this development. Mann viewed a woman teacher as "guide and guardian of young children," because in her mental and emotional make-up, he believed, affection overbalanced intellect. Providence, he maintained, had ordained the dispositions of young children, and a woman's affection made her a per-

Table 3.11. Percentage of Women Normalites at Westfield and Women Teachers in Massachusetts in the Mid-1800s

	Westfield Normalites	Massachusetts Teachers
1844	57	64
1845	61	64
1846	65	66
1847	60	68
1848	68	69
1849	72	70
1850	72	71
1851	78	72
1852	76	73
1853	71	74
1854	80	76
1868	94	89
1869	88	88
1870	88	88

Sources: Manuscript Entrance and Graduation Register, Framingham State Normal School; typescript of Early Enrollment Records; and manuscript General Record Book 1864–1876, Westfield State Normal School; and David Asher Gould, "Policy and Pedagogues: School Reform and Teacher Professionalization in Massachusetts, 1840–1920," Ph.D. dissertation, Brandeis University, p. 29.

fect match for the pupils under her control. As far as Mann was concerned, nature had made the selection of women as professional teachers par excellence. It was up to women now to prove themselves worthy:

> It is a duty imperative upon them so to improve their minds, by study, by reading, by reflection, and by attending such a course of instruction on the subject of teaching, as the recent legislative appropriation for the continuance of the Normal Schools has proferred to all, that they can answer the just expectations of the public, and discharge, with religious fidelity, the momentous duties to which they are called.

To Mann the preponderance of women among the normal school students was an asset, not a liability.[40]

As the schools' geographical locations would suggest, there were fewer students of farm background at Framingham than at Westfield. At the eastern school they amounted to about 30 percent of the student body, though when the Lexington school moved to West Newton and finally to Framingham its percentage of farm students increased. At the western school between 40 and 45 percent of the students came from farm families (Tables 3.4 and 3.9). There the share of farm women remained relatively stable. At both schools farm women outnumbered the women of the other occupational groups. Of the 1,628 students of farm background included in our survey, a little over a fifth attended the all-woman Framingham school. At Westfield the remaining 1,272 students from farm families accounted for a little more than half of the total student body (Table 3.12).

These percentages would be even higher if we were to consider the likelihood that many of the women from the unlisted category came from farm backgrounds as well. If we exclude the students with unlisted parents from consideration, then the share of farm students among all those with known parental occupations at Framingham stood at close to a third (32.3 percent), while at Westfield it reached 6 out of 10 (61.2 percent) (Tables 3.12 and 3.13).

Much of what we have found about women normalites holds true for their fellow male students as well. But there are differences. Over time, the size of the male student body decreased relative to that of the women. The slow push of the Westfield school to lengthen the required period of study and the call to arms issued during the Civil War contributed to that development. While men from farms had contributed a large share of the normal school population in the 1840s, their numbers were surpassed after the Civil War by men whose parents were professionals or other white-collar workers (Table 3.9). But even then farm families contributed a larger relative share of sons than of daughters to the normal school population. Though the total percentage of men among farm students was only a little less than 25, this was a great deal higher than the 16 percent men represented of all normal school stu-

Table 3.12. Distribution of Massachusetts Normal School Students, by Parental Occupation and School, in the Mid-1800s

	Framingham 1848–69		Westfield 1844–55; 1868–76		Total	
	Number	Percent	Number	Percent	Number	Percent
Blue collar						
Farm	356	29.8	1,272	52.1	1,628	44.8
Nonfarm	341	28.6	490	20.1	831	22.9
White collar						
Nonprofessional	304	25.5	186	7.6	490	13.5
Professional	102	8.5	132	5.4	234	6.4
Unlisted	90	7.5	361	14.8	451	12.4
Total	1,193	100.0	2,441	100.0	3,634	100.0

Sources: Manuscript Entrance and Graduation Register, Framingham State Normal School; typescript of Early Enrollment Records; and manuscript General Record Book 1864–1876, Westfield State Normal School.

These figures referring to parental occupations cover 3,634 students altogether. Of these, 1,193 women enrolled at Framingham between September 1848 and September 1869, 1,259 women and 509 men students entered at Westfield between September 1844 and March 1855, and 606 women and 67 men students did so at Westfield between the fall of 1867 and the spring of 1876.

dents. While only 4 out of 10 normalite women came from farm families, 7 out of 10 men in the two schools came from a farming background (Table 3.14). For the sons of farmers, then, the normal school proved to be a potent attraction.

For men in the rural hinterlands the normal school offered a second chance. It brought them educational opportunity. Many of the graduates would subsequently leave teaching to pursue further studies or enter upon different careers. For the opponents and some friends of the normal schools, that constituted one of the major grievances. A public institution was being abused for private gain. Others argued that these graduates were only practicing the time-honored American way of trying to get ahead in life and to climb the ladder of social mobility. They saw nothing wrong with it.

Table 3.13. Number of Massachusetts Normal School Students Checked for Parental Occupations in the Mid-1800s, by School

	Information Available	Information Not Available	Total
Framingham	1,103	90	1,193
Westfield	2,080	361	2,441
Total	3,183	451	3,634

Sources: Manuscript Entrance and Graduation Register, Framingham State Normal School; typescript of Early Enrollment Records; and manuscript General Record Book 1864–1876, Westfield State Normal School.

Table 3.14. Gender Distribution of Massachusetts Normal School Students, by Background, in the Mid-1800s

	Men		Women		Total	
	Number	Percent	Number	Percent	Number	Percent
GENDER DISTRIBUTION						
All students	576	15.9	3,058	84.1	3,634	100.0
Farm students	399	24.5	1,229	75.5	1,628	100.0
BACKGROUND DISTRIBUTION						
Farm background	399	69.3	1,229	40.2	1,628	44.8
Nonfarm background	177	30.7	1,829	59.8	2,006	55.2

Sources: Manuscript Entrance and Graduation Register, Framingham State Normal School; typescript of Early Enrollment Records; and manuscript General Record Book 1864–1876, Westfield State Normal School.

Age

As far as their ages were concerned women were ready to leave their homes, enter normal school, and begin teaching at a slightly earlier age than men (Table 3.15). This was true particularly at the Framingham school. There during the 1840s most of the women were slightly younger than their male contemporaries at Harvard and Yale. Those under 17 showed about the same proportion as at Harvard, but a much larger proportion than at Yale. On the other end of the spectrum the percentage of Framingham's students older than 21 was about the same as at Harvard and Yale (Table 3.16).

At Westfield the entrance age of women was a little higher than at Framingham, because farm and rural small-town life postponed the young women's entry to the school. As time went on, however, the average entrance age for women declined at both schools, and women found it easier to leave the farm at an earlier age (Table 3.17).

In the 1850s the picture remained essentially the same, except that the share of the older students rose considerably. The older woman, in many cases having lost her parents or her husband and the economic support that had been provided for her, turned to teaching and sought a normal education to improve her chances for employment. In many cases the Westfield records show that such women had taught before at an earlier age for one or several terms. When tragedy struck, she sought professional advice and instruction and reembarked upon teaching. Not only did the normal school provide a perfect means for reentry, it also gave a chance to combine gaining a livelihood with what later generations came to call a continuing education.

The women normalites were older than girls and women attending high

Table 3.15. Distribution of Average Entrance Age into Massachusetts Normal Schools, by School, 1839–1870

	Framingham (Women)	Westfield		Difference for Women
		Women	Men	
1839–49	18.32			−2.25
1844–49		18.73	20.57	−1.84
1850–59	19.07			−1.66
1850–55		19.47	20.73	−1.26
1860–69	18.16			−2.32
1867–70		18.31	20.48	−2.17
Average difference:				−1.92

Sources: Manuscript Entrance and Graduation Register, Framingham State Normal School; typescript of Early Enrollment Records; and manuscript General Record Book 1864–1876, Westfield State Normal School.

The data refer to the ages at entrance of 3,641 normal school students. Of these, 1,649 women entered the Lexington/West Newton/Framingham school between July 1839 and September 1869; 1,231 women and 497 men students enrolled at the Westfield school between September 1844 and March 1855, and 241 women and 23 men students enrolled at Westfield between the fall of 1867 and 1870.

Table 3.16. Percentage Distribution of Students Entering College in the 1840s and 1850s, by Age and School

	1840s				1850s			
	Percentage				Percentage			
	Younger than 17	17–21	Older than 21	Number	Younger than 17	17–21	Older than 21	Number
Harvard	33	51	16	150	21	70	9	238
Yale	19	57	24	146	16	68	16	188
Newer colleges	18	55	27	482	13	66	21	610
Framingham	31	53	16	594	19	63	18	511
Westfield								
Women	29	51	20	500	22	54	24	731
Men	0	68	32	262	1	66	34	235

Sources: Manuscript Entrance and Graduation Register, Framingham State Normal School; typescript of Early Enrollment Records; and manuscript General Record Book 1864–1876, Westfield State Normal School.

Table 3.17. Percentage Distribution of Farm Women Who Entered Normal School at Average Age of All Massachusetts Women Normalites in the Mid-1800s, by School

	Framingham		Westfield	
	Average Entrance Age of All Women	Proportion of Farm Women (%)	Average Entrance Age of All Women	Proportion of Farm Women (%)
1848–55	18.69	21.9		
1844–55			19.1	47.4
1856–69	18.43	34.8		
1860s–70s			18.31	45.5

Sources: Manuscript Entrance and Graduation Register, Framingham State Normal School; typescript of Early Enrollment Records; and manuscript General Record Book 1864–1876, Westfield State Normal School.

schools or academies, but they differed little from the students at the female seminaries at Norton and Mount Holyoke. Though Wheaton Seminary, established in Norton in 1834, admitted some of its students as early as age 13, it should be kept in mind that its 13- and 14-year-old students were usually local day students or sisters of older students in attendance. Wheaton's boarding students differed in age neither from the normalites nor from the students at the male colleges. Some of them were as old as 25.[41] Mount Holyoke Seminary, which, as Mary Lyon proudly said, was designed "to fit young women to be educators rather than mere teachers," did not want young girls as students. When it opened its doors in 1836 its prospectus read that "except in extraordinary cases none will be received under sixteen years of age," and many students in the first year were in their 20s and had already taught school.[42] In age, normal students were much like their sisters in the early female seminaries and their brothers in the colleges.

The older students at the seminaries and normal schools found that their institutions could respond better than the academies and high schools to their need for vocational preparation or continuing education. Both Wheaton and Mount Holyoke spoke directly to "adult young ladies" or "young ladies of mature age" rather than to "younger scholars or misses."[43] The normal schools had the additional advantage of being able to grant tuition release. Thus the normal school at Bridgewater, opening in 1840 at a distance of 20 miles from Norton, would attract the daughters of farm and other blue-collar families, whereas Wheaton sought mainly the daughters of business and professional parents.[44]

The Westfield normal, on the other hand, competed in western Massachusetts with Mount Holyoke for what Mary Lyon called "the adult female youth in the common walks of life."[45] Westfield students came, just as David

Allmendinger reported about Mount Holyoke students, from farms and "families associated with country occupations."[46] In antebellum Massachusetts, then, the normal school was not a competitor of academies and high schools. It functioned more like a female seminary or a college and, because it appealed to lower middle-class and working families, became what contemporaries used to call a people's college.

In the case of the men, students under 17 were strikingly absent during both the 1840s and the 1850s, but a far greater proportion of men older than 21 was present. Men enrolled not only at a later age than women normalites did, they were also generally older than their fellow students at both the traditional and the newer colleges in the interior of the country (Table 3.7). Apparently their labor was needed on the parental farm or in the household before they could turn to their studies (Table 3.8).

Class

In a state where higher education was represented by private colleges, academies, and female seminaries modelled on the liberal arts education of the Yale report, the normal schools together with the public high schools became the "people's colleges." As we have seen, the normal schools distinguished themselves from the high schools in that they were state supported, fewer in number, prepared to house and board their students, and attractive to students older than usually seen in high schools.

The normal schools' character as people's colleges was enhanced also by the waiver of tuition for those who promised to teach in the common schools and by the expectation that attendance, however brief, would improve a girl's opportunities for seasonal employment or, in case of necessity, a woman's chance to earn a livelihood. The normal schools thus appealed to children of farm and other blue-collar families. Both farm and nonfarm blue-collar students together amounted to a little more than two-thirds of all normal school students (Table 3.12). As geography would suggest, at Framingham near Boston the nonfarm blue-collar group was larger than at Westfield. In Westfield, located in rural farm and small-town country, the nonfarm blue-collar students reached less than half the strength of the students from farm families and were more strongly represented among the women than among the men (Tables 3.9 and 3.10). Put another way, the farm students accounted for slightly more than 50 percent of the Westfield and for a little less than 30 percent of the Framingham students. Seven out of 10 farm women studied at Westfield and 3 at Framingham. Of the Westfield farm students, 7 out of 10 were women and 3 out of 10 were men; nonetheless 7 out of 10 Westfield men but not quite 5 out of 10 Westfield women came from farm families (Table 3.18).

At the other end of the social spectrum we find the children of profes-

Table 3.18. Occupational Background Distribution of Massachusetts Normal School Students, by School and Gender, in the Mid-1800s

	Farm Background		Nonfarm Background		Total	
	Number	Percent	Number	Percent	Number	Percent
	OVERALL SCHOOL DISTRIBUTION					
Framingham students	356	29.8	837	70.2	1,193	100.0
Westfield students	1,272	52.1	1,169	47.9	2,441	100.0
	SCHOOL DISTRIBUTION OF FARM WOMEN					
Framingham	356	31.4				
Westfield	873	71.0				
	GENDER DISTRIBUTION OF WESTFIELD FARM STUDENTS					
Men	399	31.4				
Women	873	68.6				
	BACKGROUND DISTRIBUTION OF ALL WESTFIELD STUDENTS					
Men	399	69.3	177	30.7	576	100.0
Women	873	46.8	992	53.2	1,865	100.0

Sources: Manuscript Entrance and Graduation Register, Framingham State Normal School; typescript of Early Enrollment Records; and manuscript General Record Book 1864–1876, Westfield State Normal School.

sionals, among whom are included ministers, missionaries, lawyers, physicians, and teachers (Table 3.12). Though their numbers were not large, the daughters of professional families constituted a larger percentage at Framingham than they did at Westfield. At Westfield, on the other hand, the sons of professional families could be found at the normal school at a slightly higher rate than their daughters. Nonprofessional white-collar students were quite strongly represented at Framingham, where they accounted for a quarter of all students. At Westfield they did not quite reach 8 percent (Table 3.12).

What stands out, though, is the increase at Westfield of men from professional and nonprofessional white-collar families. It became particularly pronounced during the post–Civil War years from 1868 to 1876, though it should be pointed out that the overall number of such students was small (Table 3.19). Nonprofessional white-collar occupations moved up by 9.5 percentage points among men and by 8 among women. Farm families, on the other hand, declined by 14 points in the share of children they sent to Westfield State Normal, while nonfarm blue-collar families increased by 13.5 among men students and by 11 among women students. These shifts reflect in part the decline of agriculture in western Massachusetts during these years and in part

Table 3.19. Distribution[a] of Massachusetts Normal School Students from Professional Families, by School and Gender, in the Mid-1800s

| | Framingham (Women) | | Westfield | | | |
| | | | Men | | Women | |
	Number	Percent	Number	Percent	Number	Percent
1848–55	26	6				
1844–55			21	4	61	5
1856–69	76	10				
1868–76			12	18	38	6
All years	102	9	33	6	99	5

Sources: Manuscript Entrance and Graduation Register, Framingham State Normal School; typescript of Early Enrollment Records; and manuscript General Record Book 1864–1876, Westfield State Normal School.

[a]Percentages shown relate to total number of students in each category.

the growing tendency of the normal school to emphasize the training of male teachers for the high schools.

Failure of the Country Normal

"Father" Peirce at Lexington had complained of his normal school students as young and badly prepared, and James Greenough at Westfield had appraised them as intense, serious, and earnest. To neither had they seemed an impressive lot. Our profile tends to agree. The Massachusetts normalites of the 1840s, 1850s, and 1860s do not present a picture of enthusiastic pedagogues or dedicated scholars in training. Their motivation was not scholarly learning but basic vocational preparation. Women either desired to mark time before marriage or to rely on schoolteaching as a convenient and relatively easily attainable occupation to survive spinsterhood or widowhood. Most men planned to use schoolteaching as a springboard to leave behind a rural existence and enter the world of professional or other white-collar employment.

If Horace Mann and his colleagues had seen the early normal schools as a solution to what they considered to be a rural school crisis, they had calculated wrongly. It was true, to be sure, that most of the school children, teachers, and schools in Massachusetts were found in rural areas. The crisis here, as Kaestle and Vinovskis have pointed out, was one of quality and amount of schooling. It concerned poor physical facilities and equipment, untrained teachers, and short sessions.[47] But the appeal of Mann and his colleagues to the state to support the normal schools and to the rural population to furnish them with students turned out not to bring the desired effect. A corps of professional teachers did not begin to show.

Instead, the normal schools served the young people of Massachusetts' farming areas and small towns as vocational training centers. They prepared their students for temporary employment in the schools or future nonfarming careers elsewhere. Thus they aided—unwittingly, to be sure—what we have come to call the brain drain from the country. The normal schools did not thereby accomplish their original purpose of aiding the rural schools. If they gave help in some way, it is more likely that such help was incidental. The rural schools were not the ultimate gainers. The normalites were on the move both socially and geographically, and only few stayed or returned to play the role of country schoolmaster or schoolmistress.

Contemporaries were well aware of that fact and said so. Not all of the critics were opponents of the schools, either. One of them who was intimately familiar with the Massachusetts common schools was William B. Fowle, the editor of the *Common School Journal.* Ten years after the initial opening of the first normal school in Lexington, Fowle charged that the results of all the efforts to improve the standards of common school teaching had been meager. For this, he felt, the chief responsibility lay with the Massachusetts Board of Education. It had permitted the admission of too many immature and unqualified students into the normal schools.[48]

In 1843 the board members had rejected the suggestion to concentrate on an extended and intensive education of fewer students, and instead had placed their hopes on minor improvements in the training of a larger number of teachers. According to Mr. Fowle the board members had quite deliberately encouraged the admission to the normal schools of students "whose qualifications were not sufficiently high to enable the most assiduous teacher, during the brief period of their remaining with him, to fit them for the situation to which they aspired. . . ."[49] Thus persons "hardly competent to learn" had been sent out to teach others. The chaff had to be taken with the wheat, the board implied, and they maintained that the results of their efforts had generally been gratifying.[50]

Mr. Fowle disagreed. He pointed out that the average age of the 1,500 students who had attended the state normal schools since their inception was under 21 and, he thought, steadily going down. Too many graduates failed to repay the state's investment in their training and never entered a classroom. As far as male teachers were concerned their transient role in teaching, he argued, was due to insufficient salaries. This forced them to regard teaching as a some-time activity only. Women generally left teaching for marriage. Besides, the overwhelming majority of Massachusetts teachers had not been trained at all. They reentered the common schools as teachers immediately upon having left them as students. They grasped the rod, the editor wrote, "the moment they have ceased to feel it. . . ."[51]

Worse yet, the normal schools were forced to make up for the deficient common school education of their pupils and could devote little time to their real objective, instruction in the art of teaching. How absurd, then, Mr. Fowle observed, to complain, as some did, that the normal schools did not offer Greek and Latin and other advanced studies. "The wildness of this notion," he exclaimed, "can find no excuse in the original design of the schools, in the wants of the districts, or in the common sense of the people." Normalites needed more and better instruction in English, not an acquaintance with Latin and French. Besides, Mr. Fowle observed, there was no need for more high school teachers. Academies and colleges turned out plenty of them. What was needed were teachers for the common schools. Before the normal schools attempted to look like seminaries or colleges, Mr. Fowle suggested, they ought to accomplish their original mission.[52]

In subsequent issues of the *Journal,* the criticisms continued. An anonymous contributor, identified as a one-time teacher, wrote of his personal acquaintance with normal school students. Of some of them, he wrote, it could be said with Burns that "at their birth, God Almighty stamped DUNCE in capital letters upon their foreheads. . . ." They could never be turned into decent teachers, and they were sent to normal school "only to save the expense of getting the rudiments of an education elsewhere."[53] Apparently, there was some feeling abroad that the normal schools were being abused by parents who sought a cheap substitute for an academy education.

The *Common School Journal's* editor also found fault with the model schools connected with the normal schools. These experimental schools were counterproductive, he claimed. The normalites not only disrupted the instruction of the model school's teacher, but, because of the brief period they spent in the model school classroom, they also failed to benefit themselves from that experience. Teaching talent had to be stimulated and developed in a sustained effort. That was best done, the editor thought, on a monitorial plan in which older students taught younger students and continually improved both their learning and their teaching skills.[54] As we shall learn, this was what Principal Wells would accomplish five years later at Westfield, when the closing of the model school forced him to make a virtue out of a necessity.

Mr. Fowle's criticisms were well taken. By 1850 the district schools could not be said to have been measurably improved. But the faults decried by Mr. Fowle did not so much lie in the normal schools, their efforts, and their overall direction by the board as they did in the continuing unwillingness of the district and town school boards to contribute their share to any reforms. It was up to them to demand better qualified and more mature teachers and to offer the requisite financial incentives. The school committees were generally quite content to hire young teachers at minimal compensation. They were reluctant to persuade them through salary increases or improvements in working conditions to stay for longer than a term or year.

This unwillingness of district school boards to improve the working conditions of teachers was particularly pronounced in the rural areas of the state. There it became evident that by the 1860s when the Civil War brought increased feminization and lower wages most normalites either left teaching or moved to teach in a city school. No matter how low the entrance standards of the normal schools, under these conditions they could not possibly hope to supply the numbers of teachers needed in the country. By 1873, Gould tells us, "almost half of the teachers with normal school training taught in the eighteen cities in the state."[55] The country towns, Gould has observed, served as a farm system for the urban centers and, in the words of George Martin, the secretary of the Massachusetts Board of Education, the influence of the normalites on the rural schools was "as evanescent as a perfume."[56] The Massachusetts normal schools had not solved the rural school crisis.

4

Massachusetts and Beyond

Varieties of Teacher Education

The Westfield Approach

As the 1870s began, normal school educators faced new issues and challenges. They were on the move in three directions. They expanded their curriculum to include the preparation of teachers for high school classes, academic specialists, and school administrators. They shifted their attention from the countryside to the cities, and they opened new normal schools in states south and west of Massachusetts. The expansion of the curriculum to train high school teachers and offer professional work and the growing interest in normal education in the cities went hand in hand. It sparked vigorous debates over the purposes and priorities of teacher education.

In part these developments were prompted by the normal educators' dissatisfaction with their inability to solve the rural school crisis. To some extent the developments also followed rather naturally from the early normal educators' own experience and inclinations as college graduates who, trained as they were in academic subjects, were themselves far removed from the elementary school classroom and its setting. But even more fundamental was the effect of urbanization and the westward movement.

The history of the Barre/Westfield school illustrates the changing attitudes of the normal educators. Quite different from Cyrus Peirce at Lexington, the early Westfield principals had had no experience as common school teachers. Principal Samuel Phillips Newman at Barre had been a professor of rhetoric and political economy at Bowdoin College. His successor after the school's move to Westfield was the Reverend Emerson Davis, then the Trinitarian pastor of the town's First Congregational Church. Prior to that Davis had been a tutor and vice-president of Williams College, and had served from 1822 to 1836 as principal of the Westfield Academy, a private, tuition-charging school that was attended by boys and girls from Massachusetts, Connecticut, and New York.[1]

Newman and Davis were academic scholars at heart. Their training and experience had been in the world of academies and colleges, and their response to their students' shortcomings was not to strengthen the students' preparation in the elementary studies, but to appeal to an advanced academic curriculum and to what then came to be called educational science. They also hoped that by raising the level of their offerings and by taking on the preparation of high school teachers they would attract better-prepared and motivated students. Newman insisted that elementary teachers "should have a fund of knowledge in advance of the branches commonly taught in our schools." He promised that his students would "receive instruction in the Natural Sciences, in Intellectual Philosophy, in our Political System and in Moral Philosophy."[2]

When David S. Rowe took over from Emerson Davis in 1846 the academic emphasis continued. Rowe, a graduate of Bowdoin College, had taught in various public and private schools in Massachusetts and Maine. In his own teaching he relied primarily on lecturing. He took great pride in bringing to rural Westfield some of the world's outstanding scholars as guest lecturers. The Swiss geographer Arnold Guyot, the natural historian Louis Agassiz, and the pedagogue William Russell, the editor of the *American Journal of Education,* all spoke before Westfield audiences.[3] At the normal school Rowe introduced courses in philosophy, astronomy, history, surveying, and bookkeeping. One recent observer comments that these courses "were, no doubt, comparable to those offered at the academies and high schools of that time. However," he adds, "many of the texts covering the course contents also were the same as those used in similar courses offered in many of the colleges of that day."[4]

Still, Newman's experience with and preference for the academic approach ran against the shortcomings of normal school students and local conditions. As in Lexington so also in Westfield, the inadequate academic background of the normalites required that priority be given to a review of the elementary curriculum and instructions on how to behave in the classroom. The town's demand that the normal school contribute its share to alleviating the local teacher shortage meant that normal students usually attended the school for no more than one term before they either stopped their studies altogether or interrupted them to teach in the common schools.

Like Newman, Rowe, too, had to face the inescapable dilemma of the normal school educator: His own preference for the academic approach to learning notwithstanding, the prior preparation of his students and the demands of their future vocation dictated an emphasis on elementary work and what was called the theory and practice of teaching. That course, writes Fiorello, "was augmented by lectures . . . on such topics as methods of teaching, school discipline, obligations of teachers and school arrangements." As at Lexington a model or experimental school was utilized. Seventy-five pupils between the ages of 4 and 16 provided practice for the normalites and helped to dissuade them from leaving the school for a practice term elsewhere. Instead Westfield normal students who had finished their first term now spent an hour a day as assistant teachers in the model school. But even then, writes Fiorello, "from 1844 to 1853 . . . professional studies had but a minor role in the training of teachers. . . ."[5] Rowe saw to it that academic learning remained the heart of the curriculum.

The principalship of William H. Wells following Rowe's in 1854 brought a further increase in the academic content of the Westfield curriculum and the first sustained concern with school administration. Wells was the first bona fide schoolman and teacher educator to take over the reins of the Westfield institution. He did not have a college degree, but had studied instead in private academies, among them at Samuel Hall's teachers seminary in Andover. He also had served as an assistant to Henry Barnard, Horace Mann's counterpart in Connecticut as secretary of the state board of education, and as teacher in the teacher seminary at East Hartford, Connecticut. He left a principalship in Newburyport to take command at Westfield.[6] His academic interests were well balanced with his experience in and concern for school administration and teacher education.

Difficulties with town authorities led in 1855 to the closing of the model school and the introduction in its place of a system of "mutual instruction." Normal students taught in front of their own classmates, who in turn evaluated their performance. Wells took pride in the substitution of observation, experiment, and criticism for the traditional memorizing and book-learning. He saw the change as progress in professional work that demonstrated a growing acceptance of the theories of Johann Heinrich Pestalozzi.[7]

In 1856 Wells's reputation brought him a call to the school superintendency of Chicago and thus limited his stay at Westfield to two years. But before he left Westfield he had organized a diploma program and introduced advanced courses to be offered in the last term of a student's three-term stay at Westfield.[8] He had inaugurated elective courses in Latin and French "for the accommodation of pupils whose time and attainments enable them to pursue studies not embraced in the required course."[9] He had sponsored the introduction of experimental work in the natural sciences, he had sought to place the course in the theory and practice of teaching on a more substantial philosophical basis, and he had strengthened professional studies with a course in Massachusetts school law. His academic innovations introduced college preparatory work and opened the door to the training of teachers for the high schools. Under Wells's guidance the professional standing of the Westfield State Normal School had markedly improved.

The new departure inaugurated by Wells was continued by his successor, John Woodbridge Dickinson. A graduate of Williams College, he had begun his teaching career at Westfield State Normal, and after four years became the school's principal in 1856. A Pestalozzian par excellence, he was to remain in that office for 21 years. He stressed observation and experiment and perfected the mutual-instruction approach to practice teaching so much that it no longer appeared as a make-do solution to the loss of the model school. In fact, the practice was continued even when in 1868 a local school was again used for practice teaching.[10] After having indicated in the 1857–1858 catalogue for the first time that students could continue their studies with elective courses taken after they had finished the required three-term program, Dickinson expanded the basic course for elementary school teachers in 1864 to a full four-term program. New additions were offered in zoology, mineralogy, and geology.

By 1869 Dickinson was ready to add to the two-year course for elementary school teachers an advanced course of another two years for the preparation of high school teachers. Its subjects were to be Latin, German, French, drawing, higher mathematics, chemistry, and natural history.[11] Dickinson promoted this new departure despite the objections voiced by the board of education in Boston. Such advanced instruction, the board stated, would only divert time and attention of both students and teachers from the regular course.[12] But Dickinson prevailed. Though in 1870 Latin and French were temporarily dropped, they were reinstated in 1875 and accompanied by German as well.[13] By 1879 the advanced course included algebra and geometry, trigonometry, surveying, advanced chemistry, physics, botany, English literature, and general history. The board of visitors was free to decide whether it wanted to offer German and Greek.[14] Westfield, like all the other Massachusetts normal schools, had entered upon the task of training teachers for the high schools.

These developments at Westfield were not without their critics who saw in them a tendency to abandon unsolved problems, to betray the elementary school teacher, and to scuttle the old Massachusetts normal school. They had provoked Mr. Fowle's wrath as early as 1849.[15] He had then excoriated Westfield as well as the other normal schools for their failure to provide well-trained teachers for the rural common schools and had scorned the idea of offering the study of French and Latin. He had also surmised that unless a halt were put to these moves, the day would come when a second grade of normal schools would be established to offer advanced work for the training of high school teachers. According to him, there was no way that could be avoided. The only question was when it would happen.

During the 1850s and 1860s critics condemned the arguments of the Westfield principals as self-serving. While the principals stressed that elevating the curriculum of their normal school would raise the quality of their students and the morale of their faculty members and discourage those concerned only with vocational preparation, the critics pointed out that educators always tried to lighten their burden of having to teach elementary subjects. They always asked for an extension of the required time in which to cover the curriculum and demanded the introduction of higher studies.

In 1863 the principals of all the Massachusetts normal schools then met with a committee of the board of education. The committee concluded that, although it was not advisable to enlarge the general course of studies at the normal schools, it seemed wise that several of its branches should be extended. Thus they recommended that Principal Dickinson's policy at West-field be adopted statewide and a fourth term be added to turn the regular course into a full two-year sequence. This went into effect in 1865.[16]

The development that was now set in motion was not easily deflected or stopped. In a feeble attempt to backtrack, the board warned in 1866 that it did not object to the offering of Latin and French as optional, "but not to the neglect of the English course." It added that it deemed it "unwise to encourage the formation of regular advanced classes, whose instruction can not fail to divert a considerable amount of the time and attention of the teachers from the under-graduate course."[17] But what was to prevent the normal school pedagogues from eventually turning their optional advanced work into regular required offerings?

The answer, then as now, was rather obvious, and three years later the board accepted the inevitable, and college-level instruction began in the fall of 1870.[18] A new philosophy had begun to take hold in the Massachusetts normal school establishment. It did not seem to matter that students in far too many cases continued to look upon their sojourn in the normal schools as but a stepping stone to marriage or business or might now use it to gain entrance to college or professional school. It did not appear to bother the normal school pedagogues that most of the state's elementary school teachers continued to regard their work as a temporary activity. Board members and normal school instructors had begun to deny the reality of the citizen-teacher and refused to look upon their program as a vocation-oriented training course. They now began to demand a scientifically based professional education.

For the majority of the Massachusetts normal educators the goal became the experimental and advanced work that Wells and Dickinson had introduced at Westfield. They sought to develop it into a scientific speciality of their own in the hope that this might bring glamor to an otherwise low-reputed enterprise. For their more promising students and particularly for the men among them, they recommended high school teaching and perhaps even a principalship or superintendency. Already in the 1860s at the Salem State Normal School—established in 1854 for women only, the fourth normal school in Massachusetts—the catalogue read like an advertisement for college: "The great object of the school is to make the pupils investigate, think, and speak for themselves; to make them independent, self-reliant, and ready to meet whatever difficulties may arise."[19] However progressive in the spirit of Pestalozzi and Diesterweg these sentiments may sound, they should not deceive us into forgetting that they were bought at the expense of the education for the female elementary school teacher. Scholarly and professional advance was introduced while there remained much work to be done on the foundations.

The City High and Normal Schools

Critics of the normal schools pointed to the newly appearing high schools as possible alternate and better suited centers for teacher training. The board of education considered that suggestion in 1869.[20] But because most of the state's high schools were located in larger towns and cities, their graduates rarely left to teach in rural schools. In fact, when in 1852 Boston had opened its city normal school, Nathan Bishop, the city's superintendent of schools, had asked that it be used to train women teachers for the Boston grammar schools.[21] The first public normal school administered by an American city was not meant to help alleviate the rural school problem.

What must have intrigued the members of the Massachusetts Board of Education in 1869 was that in 1852 girls who had graduated from the city's common and grammar schools and their parents had shown little interest in normal schooling. They had much preferred high school education for girls. This had been true ever since the city in its parsimony had closed the Girls' High School in 1828 and supported only the English High School for Boys. So when more and more women appeared as teachers in Boston's elementary and grammar schools and the demand for their better preparation was raised, a call for a city normal school provided a perfect cover for what was really wanted—a high school. Larkin Dunton, subsequently to be Boston Normal's fourth headmaster, admitted that much when he reported that the normal school was asked for in Boston only because people were reluctant to revive the old high school controversy.[22]

Once the institution was established as the Boston Normal School and its students had been found to be insufficiently prepared for teacher training, a two-year high school curriculum was introduced to precede the third-year normal work proper. By 1854 public pressure forced a change in name and curriculum, and the school became in name what it had already been in fact: the Boston Girls' High and Normal School. "But the normal features were soon quite overshadowed by the high school work," wrote Larkin Dunton.[23] Whether that occurred by necessity or by design is now a moot question. Suffice it to say that for 18 years the Boston Girls' High and Normal functioned for all practical purposes as a high school.

The actual beginning of the school as a teacher training institution then occurred in 1872. In that year, finding that "the normal element had again been crowded out by the high school work and that the school had almost lost its distinctively professional character," the Boston School Committee separated the two schools.[24] The Boston Normal School thereafter led an independent existence. It continued its one-year normal course, begun in 1852, for 36 years. In 1888 that course was extended to 1½ years and in 1892 to 2 years. By 1924 the school became the Teachers College of the City of Boston, and eventually the Boston State Teachers College and the Boston State College.

The Boston story showed that the high school as city normal school was an unqualified success. By 1894 Larkin Dunton could report that, since 1873, 1,018 of the 1,368 graduates of the school had been appointed to Boston public schools and 738 were still teaching.[25] Whether one focusses on the 54 percent of all the graduates or the 73 percent of those appointed to teaching positions, the rate of Boston normal graduates teaching in the public schools in the city in 1894 was substantially higher than the 31 percent of all the state normal school graduates teaching in the public schools of Massachusetts.[26] Quite obviously, it was easier to train teachers for and to keep them in city schools than to be similarly successful in the country.

Another Massachusetts city had also embarked on the training of its elementary teachers in a normal school of its own. In 1868 Worcester opened such a school, but transferred it six years later to state control. After 1881 the Worcester State Normal School not only offered the standard two-year general and the two-year advanced course but also provided one-year courses for college graduates and practicing teachers. Like the Westfield principals Wells and Dickinson before him, Worcester principal E. Harlow Russell believed in scientific observations of teaching. When G. Stanley Hall, the pioneer leader of the child-study movement, assumed the presidency of Clark University in Worcester in 1888, Russell offered the Worcester State Normal School and students as a laboratory for this new departure in scientific pedagogy. Just like the Boston school, the Worcester school built an impressive record of its graduates' employment in the elementary schools of its city. The urban environment made it possible to train teachers in modern educational science, and urban salary scales helped to keep them in the schools as well.[27]

The question that presented itself to the members of the Massachusetts Board of Education in 1869 and to educators elsewhere concerned about teacher éducation was whether it wasn't the urban environment that had made the normal schools in Boston and Worcester so successful? Was it the two years of high school education preceding the third year of normal training and the age difference implied by the two years which distinguished the graduates of Boston Girls' High and Normal from the students that had come to Cyrus Peirce's school in Lexington? Was it the availability of students able to take the advanced course and of graduates of high schools and colleges as well as the availability of practicing teachers that spelled the difference in Worcester? Was not this the lesson taught by the urban experience: Before teachers embarked upon normal training, they needed an extended general or liberal education in grammar and high school and a few years of growing and maturing? Too many of the common school teachers educated in the rural state normal schools of Massachusetts had been too young and immature. No amount of vocational or professional training could ever have replaced or made up for that liability.

Could the city approach of prolonging teacher training through adding grammar or high school years be applied to the state normal schools in the country? The experience in Massachusetts and other states suggests a negative reply. Boston and Worcester taxpayers were willing to provide educational opportunities for their sons and daughters beyond the common schools, though it is a safe guess to say that they did not envisage their daughters seeking employment in the country, least of all as country schoolmistresses. But rural school committees were no more eager to push vigorously for country high schools than they had been to improve working conditions for their teachers in the common schools. Massachusetts educators had to look for other ways to improve teacher preparation and performance.

The Bridgewater Tradition and Teacher Education in the Midwest

The inception in the 1870s of the advanced course at Westfield signalled the end of the early period in the history of the Massachusetts state normal schools. Although the normal pedagogues had been unable to solve the problems of the rural schools and their teachers, they had found that the rise of the high school and the increasing urbanization of the country offered, if not a solution to their problem, then new challenges that allowed them to move off in different directions.

Geographical expansion provided another such challenge. From Massachusetts the public school movement and teacher education spread across the United States. During the 1840s state normal schools were opened in New York and Pennsylvania. In the next decade Connecticut, Rhode Island, and New Jersey followed in the East, and Michigan and Illinois added theirs in the Midwest. Kansas and Wisconsin followed during the 1860s, and Iowa in the 1870s.

As in New England, teacher education in the Midwest was not necessarily or solely a matter for state normal schools. In many midwestern states the public school movement relied for the education of its teachers on private academies and colleges and on state universities. Besides, there was an insistent demand for agricultural and mechanical education that many thought was more suitable to the sons and daughters of the settlers on the prairies and the plains than the traditional academic fare offered by the colleges. Teacher education, they thought, could well be offered in these institutions also.

Different states followed different paths. Michigan kept the eastern model and opened its state normal school in Ypsilanti in the spring of 1853. The school served as a state-supported alternative to teacher education in private academies and public high schools. It did so as a specialized institution separate from the state university at Ann Arbor and the state agricultural college that was to begin its work in East Lansing in 1855.[28] But when in the late 1840s educators in Iowa and Wisconsin discussed the legal steps required for founding institutions for teacher training, they thought of their state universities as the logical place to begin this work.

In Illinois yet another tack was taken. During the 1850s the Illinois State Normal University was projected as a full-fledged state institution offering instruction in all vocational fields as well as all the traditional academic areas. The founders seized upon the insistent demand that practical training be provided in agriculture and mechanics. Because they distrusted the ability and the willingness of the private colleges and a traditional state university to supply this demand, they created a separate institution that would combine practical instruction in agriculture, in the mechanical arts, and in teaching as well.

But more was involved in Illinois than the creation of an unconventional institution. The founders viewed the normal university as different from the normal schools of Massachusetts. To them it was a people's university open to young men and women from all walks of life. Its early historian, Charles A. Harper, denounced eastern normal training as class-based education and argued that the Illinois State Normal University "was not a plebeian thing, an upper class gesture of philanthropy to the poor and ignorant. . . ." It was "a beacon of progress," an institution created to respond directly to the educational needs of the people. It did not have to compete with academies and colleges, and "there was no State University nor outstanding institution of higher education" to dispute its claim to educational leadership in the state.

By contrast, he continued, the New England state normal schools were "clearly enough due to the Prussian influence and . . . much the same in spirit." They were "training teachers for the common, elementary or folk schools . . . by 'methods' which could be applied rather mechanically, [and] they had no connection or affiliation with any other grade of education." The Illinois State Normal University, however, was free to respond to the needs of local communities and their common and high schools for properly prepared teachers and to develop advanced curricula in professional and academic studies.[29]

Harper's view, though correct in its general outlines, oversimplified a more complex historical development. His reference to the early days of Massachusetts normal schools was unduly critical. To be sure, Cyrus Peirce and Horace Mann had relied on the Prussian model to infuse the common schools of rural Massachusetts with some semblance of Pestalozzian pedagogy. But it had been neither Peirce's nor Mann's fault that the abysmal ignorance of common school graduates required instead a review drill in the elementary curriculum. It wasn't so much that the New England normal schools were limited in their scope by the academies and colleges or by the intent of their founders as Harper claimed, but that the needs of the common schools cried for relief on a quite different level.

Harper also overlooked subsequent developments. He did not credit the honesty of his eastern colleagues when they concluded—some sadly, some gladly—that they could never meet the needs of the rural common schools with the resources at their command. Many of them, we know, followed the Westfield principals and began to train young men from lower middle-class backgrounds as administrators and teachers for city schools and high schools They wanted to break out of the essentially Prussian mold that had assigned the sons and daughters of farmers and industrial workers to the nonacademic teacher seminaries and reserved high school and administrative careers to university graduates. As we have pointed out, they preferred academic and professional education over the basic review of the elementary curriculum and the low-level "theory and practice of teaching." Despite the assertions of their critics to the contrary, they meant to benefit their students as much as themselves. Harper, however, implied that their own academic proclivities made their aims self-serving.

Harper also paid little attention to those of the eastern normal schoolmen who dissented from their colleagues in the Westfield tradition and continued to hope against hope that they might be able to keep alive the normal schools' initial aim of improving the training of the largely female teachers in the elementary schools. That had been the special concern of Colonel Nicholas Tillinghast at Bridgewater. A West Point graduate, Tillinghast had spent a term at Mr. Newman's school in Barre to study the methods of teaching before he took over the reins at Bridgewater. He vigorously championed a less ambitious but more thorough course than proposed at Westfield. "A very few studies and long dwelling on them—this is my theory," he wrote in 1851.[30] He reminded his students that normal schools were to train teachers for the *elementary schools* and that their academic concern was to be with the "foundation on which to build an education." Latin and French, he might have said, were part of the superstructure that for its erection would have to wait for the careful completion of the foundations.

While Tillinghast and like-minded colleagues sought to remain faithful to the initial aims of Mann and Peirce, they did not mean to reject altogether the new direction toward academic and professional studies. They favored a balanced approach that would yet keep the education of elementary teachers as the normal schools' primary task. Though many normal school educators now found the older concerns uninspiring and frustrating, the dissenters were unwilling to write off the rural elementary schools and their women teachers. They refused to allow themselves to be captured altogether by the proponents of scientific pedagogy and professionalization. At Bridgewater and in city normal schools like Boston and Worcester they felt that they could continue to combine the training of elementary school teachers with the new departures in the science of education, school administration, and the training of high school teachers.

It was to prove difficult and, as it would turn out, impossible to keep the two goals in balance. Eventually, the new dispensation of scientific pedagogy and training for high school and administrative positions would dominate the field. But for a time the Bridgewater tradition, defined as a combination of instruction for classroom teaching and preparation for advanced career goals, successfully competed with the Westfield idea for the loyalties of the normal school pedagogues.

As will be shown in greater detail in a later chapter, this was particularly true in the new normal schools in the Midwest. There the need for teachers in rural areas was especially pressing. Charles Hovey, the first principal of the Illinois State Normal University, vigorously promoted training in both academic subjects and teaching: "Those schools that teach the subjects as well as the way to teach them, turn out the best teachers."[31] As his first faculty member he chose Ira Moore, a graduate of Bridgewater and then head of the Chicago High School's normal department. Both Hovey and Moore were steeped in the Bridgewater tradition and thoroughly convinced that the normal university's first duty was the education of elementary school teachers. They thought this ought to be done with rigorous attention to the elementary subjects that lay "nearest the people and . . . will be of most service to them."[32] Pedagogical methods, ethics, and discipline were next in importance. Future teachers needed to know their subjects and be in command of the methods by which to teach them. They also needed to understand the reasons why a particular approach was chosen for teaching a subject.

Under Hovey's successors the Bridgewater tradition continued to dominate the Illinois State Normal University until the 1890s. Richard Edwards, a graduate of Rensselaer Polytechnic Institute, one-time student and instructor at Bridgewater and principal of Salem State Normal School, came to Normal, Illinois, in 1862 from his post as principal of the St. Louis Normal and High School. At Illinois State Normal he presided over a faculty that held three other graduates of Tillinghast's Bridgewater: Edwin C. Hewett, instructor of geography, Thomas Metcalf, instructor of mathematics, and Albert Stetson, Harvard graduate and instructor in Latin, rhetoric, and grammar. When after 14 years Edwards passed the reins on to Edwin Hewett, the Bridgewater tradition remained unbroken. Tillinghast could have written what Edwards submitted to the National Teachers Association in 1865: "The proper work of the Normal School cannot be performed unless the mastery of the subjects has first been obtained."[33] He would have endorsed Hewett's sentiment of 1871 that it "ought always to be fundamental" that "the common branches will receive much attention."[34] The Illinois State Normal University of the 1860s was the Bridgewater of the West.

Teacher Educators Debate Their Trade

The spread of normal schools beyond New England and the differences among normal pedagogues in their approach to teacher training impressed them with the necessity of familiarizing themselves with each other's work and of debating their various views and philosophies. They met on a nationwide basis for the first time in 1859 at Trenton, New Jersey. From the start, members argued that men teachers trained in advanced courses in normal schools should be able to climb to the top of their profession. William Franklin Phelps, the first president of what was to become the American Normal School Association, declared that "there is but one salvation for the Normal Schools, and that is, they must be truly professional schools for training teachers."[35]

His colleague Alpheus Crosby of the Salem normal school interpreted this to mean that state normal schools should offer work of collegiate quality to men through advanced courses and didactics. Women normalites should continue to give greater attention to primary education in the basic course, though advanced courses should be open to them also. Crosby reported proudly that at his Salem school 10 women were now enrolled in the advanced class to prepare themselves for high school teaching.[36]

At its conclusion the convention resolved that the normal schools' object was "strictly professional, viz., the direct preparation of teachers for their great work. . . ." Therefore,

> pupils should not be received until they have attained such maturity of mind and amount of knowledge that they can at once enter profitably upon the proper professional course of the school. . . . While the labors of the Normal School must be chiefly directed, for the present, to the right preparation of common school teachers, it ought not to omit from its plan the professional education of teachers of any grade. . . .[37]

Members at the convention were no longer willing to spend their time on remedial education of common school graduates. They were in no mood to restrict their activities entirely to the education of elementary school teachers. They were ready to push ahead into new territories of professional work.

Eleven years later at the 1870 convention in Cleveland the normal educators were even more determined to follow the professional course and to
reject the education of elementary teachers as their primary task. New professional vistas were beckoning. Professor Phelps, who by now had moved from
the New Jersey State School at Trenton to the Minnesota State Normal School
at Winona, was clearly worried about this trend. When he delivered his
report "The Course of Study for Normal Schools," it was the last time that an
ex-president and major influential voice among the normal school educators
sought to stem the tide and put in a word for the training of teachers for the
elementary schools. "The schools forming the lower parts of our system are
deplorably deficient," he said. "They are mainly in the hands of ignorant,
unskilled teachers."[38]

This was not and should not have been a new revelation. Everyone in the
assembled convention either knew or could have known that, but few were
willing to admit it. The normal schools had never managed to conquer the
problems of preparing teachers for the rural elementary schools. These lower
schools, Phelps said, "present altogether the most difficult problems in respect to methods of instruction and administration with which educators are
obliged to deal. . . ." By comparison, training teachers for high school and
college teaching was an easy matter. Primary school teaching, on the other
hand, "is so distinctive and peculiar in its character and aims as to demand a
distinctive and peculiar training. . . ."[39]

Phelps pointed directly to the share of blame that normal school pedagogues carried. The normal schools, Phelps argued, had been diverted from
their original task of training teachers for the elementary schools. They were
now far more interested in the preparation of instructors for the high schools.
This had diminished "their influence and usefulness as agencies for the professional training of teachers." What was needed at this point, suggested
Phelps, was a new departure: the introduction of a graded system that would
establish and distinguish two separate kinds of normal schools, one "for the
preparation of elementary teachers, and another for school officers and instructors in the higher departments."[40] The Bridgewater tradition of a balanced emphasis in every normal school had to be modified.

In presenting this proposition Phelps's chief concern remained for the
elementary schools and their teachers. The great mass of students in the country spent their time in elementary schools and were taught by teachers who
themselves stood in need of further education. Thus the association should
turn its attention to the area of greatest deficiency and need—the normal
schools training elementary teachers. These teachers had to deal every day
with students of whom only "few are able to ascend so far as to claim the
privileges of the higher institutions. . . ." Thus, Phelps emphasized, "the
courses of study for the elementary schools should be selected less with refer-

ence to a preparation for the higher courses, if need be, than for the duties of life."[41] The same policy should then be followed with regard to the curriculum for the normal schools that trained elementary school teachers.

County Normals and City Training Schools

Phelps's suggestion to improve the education of elementary school teachers by creating a graded system of normal schools met with favorable response from his colleagues in the Midwest. Professor Samuel W. White of the county normal school in Peoria, Illinois, urged the normal educators at the Cleveland convention "to go down to the mass of the teachers and take them by the hand and help them. . . ." He reminded his colleagues that normal school students everywhere rarely finished the full normal course. What, then,

> is the advantage of establishing schools with a two or three years' course for them to attend? . . . It is apparent that the experience of the country demands the establishment of a system of normal schools which shall embrace in their course of study only branches taught in common schools, with some instruction in methods and school management. . . .[42]

Being an instructor in a county normal school, White knew whereof he spoke. Normal school students, he added, do not travel far to go to school. Therefore normal schools should be located near their homes, and a system of county normal schools would accomplish that. Furthermore, primary school teachers usually do not teach much longer than one year. That was convincing proof, argued White, "that they look upon the business of instruction as a mere make-shift and that they will make no greater effort to fit themselves for it than public opinion requires."[43] Phelps's proposal, White thought, was an appropriate and inexpensive means to reach the largest number of elementary school teachers with a modest, but adequate, amount of training. The county training or county normal school provided just what was needed.

From Iowa, Professor W. E. Crosby added support when he spoke of a variation on Professor White's county normal school. In Iowa, Crosby reported, a legislative provision had already been made for county high schools with teacher training departments. "I think," said Crosby, "that when this law comes to be worked out properly, it will be seen that the training or normal school may be properly and with great advantage, attached to the county high school." This was to be a great boon to women. "Every young lady that enters a high school should be able to train children; and the one who is prepared for that work of teaching in the school, is all the better prepared for the duties of life."[44] Teacher education would then go hand in hand with secondary education and take care of the country's need for elementary school teachers.

Three years later at the 1873 meeting of the National Education Association in Elmira, New York, Delia A. Lathrop, a Cincinnati teacher, took up the suggestion of the training school. She complained that the state normal schools neither sent their graduates as teachers into the rural elementary schools nor supplied the required number of trained administrators for these schools. As a result administrative positions were usually taken by college graduates who had never served an apprenticeship in teaching, knew nothing of any philosophy of education, and only scorned the normal schools and their mostly female graduates. So it happened, she continued,

> that in many instances the keen-sighted, professionally educated women in subordinate positions are thwarted in all their superior plans by the stupid conservatism or conservative stupidity of time-out-of-mind principals or superintendents, or by the ignorant assumption of book-crammed boys placed in authority over them.

Since, she concluded, the state normal schools did not produce the needed elementary teachers anyhow, they might allow the county training schools to take over the education of elementary school teachers while the state normals devoted their energies "to the work of educating school superintendents, teachers of high schools, [and] principals of training schools. . . ."[45]

The county training schools, Lathrop argued, were far superior to the annual teacher institutes in which local committees exposed the participants to academic and professional inspiration through guest lectures and an exchange of experiences.[46] Better work could be done with and for the mass of teachers in small towns and rural areas. There, Lathrop said, young women will teach for four or five years and can never be expected to become professional teachers. Yet the state could not afford to have them spend any part of their teaching years "in unskilled work or foolish experiments. . . . We have a right," she insisted, "to demand excellent qualifications, educational and professional, from these temporary teachers."[47] A new effort needed to be made to rescue the rural schools, their students, and their teachers. The county training school was the answer.

Lathrop pointed to the city training schools in the Oswego tradition as models and recommended that they be introduced in rural locations where they could be combined with township high schools.[48] The county superintendents were to be their supervisors, and high school graduates aspiring to teach for a few years could there receive a one-year training course. The danger to be avoided, she counselled, was that, under the pressure of parents and instructors who sought heightened academic standards, the training course become nothing more than an additional year of high school education. Lathrop, however, wanted students of excellent academic preparation who were to receive strictly professional training.[49]

Lathrop's proposal sought to bring as much of the Bridgewater tradition as possible into the twentieth century. But, like Phelps's, it broke with Tillinghast's concern for the unity of the teaching profession when it sundered the teacher education enterprise by separating the training of temporary rural elementary teachers from that of the "true professionals" in city schools and administrative offices. It may well be argued that, instead of Lathrop's proposal being seen as another instance of deepening and hardening the rift among America's public educators, it should be appreciated as but a realistic recognition: As long as America's rural schools were governed by local boards and their teachers were subject to lay direction in professional matters, neither could rural teachers regard themselves as professionals nor would they serve in any other capacity than as temporary schoolkeepers. The meaning of Lathrop's proposal as well as that of many other contributions to the on-going discussion on teacher education hinged on the place the American teacher held in the estimation of her countrymen.

Professionalization Takes Command

However one may interpret the proposals debated at Cleveland and Elmira, the pleas for graded normal schools and separate training schools for elementary teachers did not find ready acceptance among the educators assembled at their conventions. In 1870 Phelps's eastern colleagues objected to his report because they felt he had exaggerated the deficiencies of the country's elementary schools, and they were unwilling to modify the system as they knew it. Each respondent complained that Phelps had not paid enough attention to whatever subject the respective speaker favored—drawing, mental philosophy, object teaching, government, or some other field.

Phelps replied that because of financial pressures alone the western states could not plan on training every kind of teacher. With only moderate means available in Minnesota, Illinois, Indiana, Kentucky, Louisiana, and the Southwest a choice had to be made and priorities had to be defined. The eastern model could not be adopted everywhere. Phelps was very clear on his recommendation. He wanted to place the accent on the primary schools. "I claim," said Phelps, "that the system in New York is too complex for the newer states. Why should our normal schools attempt at the same time to train primary teachers, high school teachers, and teachers for the colleges?"[50] A graded system where schools would be distinct in their functions and where greater attention would be paid to the lower grade and smaller schools that served a dispersed rural constituency across the country—that was Phelps's proposal in 1870. If he rejected the Westfield approach, his sympathy for the elementary teacher did not prevent him from counselling a modification of the Bridgewater tradition.

Phelps's colleagues did not appreciate his message. Despite the favorable words of some of the western county and high school normal advocates, the 1870 convention was about to turn Phelps down. Debate grew heated, and at one point Phelps remonstrated emphatically that the subject of his report was the normal curriculum for teachers of the elementary schools. He did not wish to have it diluted with concerns of the training of high school and college teachers. "No, sir," he said, "I consider primary education to be as high as any grade. I am not willing to admit that it is lower than college education."[51] Alas for Professor Phelps. The convention decided to submit the entire question of curriculum and type of training to a committee that was to report at the 1872 meeting in Boston.[52]

When the committee submitted its work, little was left of Professor Phelps's concern for the elementary schools and their teachers. As the members stated with disarming honesty: "A little reflection . . . will show that . . . we have broached nothing that is new." The committee just brought everything together that had, at one time or another, been recommended as being good for teacher education. Referring to the many schools, professorships, and institutes listed in the report, it said:

> Each of the agencies named exists here and there, and many of them are acting with vigor and efficiency. What we need is that they should come into general use, that they should all act with energy and effect, and that they should be supported with a liberality proportionate to the wants of the nation.[53]

Phelps had been overruled. Concerns for affordability were no longer heard. Everything was to be had in spades.

Just what were the "agencies" the committee recommended? Starting at the top, there was to be a school or faculty of education at every university and a professor of education for every college and high school. Next, every state should have at least one, if possible two or more, higher normal schools for the training of teachers for high schools and for elementary normal schools as well as for the preparation of city and county school superintendents. Then should come elementary county normal schools for the training of teachers for primary and intermediate grades and for rural schools. Finally, every county should be encouraged to run a normal institute for two to six weeks every year. Mr. Phelps's great concern for the rural schools had been absorbed as only one item—and as such neither a very important nor exciting one—in a grand shopping list in which every one could find something of interest.[54]

As if to bring home the orchestrated performance to the group and to underline that here, indeed, the convention was confronted with a finely balanced grab bag, the presiding officer, after noting that Mr. Phelps had spoken from the Northwest, called for comment on a representative from each the East and the South. Principal Hagar of Salem Normal School endorsed

Phelps's report but added that he did not favor the elementary county normals. President Hodgson of the University of Alabama moved in the same direction. He informed the group that normal education in his state was carried out at the university only. That meant women did not receive any teacher training. "We have begun in the university and expect to work downward," he added.[55] Everyone seemed eager to keep the lid down on Professor Phelps's earlier concern for the rural elementary schools and their teachers. As far as the American Normal School Association was concerned, training teachers for the rural elementary schools had decidedly gone out of fashion. Now the future lay with the creation of an educational professional elite. The preparation of high school teachers, normal school instructors, and superintendents was the goal.

From Boston the new dispensation spread in speeches, addresses, and editorials all across the land. One of the most colorful speakers in this professional circuit riding was the Reverend Amory Dwight Mayo, a Massachusetts-born Unitarian and staunch advocate of public and normal schools. During the late 1870s his essays expressed his despair over the normal schools as they had existed in the past. They could never, he argued, remedy the rural teacher problem. They were clogged

> with young women of every stage of academical unfitness; indeed, [Mayo continued,] a considerable number of their students could not obtain admission to a superior high school. . . . It is almost impossible that a green country maiden, with a poor grammar school outfit, even after a year's severe application, should be competent to appreciate the profound system of normal methods so admirably elaborated in schools like Westfield, Mass., and Oswego, N.Y.

What was needed was a complete remodelling of the whole teacher education process. State normal schools should become "true normal colleges. . . ."[56] This would ultimately result in the improvement of the rural common schools and their women teachers.

The new, improved normal colleges should accept neither the young common school graduates nor the older but inexperienced and untrained teachers, but send them to the county normals and institutes. Instead, the normal colleges should seek to educate a new breed of master teachers, department heads, and principals. These in turn could then transmit their knowledge of the principles of scientific pedagogy obtained in the normal colleges by coaching and supervising the elementary teachers in the classrooms of the common schools. Mayo's assumption, not always made explicit, was that the supervisors would make up a largely male corps of professional pedagogues directing the activities of an overwhelmingly female teaching force in the elementary schools.

In all of this Mayo was very concerned that this new scientific professionalism of the supervisors and the semiprofessionalism of the classroom teachers be under the exclusive control of the scientific pedagogues. "The heart of the new education is its reverence for the true scientific spirit," and it must prevail in every teacher.[57] Just as the master teacher was to receive his education in the state normal schools, so the great majority of the classroom teachers needed to attend only a basic one-year introduction in one of the county or city training schools. In effect, these new training schools would take the place of the old but now upgraded normal schools. They would offer a program similar to that of the Boston Normal School.

Mayo vigorously opposed the college and high school as they then existed as sources of teachers for the common schools. He berated the high school that sought a college graduate "absolutely untaught and untested in teaching" as its principal.[58] Echoing Delia Lathrop, Mayo painted a picture of open or smothered conflict in hundreds of classrooms in which "the learned young man, contemptuous of the academical inferiority of his girl assistant" was pitted against "the bright girl-graduate of the normal school, electric with tact, and on edge with the new methods, poking fun at the pompous, pedagogic incapacity of her principal."[59] It was Mayo's belief that their past sins notwithstanding—the deference so often shown to the academic approach of lecturing and classroom instruction—only the normal schools had caught a glimpse of the spirit of modern, scientific pedagogy. They alone were able to convey it.

For men like Mayo the elevation of the normal school to be teachers colleges of truly scientific standing and devoted to the training of competent teachers meant the creation of a selective, centralized system of teacher education in each state.

> Instead of multiplying the state normals, the efforts should be made to raise the qualifications for entering, and so enlarge their facilities and extend their course of study that they may furnish, even in greater measure than now, the leaders of superior school-keeping. . . . Here may be educated an increasing number of experts who, after suitable experience, will naturally fall into the management of the department of pedagogics in every institution of learning.[60]

The normal schools, instead of being schools for teachers, would become colleges for the teachers of teachers.

In his many speeches and articles Mayo built on the resolution of the 1872 normal school convention in Boston. He envisaged an all-inclusive system of scientific pedagogy topped in each state by one central state normal university. Its staff would be responsible for the training of professors of teaching for all educational institutions. These new pedagogical experts would hold the chairs of pedagogy in universities, colleges, and state normal schools and also in the training schools, high schools, and academies. Once the system was in place, high school teachers could again safely be educated in universities and colleges. The new professors of education trained at the state normal universities would see to it that scientific pedagogy would be taught there as well.[61]

Old Debates and New Issues

However grand Mr. Mayo's prospect, it did not go entirely unquestioned. Occasionally, voices of protest could still be heard that sought to call Americans down to earth to the world of teacher education as it existed, not in the blue prints of committees and enthusiasts like Mayo, but in the rural and urban normal schools themselves. We read one such presentation in the remarks of George E. Gay, in 1897 superintendent of schools in Malden, Massachusetts, as he debated with Albert G. Boyden, principal of the Bridgewater State Normal School. Gay took the Horace Mann–Cyrus Peirce point of view of normal education as the preparation of teachers for the elementary schools. Boyden sought to fuse a version of Mayo's new scientific pedagogy approach with aspects of the philosophy of his Bridgewater predecessor Tillinghast.

In Gay's view the normal schools' departure into the academic and professional training of high school teachers and administrators was a waste of money. That effort diverted "the time and strength of principals and teachers from what should be the regular work of the schools." Only very few students took that instruction anyway, and "the money spent upon them is altogether out of proportion of the good accomplished." Gay cited a joke told in Westfield of a normal school teacher earning $2,000 per year to teach three pupils to speak Latin.

That effort was not only expensive, said Gay, it was also pointless. There were now enough college graduates available for high school teaching, "and the normal graduate *per se* is no longer in demand for high school work." Besides, he added, the high school graduate who chose to take a four-year advanced course at a normal school and then wanted to enter a university found that he was qualified to enter no higher than the junior class in college. "It is a perfectly safe conclusion," remarked Gay sarcastically, "that the academic work of our normal schools can not be justified on account of its preeminent excellence."[62] No, the normal schools should stay with their traditional task and bend all their efforts to prepare their students to teach in the elementary schools.

Boyden's response played on the theme of professionalism. From Tillinghast, Boyden took the assertion that normal schools should educate elementary teachers as educators who were thoroughly trained and had learned to think for themselves.[63] For that reason, Boyden wrote, a four-year course with its strong and deep foundation in academic subject matter and principles of teaching and school administration was preferable to a mere two years of training. That Boyden had paid heed to Mayo's message became apparent when he proudly related that at Bridgewater a course "was established and is now maintained for the better preparation of teachers for the upper grades of the common schools, principals, assistants and teachers for departmental work. . . . As a matter of fact," Boyden added, "some of the abler graduates . . . have become teachers in high schools, and some have become superintendents and supervisors. . . ." Still, he went on, "it is no part of the purpose of this course to fit for college, but it has so increased the desire for more extended study that many of the graduates from it have gone to college and are now filling influential positions. . . ."[64] Under Boyden, Bridgewater meant to uphold both the Tillinghast tradition and the commitment to professionalization.

Was all, then, well and good in the world of Massachusetts normal schools? Hardly, one would think, if one looked once again at what actually happened to the students of the state's normal schools. There was something curiously incongruous about the developments after 1870. At the very time that the normal school principals sought to make the study of pedagogy scientific and to march in a collegiate direction, playing down the training of women teachers for the elementary school and introducing instruction for men in high school subjects, nearly 9 out of 10 Massachusetts teachers were women.[65] Twenty-nine years later in 1899 the United States commissioner of education would report that in the then 10 public normal schools in Massachusetts 56 (i.e., 4 percent) of the 1,421 normal students were men.

Did the new trend toward high school teaching exist for the benefit of these 4 percent? Was it but a ploy to stem the tide toward ever-increasing feminization in public school teaching and to save and keep the few remaining men by promising them a more attractive future in secondary education and in administration? Were the normal pedagogues ready to write off the many hundred women who wanted to be prepared for elementary school teaching?

And how successful were normal educators like Boyden with their students? Apparently they did not convince many of their students to enter upon a professional educator's career from high school teacher to principal and superintendent or normal school president. Many of the male graduates used their prolonged training at Bridgewater as a platform from which to enter business, law, or other white-collar and professional careers. In very few cases, if any, did anyone with either Boyden's or his students' outlook regard elementary teaching as a career in itself. The rural classrooms would not see these graduates, at least not as teachers.

Yet as the last quarter of the century wore on, something new did appear on the educational horizon and began to deflect attention from the problems of the rural schools. Immigration from Europe and the population movement from the countryside into the cities called for an increased supply of elementary teachers for city schools. Neither were the untractable problems of the rural schools solved nor did they disappear from the scene. But they vanished from the attention of contemporaries and came to be by-passed in favor of the urban issues.

For normal educators in Massachusetts these new departures had manifested themselves in the struggles over the opening of city normal schools. In Worcester and Boston, as we know, city normal schools separate from the high schools had gotten underway in 1868 and 1872. Similar development had occurred in other states. Philadelphia witnessed the opening of a normal school for girls as early as 1848. In Baltimore, Saturday normal classes for teachers had been added to the high schools in 1851, and by 1864 a fourth-year normal class was added to the two female high schools. When the Maryland State Normal School opened two years later in Baltimore, a city normal school was then no longer thought necessary.[66] In Chicago a normal department was opened at the high school in 1856.St. Louis reported opening its normal school the following year, Cincinnati did so in 1868, and Cleveland in 1874.[67]

The growth of city schools and the attendant demands on the supply of teachers soon overshadowed the unmet needs of rural schools. By 1870 Massachusetts educators could persuade themselves that whatever training was necessary for the teachers of rural schools could be given in the state normal schools and in the one-year course of the training schools. But that training was no longer the normal educators' chief concern. The more demanding problems and issues, they thought, now lay in the cities. Here city normal and city training schools could take on the task of furnishing teachers, while the state normal schools should now be focussed on the training of high school teachers, school administrators, and teacher educators. State normal schools would become the scientific centers for the study of pedagogy and school administration on every level. There would lie the future of the profession.

5
Teacher Education in the Midwest

Normal Training Comes to Illinois

Charles Harper said it emphatically: The midwestern state normal schools—
and particularly the Illinois State Normal University—were democracy's
institutions. Unlike their earlier cousins in New England, they no longer were
held by bonds of indebtedness or sympathy to the teacher seminaries of Prussia's class-bound society. Unlike the New England normal schools, too, not all
of them had to appear on a scene already dominated by private academies
and colleges or private and public universities. To them to ask for public
support was not a matter of asking for charity but of claiming a public right.[1]

In Illinois in the 1850s habits and traditions of schooling were still very
much in flux. Public taxation for the state's common schools became law only
in 1855. While during the next five years the state's population increased by
31 percent, the number of schools leaped by 106 percent, students by 172
percent, and teachers by 159 percent.[2] There was neither a state university
nor enough academies and high schools to supply a sufficient number of
trained teachers. The schoolmen interested in creating a state normal school
maneuvered in an open field, and their chances of success were good.

Proponents of normal education were not the only ones seeking public
support for educational ventures in the new state. Illinois had witnessed a
lively agitation by the Industrial League and the State Agricultural Society
for industrial and agricultural education. When the first annual meeting of
the newly created Illinois Teachers' Institute took place in December 1854,
the assembled members endorsed a suggestion voiced by State Superintendent Ninian W. Edwards that, in a projected state normal school, "the courses
of instruction . . . must be materially modified" because of the dominance
in Illinois of so many agricultural, mechanical, and commercial interests.[3]
Edwards maintained that the cause of normal school education could benefit

109

from more widespread support only if it were tied to the growing demand for practical and utilitarian instruction.

The teachers were correct. The alliance of proponents for agricultural, industrial, and normal education persuaded the legislature, and in 1857 it authorized the founding of the state normal university at what was to become Normal, Illinois. The institution's charter, however, was not modelled on those of the New England normal schools. The state normal university's assigned duties were to go beyond the usual normal school subjects of the theory and practice of teaching and the elementary school curriculum. They were to cover instruction "in the elements of the natural sciences, including agricultural chemistry, animal and vegetable physiology, in the fundamental laws of the United States and of the state of Illinois in regard to the rights and duties of citizens, and such other studies as the board of education may from time to time prescribe."[4]

It is a moot question whether this formulation was meant to endear the institution to the continuing goodwill of the industrial and agricultural interests, or whether, as an anonymous contributor to the *Illinois Baptist* wrote, it was used to allow the state to draw on the federal government's university fund, or whether, as Superintendent William H. Powell remarked, it was chosen to permit the school readily to be "swelled into the full proportions of a university, should the people of the State and the Legislature desire it."[5] But it did demonstrate rather clearly that Illinois legislators and schoolmen desired to emphasize the intimate connection of the common schools to the state's principal economic concern. "It is as necessary that the boy in our Common Schools, destined to the life of a farmer, should be taught the scientific admixture of soils, and the principles of practical horticulture and arboriculture, as it is that he should be instructed in the art of framing sentences, or the solution of difficult mathematical problems," wrote Superintendent Powell.[6]

As subsequent developments would show, circumstances dictated that the Illinois State Normal University was to base its appeal to the citizens of the state on its comprehensive approach. Charles Harper's view was to prevail. The Illinois Industrial University was not going to imitate "the spirit of the New England normal. . . ."[7] While the founders saw the training of elementary school teachers to be the school's primary object, they rejected a restrictive view of this mission. Instead they hoped to expand and elevate teacher training until it would include the best and the latest of new pedagogical insight and wisdom.

As indicated in the preceding chapter, the educators at Normal, Illinois, remained faithful to the Bridgewater tradition and spoke up as defenders of the largely female elementary teachers and their needs. Like Nicholas Tillinghast they were determined to preserve the unity of the teaching profession. Their first principal, Charles Hovey, though a graduate of Dartmouth

College, was much experienced in public education. Before he assumed his duties at the Illinois State Normal School he had pursued a distinguished career as a public school teacher, principal, and superintendent. When he arrived in Normal he served as the editor of *The Illinois Teacher* and president of the State Teacher's Association.

Hovey did not limit his vision of the normal university to the circumstances of 1857. Writing in that year and acknowledging the advice of William F. Phelps, he endorsed Phelps's suggestion of a graded system of normal schools. Preparatory normals would offer a "thoroughly elementary training" and a testing of the pupil for "his adaptation for the profession of teaching." Their graduates should be qualified to teach in primary and small schools. The normal schools proper would admit graduates of the preparatory normals or of a high school and turn out teachers for grammar, union, and large city high schools.[8] Like Phelps, Hovey advocated graded normal schools without lessening in the slightest his insistence that the state normal schools had as their primary duty the training of elementary school teachers.

Two years later at the Trenton convention of the American Normal School Association, Hovey elaborated on his conception of a thorough training of elementary school teachers. He told the convention that his colleagues in Illinois wanted to accomplish more than supplying the normal department of a state university. "We mean," he said, "that it shall be a university in fact as well as in name."[9] For elementary school teachers to have a firm knowledge of their subjects they should study them at their advanced as well as at their introductory level. The study of grammar, for example, should move beyond the memorization and repetition stage and be based on a study of English classics. For the English language to be understood fully, Hovey wrote, "its father, the Latin, and its mother, the German, may well be introduced to the acquaintance of the student."[10]

Yet during the school's early years the emphasis on the advanced subjects had to be muted. It was difficult enough to persuade the Illinois State Normal men and women students to pass through the full three-year course, let alone entice them to take advanced academic subjects. During the school's first five years of instruction relatively few students graduated from the three-year course. By 1862 a total of 506 students had passed through the school and only 52 had stayed for three years and graduated. Nineteen of these had been men, and 23 women.[11] As late as 1907 only 1,760, or 7.33 percent, of the 24,013 normal school students had attended for three years and received their diploma.[12]

The low percentage of graduates speaks in part for the high demands and expectations set by the school from its very beginning, but even more so for the background, intentions, and aims of the students attending the normal university. Almost all of the normalites came from farm and lower middle-class homes. President Edwards reported in 1874 that 52 percent of the 2,822 students whose parental background was known and who had attended the university since 1857 had been children of farmers, 13 percent took care of themselves, and 9 percent were children of widows. Most in the latter two groups, he said, had also come from farm families, thus increasing the contingent to about 7 out of 10 students. Seventeen percent of the students came from white-collar families, and 9 percent were of a nonfarm blue-collar background.[13]

As we found in Massachusetts, the students at the normal university in Illinois, too, were generally unable to finance their studies for a long period, and not everyone expected to make teaching his or her life's work. Many were older and had already taught. They came to the university to improve their skills rather than to begin a full course of studies. During the 30 years from 1858 to 1888 the average age of the students in the normal university graduating classes was 26 years and 3 months.[14] These men and women appreciated the opportunity to brush up on their skills and knowledge for as long as they could afford it. They were not necessarily interested in diplomas, but they were eager to get back to work and support themselves through their teaching.

The People's Universities at Normal and Carbondale

During its first 10 years, from 1857 to 1867, the normal university was for all intents and purposes the state university of Illinois. As such its spokesmen had to learn early to listen to what newspaper editorials and legislative committee reports had to say, and, if need be, to play down their own professional interests. To be sure, they remained intent to offer the best possible professional education for their teachers and administrators, but they had to listen to lay people who thought of the normal schools as community colleges or people's universities that would serve the largest number of students with the greatest variety of academic and vocational subjects.

The Illinois State Normal University expressed this ambition in its very name, though in its practice during its first decade it reached a varied and relatively unsophisticated clientele that forced it to be content with rather modest achievements. Its first three presidents, Charles Hovey, Richard Edwards, and Edwin Hewett, had been well aware that it was the school's ability to respond quickly and directly to the needs of its constituents rather than its faithful adherence to the Bridgewater tradition that had earned it its popularity and support. The question that it and other state normal schools had to confront, however, was just who these constituents were. Were they the people of the state of Illinois or of the Bloomington-Normal region, or were they the state's educators: the teachers, school board members, and superintendents? For the normal university's presidents it became a question of how best to serve the state's educational interests while gaining the widest possible support for the school from the tax-paying public. They knew that, however much they may have wanted to pursue single-mindedly the goal of transforming the state's teachers into a truly professional organization whose members were committed to life-long service, they had to take the views and needs of a large community into account. Flexibility and adaptability to popular demands had to be their prime characteristics.

One area in which these qualities became quite apparent concerned the model school associated with the normal university. The model school with its high school department did not fit the Bridgewater pattern. But it filled various needs. It offered opportunities for demonstration, practice, and experimentation in teaching the elementary and intermediate grades. In addition, from 1860 to 1868 it served the town of Normal as a regular district school and aided the normal university financially through tuition payments from out-of-town students and through tax revenue received from the town of Normal. By 1862 a high school was added and two years later a grammar school department to increase the model school's usefulness even more. In that year the school enrolled 153 pupils, of whom 44 were in the primary and intermediate departments and 109 were in the high school.[15]

The growth of the high school occurred despite the normal university's primary commitment to the training of teachers for the elementary schools. It was a direct response to the wishes of the people in Normal and the surrounding area. President Edwards quickly recognized the high school as a cultural and academic magnet to attract older, more mature students who could take up advanced work in mathematics and the natural sciences and, after graduating, could be persuaded to enroll in the normal university. Regular normal school students could be encouraged to sign up for an optional fourth year to prepare themselves for high school teaching. They would then sign up for a program of Latin, Greek, German, French, and advanced English.[16] The fact that the high school acquired nationwide fame as a well-reputed preparatory school for eastern colleges did not harm the normal university's reputation either.[17]

Another area where response to local needs paid dividends concerned continuing education and refresher courses for teachers. Edwards encouraged his faculty to participate in the numerous teachers' institutes of the counties. By 1863 he introduced the normal university's own state teachers' institute, a four-week in-service review of philosophy, methods, and instructional, disciplinary, and legal problems of school management. It was to become an annual affair.[18]

The dependence of the school on popular support brought its own drawbacks as well as benefits. At predictable intervals Principal Edwards had to defend the normal university against attacks that accused it of unfairly competing with other high schools, academies, and colleges in Illinois. In 1868 one critic wanted to restrict the school's offerings to professional matters. The first-year course should no longer be devoted to perfecting and increasing the students' knowledge of subject matters, "but of showing how they can best be handled, taught, learned, and applied."[19]

This charge touched the sensitive issue of the school's graduates who had never taught in the public schools or had done so only briefly. Like the Massachusetts normal schools, the university had required all entering normal students to commit themselves to teaching in the public schools and, to enforce this provision, had also mandated that for three years after graduation they had to report their employment to the state superintendent.[20] Legislators expected the school to furnish from one to three teachers for each county. To provide the necessary incentive, at least one assemblyman had urged the state to consider paying teachers "a reasonable compensation" to keep men in the job for which they had been prepared.[21]

Nothing, of course, came of that suggestion, but Edwards felt compelled nonetheless to reiterate the university's commitment to the pledge of its students. Based on that commitment he felt justified in defending the instruction in the elementary school subjects. "The normal school," he argued in 1867,

> is pre-eminently a democratic institution. The good it does is diffused throughout the common schools taught by its graduates and pupils to the remotest nooks of the State. . . . I, therefore, know of no more legitimate expenditure that a State can make in the interest of the masses of the people.[22]

Besides, he added in 1870, the 13-year record spoke for itself: 2,084 students had passed through the normal university, and 145 of them had graduated from the three-year course. Of the 145 graduates, 116 were still teaching. In addition, 2,360 students attended the model school, and 15 of these graduated from the high school. He estimated that of all those who attended the normal, grammar, or high school course for any length of time, about 1,000 were then teaching in Illinois.[23]

The issue was revived again when in 1873 a census by the state superintendent revealed that the number of the alumni of the normal university then teaching in the state was far smaller than Edwards had proclaimed. It came to 120 graduates and 489 nongraduates. Edwards protested these figures. The census was taken in February, he said, when many women teachers were not employed. Many of the reports from the counties were "evidently understatements," he added. By 1874, he maintained, about 4,000 former students of the university "must have become teachers for a longer or shorter time. . . ."[24] Inasmuch as State Superintendent Bateman's 609 teaching alumni in 1873 amounted to 14.6 percent of the 4,171 Illinois State Normal alumni of 1872 and Principal Edwards' 4,000 former students amounted to 87 percent of the 4,608 alumni in 1873, the discrepancy was quite disconcerting.

However one may read these figures and arguments, the university's comprehensive record indicates that a considerable portion of the graduates taught only very briefly or not at all. Of those who graduated from the three-year normal course during the 1860s—no more than 7 percent of all students—only a third (30.3 percent) spent any number of years as teachers or supervisors in the public schools or as administrators of or professors in normal schools. As one might expect, of the women who went into education, the largest group (18 out of 23, or 78 percent) served as classroom teachers, whereas of the men only 29 percent (6 out of 21) ended their education career in the classroom. A little more than half of the men (11 out of 21, or 52 percent) became public school administrators, and almost a fifth (4 out of 21, or 19 percent) served in normal schools (see Table 5.1). Revealing also are the figures showing that the men devoted an average of 46 years of their lives to education compared with the women's 32. Of these 46 years, men averaged 8.6 in the classroom and 37.5 in an administrator's office. The women's 32-year average is composed of 22 years as teachers and 10 as administrators (see Table 5.2).

Edwards could not admit this record. He insisted repeatedly that the

Table 5.1. Gender Distribution of Illinois State Normal University Alumni, by Graduation and Occupational Statuses, Classes from 1860 to 1870

	Total		Men		Women	
	Number	Percent	Number	Percent	Number	Percent
Alumni	2,084	100.0	—	—	—	—
Nongraduates	1,939	93.0	—	—	—	—
Graduates of 3-year normal course	145	7.0	70	48.3	75	51.7
Graduates	145	100.0	—	—	—	—
Gone into fields other than education	101	69.7	—	—	—	—
Gone into education	44	30.3	21	47.7	23	52.3
Graduates gone into education	44	100.0	21	47.7	23	52.3
Public school principals	9	20.5	5	55.6	4	44.4
Public school superintendents	6	13.6	6	100.0	0	0.0
Normal school presidents	2	4.5	2	100.0	0	0.0
Normal school professors	3	6.8	2	66.7	1	33.3
Subtotals						
Administrators and normal school faculty	20	45.5	15	75.0	5	25.0
Public school teachers	24	54.5	6	25.0	18	75.0

Source: "Alumni Register," *Semi-Centennial History of the Illinois State Normal University, 1857–1907* (Normal: David Felmley, 1907), pp. 251–261.

Note: The percentages in the Total column refer to the total number in the three major categories—alumni, graduates, and graduates gone into education. Each of the percentages in the Men and Women columns refers to its respective number in the Total column.

Table 5.2. Gender Distribution of the Number of Years Spent in School Service by Illinois State Normal University Graduates in Education, Classes from 1860 to 1870

	All Graduates		Men Graduates		Women Graduates	
	Total Number	Average Number per Graduate	Total Number	Average Number per Graduate	Total Number	Average Number per Graduate
Years spent in education	1,699	38.6	967	46.0	732	31.8
Years spent as teachers	689	15.7	180	8.6	509	22.1
Years spent as administrator or normal school faculty member	1,010	23.0	787	37.5	223	9.7

Source: "Alumni Register," *Semi-Centennial History of the Illinois State Normal University, 1857–1907* (Normal: David Felmley, 1907), pp. 251–261.

Note: Columns may not add to totals shown because of rounding.

normal university had been eminently successful in instilling in its students an enthusiasm for and commitment to teaching. The students were pledged to teach, he reminded his readers. "It is their duty, as honorable men and women, to carry out that pledge. As far as known, with very few exceptions, they do it."[25] President Edwards protested too much. His successor, Edwin C. Hewett, was more forthcoming. He admitted that "the very constitution and management of a majority of our schools precludes" a majority of the university's students from devoting their lives to teaching. "Unless one expects to obtain a place in the schools of our large towns and cities, or is willing to be a wanderer on the face of the earth, working six months in a place, he cannot anticipate making teaching a life-long business."[26] As had been true in New England, in the Midwest, too, the problem lay not in the normal school but in the unwillingness of local communities to improve their teachers' working conditions.

What had taken place in Normal was to repeat itself with only minor variations in "Egypt," that is, the southern part of Illinois. On March 9, 1869, a bill for the establishment of the Southern Illinois Normal University was passed in Springfield. There, too, the intentions of the normal schoolmen to provide teacher training had to be squared with the lacking preparation of the students and their unwillingness to commit themselves to a career of schoolteaching. When in 1873 the first students were admitted to their classes, it soon became evident that much elementary work needed to be done to make up for the defects in preparation. "By far too many found their primary education had been imperfect and very superficial," wrote President Allyn. "Hence we have been doing the teaching which ought to have been done in the district school years ago."[27]

In rather stark contrast to this picture of ill-prepared applicants necessitating remedial instruction, however, stood the faculty and the curriculum they proposed. Besides Allyn, who was the former president of McKendree College and a one-time legislator and state superintendent of Rhode Island, Cyrus Thomas, an explorer-scientist and ethnologist, added lustre and scholarly reputation to the institution. All their colleagues had had public school experience, and together they designed a preparatory course for those not ready to take up the normal work. A plan to develop the course into a high school had to be given up when the board demurred. The normal work proper was offered in a classical and a scientific version for three or four years. The goal was to offer everything that might be taught in the state's common and high schools, "from the alphabet to the highest range of philosophy."[28]

The Southern Illinois Normal University thus did the best it could with the means it had at hand. Its students, President Allyn reported in 1876, came largely from the "productive employments." Not unlike those at Illinois State Normal, 51 percent hailed from farm and 12 percent from nonfarm blue-collar families; the fathers of 15 percent of the students represented professional employment and 22 percent other white-collar employment.[29] At the end of the school's first three years not quite 40 percent of the students reported that they were teaching in the common schools.

The school's historian, however, points out that many of the school's students never intended to prepare themselves for teaching. They paid tuition fees and thus avoided the pledge to teach. And even those who did teach used that experience as a stepping stone to other careers. Of the 241 graduates of the school's first 20 years, only 20 remained in teaching. The others, writes Lentz, "became leaders in law, medicine, dentistry, the ministry, politics, government service, journalism, farming, business, homemaking."[30] The training Allyn and his faculty provided served for most of his students as general academic preparation for a great variety of fields.

Throughout the 1860s the Illinois State Normal University sought hard to serve a variety of ends: to continue to prepare the much-needed teachers for the state's rural elementary schools; to supply the teachers and administrators for the new high schools; to lead and direct the summer institutes for teachers already at work; to answer its neighborhood's calls for a high school, and to develop the new educational professionalism. It was fortuitous for the school's ambitious leaders that for 10 years the normal university was spared the competition of a state university, and thus dominated the field as the state's major public university. But the question that would not go away was whether an institution that in the tradition of a community college or people's university tried to answer every educational need of everyone who knocked at its doors could fulfill the demands for which it was created: to train a state's public school teachers.

The Beginnings of Teacher Education in Kansas

In Kansas, teacher educators sought deliberately to create a comprehensive state normal school on the Bridgewater-Illinois model. But their efforts were beset with difficulties. Neither did Kansas legislators permit the development of a program on the Illinois model, nor were they willing to support the Bridgewater program. They opted for the Michigan model of the separate establishment of three public institutions: a state normal school, a state agricultural college, and a state university. Motivated primarily by financial considerations, they wanted to keep the normal school on the level of a training school that would prepare teachers for the elementary schools only.

Kansas teacher educators, like their colleagues everywhere, debated long and hard by what strategy they might best turn schoolkeeping into a profession. Could this be done by following the Westfield pattern and placing major emphasis on the training of high school and special teachers and of administrators, or should they try the Bridgewater tradition of joining in one institution and in one profession the pedagogy of the classroom teacher and the science of the administrator? If they followed the Westfield course, did this mean inevitably and necessarily that they must abandon the concern for the elementary classroom? If they adhered to the Bridgewater tradition would not the university want to restrict them to the training of elementary teachers and demand for itself the education of high school teachers, specialists, and administrators? And how could they make themselves heard in the legislative halls in Topeka?

At the very beginning the Illinois example was held up to Kansas educators and politicians. Late in 1856, W.F.M. Arny, a member of the Illinois State Board of Education, urged John W. Geary, governor of Kansas Territory, to set into motion the establishment of a university consisting of a normal school, an agricultural and horticultural school, and a mechanical school. Obviously, the Illinois State Normal precedent was in Arny's mind.[31] But it was not to prevail. Instead, the normal school opened its doors in February 1865 in Emporia, 7½ years after the Illinois State Normal University had done so in Normal. An agricultural college was placed in Manhattan and a university in Lawrence. Two private seminaries chartered by the territorial assembly in 1858 to "promote the education of agricultural and professional teachers for common and high schools" had never opened.[32]

The Kansas State Normal School in Emporia was to train men and women in the art of teaching, husbandry, agricultural chemistry, mechanic arts, the fundamental laws of the United States, "and in what regards the rights and duties of citizens. . . ."[33] The state superintendent asked that it end what he termed "the failure" of teaching. "Hitherto," he wrote, "most of our teachers have only taught as a temporary employment—as a mere stepping-stone to something that *pays* better." Though women teachers earned only about 80 percent of the salary of men teachers, the superintendent pointed out that Kansas paid women teachers far better than other states. Now, he added proudly, the normal school would improve matters even more by turning teaching into a profession.[34]

The opening festivities in 1865 bore a decidedly Christian tone. They were presided over by the Reverend Mr. Grosvenor C. Morse as secretary of the school's board of directors. Morse, who was to play in Kansas the role Charles Brooks had once played in Massachusetts, was a graduate of Dartmouth College and the Andover Theological Seminary as well as an agent of the American Home Missionary Society.[35] The parable of the sower was read and everyone present recited the Lord's prayer. The ceremony underlined the then-general Christian tenor of the public school movement. Three years later the board affirmed it once more when it resolved that it was "the duty of the faculty to impress upon the minds of the students the fundamental principles of the Christian religion. . . . Yet," the members cautioned, "as the institution is not in any respect denominational, the faculty or any member of it will not be justified in inculcating denominational peculiarities in speaking to students for or against any church organization."[36]

Speaking a year later before the American Normal School Association the school's first principal, Lyman B. Kellog, provided the "pagan" backdrop against which the "Christian" normal school came into existence. "My story is," he told his listeners,

> that of a normal school on the extreme frontier, where Indians are, where revolvers are every day companions; and where the people hang horse thieves without waiting the intervention of courts of justice. Its location is included in what used to be marked on the maps as the "Great American Desert." . . .

Kellog referred to the vicious fratricide in Kansas during territorial days. Kansas had experienced "a baptism of fire and blood" and a "record of fierce passion and atrocious crime mingled with heroism, and long suffering, and stern devotion to principle."[37] With these horrors scarcely receding into memory, was it any wonder that the normal school became a rallying point for the disciples of education and nonsectarian religion?

Before coming to Kansas, Kellog had been a student of Richard Edwards and model school teacher at the Illinois State Normal University. Acutely conscious of the Bridgewater tradition he insisted that "the primary object and purpose of the Normal School . . . [was] the instruction of both men and women in the art of teaching. All else clusters around this idea of teaching the teachers." He fully agreed with the superintendent in endorsing the state constitution's mandate in all matters concerning schools not making any "distinction between the rights of males and females." The minds of male and female teachers were "to be improved by an enlarged and liberal course of study; but," he insisted, "it is all for the purpose of adding to their efficiency as teachers."[38]

Kellog's indebtedness to Edwards becomes apparent in his formulation of the curriculum. "The studies pursued," he announced, "will be those taught in the Public Schools, to which will be added the different branches of a complete English education, together with so much of Latin and Greek as are necessary to a full understanding of our own language." As at Illinois State Normal, a three-year course was necessary to graduate, and students who received free tuition had to pledge that they would teach as many years in the state schools of Kansas as they had attended the normal school. "The honor of the pupils is at stake regarding its fulfillment," wrote Kellog.[39] When looking for faculty members to join him at Emporia, Kellog relied on Illinois State Normal to supply him with his assistant principal, Henry B. Norton, and model school principal, Mrs. J.W. Gorham.[40]

At the end of the 1860s, neither Kellog nor the state superintendent were entirely satisfied with the school's performance. Although it had shown an average annual attendance of 90 students in its normal department, only 7 men and 13 women had graduated from the three-year course (see the data through 1870 in Table 5.3). The others had attended the school for shorter periods, many of them having been teachers who came to refresh their knowledge and hone their skills. Principal Kellog reported in 1870 that a "large number of the students leave the school at the close of the first year. Some begin teaching after they have been in attendance but a single term. . . ."

Principal Kellog sought to overcome this disappointing record by suggesting a modification of the original program. He reduced the regular course for elementary school teachers from three to two years and he added a four-year course for future high school teachers.[41] The superintendent argued that "the educational growth of the State . . . has made the need of classical instruction in the Normal School imperative. . . ." The normal school, he maintained, was called upon to supply teachers not only for the common schools but for academies and high schools as well.[42]

But this step in the direction of the Westfield program met with failure. The legislators' reaction, an economic depression, and natural as well as human disasters nearly closed the school for good. Principal Kellog resigned in 1871, a tornado hit, a fire destroyed the school building, and a financial scandal involved the school's treasurer. Upset over the introduction of the high school

Table 5.3. Gender Distribution of Enrollees at Kansas State Normal School at Emporia, 1865–1900

| | Total Enrollment | | | Model School (Elementary) | | | Normal School (Secondary) | | | | | | Percent Graduating from Normal School |
| | | | | | | | Enrollees | | | Graduates | | | |
	Men	Women	Total	Men	Women	Total	Men	Women	Total	Men	Women	Total	
1865	—	—	43	0	0	0	—	—	43	0	0	0	0
1866	31	54	85	0	0	0	31	54	85	—	—	0	0
1867	—	—	75	0	0	0	—	—	75	—	2	2	2.67
1868	75	78	153	15	12	27	70	55	125	—	4	4	3.20
1869	76	74	150	18	19	37	58	55	113	5	4	9	7.96
1870	96	102	198	—	—	32	—	—	95	2	3	5	5.25
1871	111	132	243	31	32	63	79	99	178	—	—	0	0
1872	72	118	190	0	0	0	64	103	167	1	1	2	1.20
1873	89	129	218	0	0	0	66	105	171	—	3	3	1.75
1874	—	—	236	—	—	45	—	—	191	4	11	15	7.85
1875	—	—	375	—	—	230	—	—	145	8	10	18	12.41
1876	—	—	345	—	—	—	—	—	—	7	10	17	
1877	—	—	125	—	—	—	—	—	—	4	1	5	
1878	—	—	130	—	—	—	—	—	—	—	2	2	
1879	—	—	90	—	—	50	—	—	40	—	7	12	30.00
1880	—	—	199	54	82	136	29	34	63	8	3	11	17.46
1881	—	—	366	93	109	202	68	96	164	—	—	21	12.80
1882	—	—	402	92	110	202	83	117	200	—	—	44	22.00
1883	—	—	456	91	111	202	100	154	254	—	—	36	14.17
1884	—	—	534	95	156	251	114	169	283	—	—	20	7.07
1885	—	—	605	126	178	304	109	192	301	—	—	18	5.98
1886	—	—	724	86	242	328	112	284	396	—	—	33	8.33
1887	—	—	746	119	160	279	158	309	467	—	—	23	4.93
1888	—	—	875	107	125	232	231	407	638	—	—	41	6.43
1889	—	—	930	120	125	245	282	403	685	—	—	41	5.99
1890	—	—	1,120	114	144	258	275	587	862	—	—	—	
1891	—	—	1,306	110	149	259	390	657	1,047	—	—	—	
1892	—	—	1,404	86	122	208	409	787	1,196	—	—	—	
1893	—	—	1,388	66	97	163	452	773	1,225	—	—	—	
1894	—	—	1,348	51	75	126	442	780	1,222	—	—	—	
1895	—	—	1,650	53	104	157	468	1,025	1,493	—	—	—	
1896	—	—	1,840	75	124	199	586	1,055	1,641	—	—	—	
1897	—	—	1,927	84	119	203	657	1,067	1,724	—	—	—	
1898	—	—	2,096	91	126	217	702	1,177	1,879	—	—	—	
1899	—	—	1,904	61	126	187	645	1,072	1,717	—	—	—	
1900	—	—	1,993	71	145	216	642	1,135	1,777	—	—	—	

Sources: Based on Everett D. Fish and Kathryn E. Kayser, "An Outline of the History of the Kansas State Teachers College of Emporia 1865–1934," M.S. thesis, Kansas State Teachers College, n.d. The numbers of graduates were taken from *A History of the State Normal School of Kansas for the First 25 Years* (Emporia, 1889), p. 144. The incompleteness of these data account for the blanks in the percentage column. Discrepancies are due to inaccuracies in sources.

course and seeking to economize, the legislature intended to have the Emporia school be Kansas' only state normal school and to restrict it to the training of elementary school teachers. In 1876 it withdrew support of its two other state normal schools at Leavenworth and Concordia and ordered that grammar school teachers henceforth be educated in a normal department at the University of Lawrence.[43] In Emporia the enrollment fell from its 1875 high of 230 in the model school and its 1874 high of 191 in the normal school to its 1879 low of 50 in the model and 40 in the normal school. For all intents and purposes the state legislature had mandated the Kansas State Normal School in Emporia to function as a training school for elementary school teachers only.

Professionalization at Emporia

The 1880s, however, brought a reversal in fortune. In Emporia as elsewhere the drive toward professionalization in teacher education began. Albert R. Taylor, the new principal, added training in such areas as kindergarten education, psychology, child study, school law, methods and management, and the philosophy and history of education. The two-year course was abolished; the training of high school teachers resumed and was further strengthened with the addition of courses in elocution, music, French and German, art, gymnastics, drawing, science, and manual training. Enrollments climbed steadily until by 1900 they reached almost 1,800 students. The legislature took note and, as if to make amends for past injuries, reversed itself and, in 1885, ordered the university to close its normal department.[44]

Principal Taylor's success rested in the main on his adoption of the professional course that was being pursued in other normal schools as well. The training of special and high school teachers received his greatest attention. The school's own very positive self-evaluation was subsequently reflected in the 1916 report of the new Kansas State Board of Administration that had replaced the separate boards of regents of the university, the state agricultural college, and the state normal school. That centralized board endorsed the goals the Kansas State Normal School in Emporia had set for itself. It approved its pursuit of a liberal education, its keeping pace with "the newest thought in the educational world," and its holding on to "the old elemental things that have been proven educationally."[45]

But applause was not universal. Criticism soon came from both within and outside the state. The vast majority of Kansas rural elementary school teachers, it was charged, had never set foot in a normal school and those who had, had not remained long. Judging from the admittedly unreliable numbers we have, only 4.2 percent (58 out of 1,388) of the normal department students had graduated at the Emporia school during its first 11 years. Not until the early 1880s did the absolute number of graduates increase, though the percentage remained low even then. For the entire period from 1865 to 1889 a little less than 8 percent (382 out of 4,879) of the normal department's students graduated (see Table 5.3). As a result, a critic would subsequently point out, from the 1880s to the beginning of the 1920s Kansas teachers "gave mediocre service which produced a mediocre product." They lacked a sound academic preparation and courage "to fight the politicians and vested interests that blocked school progress."[46]

The critic, an assistant superintendent who served from 1926 to 1954, pointed out that far from being able tŏ put its major effort on the thorough training of the state's future elementary and high school teachers, the Kansas State Normal School at Emporia functioned primarily as a high and continuation school. It permitted already employed teachers to stay for one or two semesters and brush up on their skills before they returned to their schools, moved from the elementary to the secondary level, or left teaching for some other occupation. A federal report pointed out that all the Kansas normal schools were crowded only during their summer sessions. Their most avid students were men and women on the career advancement track who hoped for administrative positions in education or sought academic credentials for noneducational employment.[47] In Kansas as elsewhere professionalization arrived at the expense of the education of beginning classroom teachers.

Slow Start in Wisconsin

Not everywhere in the Midwest could teacher educators begin their work in normal schools or universities. In Wisconsin their concerns were overridden by the interests of private academies and colleges, and they were submerged in the more comprehensive claims of the advocates of the state university. At the constitutional convention of 1846 the spokesmen for private academies and colleges defeated an appropriation of income from the state's university fund for a normal school and effectively prevented the inauguration of normal training at the state university. For many years thereafter they succeeded in staving off separate appropriations for such a department at the university and delayed the creation of separate state normal schools. Teacher education, they argued, was more properly the task of private academies and colleges. They, after all, had been on the scene already and depended on normal training as a source of students and public support.

This did not prevent the legislature from declaring in 1849 that the university was to have a normal department and that normal students who passed a special examination were to be given teaching diplomas. The university regents heartily approved the legislature's promise that, if graduates of the normal department were to commit themselves to teaching in the state's common schools, they could attend the university without paying tuition. The regents also stated unequivocally that they viewed teacher training as a province of the state university and that they intended to make the university through its normal department "the nursery of the educators of the popular mind. . . . It is by making our University the *school of the schoolmaster*," they said, "that a corps of competent instructors is to be best provided, and that all the educational agencies of the State, from the highest to the lowest, may be made tributary to the great end of training up the mind of Wisconsin to intelligence and virtue."[48]

There was, then, in Wisconsin just as in Illinois some sentiment to harness all the educational resources of the state at one central institution and to offer there practical training in agricultural, mechanical, and normal education. Only this institution was to be the state university. Yet there was preciously little follow-up to the grand proclamation. The normal professor, who was also responsible for instruction in mental philosophy, logic, rhetoric, and English literature, was not appointed until 1854. In the next year he offered an optional course in "the art of teaching" to be taken during a student's senior year. To observers it appeared as though the university was unwilling or unable to respond to the demands for a practical education for farmers, mechanics, and teachers. Instead, the *Southport Telegraph* complained, the university was being turned into "a hot bed of literary aristocracy. . . ."[49] It was steeped in academic tradition, and both faculty and students sought to emulate the curriculum and prestige of eastern colleges. Its pride and aim appeared to be a liberal education that prepared young men for future careers in the traditional professions of the law, ministry, medicine, and higher education.

The university thus faced the opposition of the friends of the private colleges as well as of the supporters of practical instruction. While the former accused the university of lacking a Christian atmosphere, the latter objected to its stress on the liberal arts and the neglect of instruction in agriculture and mechanics. Both groups joined forces and found a convenient expression of their sentiments in an act of 1857 which established the nine-member Board of Regents of the Wisconsin State Normal Schools and allocated 25 percent of the income from the swamp land fund to such academies, colleges and universities as should establish normal classes. Only the state university, having originally been aided by a congressional land grant, was pointedly excluded from this largesse. Let there be normal training, the legislators said, but not in the university.[50]

Not everyone greeted the act of 1857 with applause. As in other states, supporters of the public school movement in the tradition of Horace Mann and Henry Barnard resented the reliance on private institutions. They felt that by using academies and colleges that were not primarily interested in the training of teachers the act diluted the effort to professionalize public school teaching. These critics wanted a system of graded normal schools where high school teachers could be trained in a strong, centrally located state normal school and elementary teachers were prepared in normal academies. As it was, these critics carried no brief for the university either.

But for another decade the public school reformers complained in vain. The Reverend Mr. J.B. Pradt presented their view at the Wisconsin State Teachers Association meeting at Portage on August 3, 1858:

> What we want is not a normal school law so loose as to induce every college and academy and high school in the state to seek, and so loosely interpreted as to enable them to gain, a portion of the school fund, without rendering an equivalent service in return; but we want half a dozen or more institutions that shall, in some just or honest sense of the term, be teachers' seminaries; schools, the leading feature of which shall be to prepare young persons for the school room, while at the same time they shall furnish sound and wholesome academic instruction.[51]

When Pradt and his friends received no satisfaction, they could only complain: "We have the Board of Regents of the Normal Schools; but strange to say, only the Regents and not the schools."[52] That situation remained unchanged until after the end of the Civil War.

Normal instruction did begin, however slowly, in the university. The presence of a competing board of normal regents had proved a burr under the saddle of the university regents and stirred them into action. In 1859 they contemplated the appointment of Henry Barnard as both chancellor of the university and agent of the normal regents. Barnard's fame as organizer of the public schools in Connecticut and Rhode Island and as editor of the *American Journal of Education* had raised high hopes in Wisconsin. Many expected him to consolidate the state's efforts in teacher training. Barnard, however, never actively assumed his post, though he initiated the organization of the university's normal class in conjunction with the Madison high school. That step was taken in 1860. It represented a compromise for those who wanted to see teacher training carried out in Madison under the aegis of the university, yet also maintained that normal training was not properly a university matter.[53]

The Civil War and the departure of many young men from the state dramatically brought home the need for teachers, and in the spring of 1863 caused a marked, though only temporary, increase in normal students at the university. Thirty-six men and 76 women availed themselves of the opportunity, more than doubling the attendance of the university non-normal male students (see Table 5.4). But already in the next year the number of men fell from 43 to 3, or from 39 percent to 1.66 percent of the total male enrollment; the 57 normal women then accounted for 32 percent of all university women, whereas in the preceding year all university women had been normalites. The

Table 5.4. Distribution of University of Wisconsin Enrollments, by Program, in the Mid-1800s

		Non-Normal	Normal			Percent
	Total	Total	Total	Men	Women	Normal
Winter 1862/63	63	63	0	0	0	0
Spring 1863	177	65	112	36	76	63
Winter 1863/64	229	67	162	43	119	71
Spring (?) 1864	361	301	60	3	57	17
Winter 1864/65	306	240	66	0	66	22

Source: University of Wisconsin Board of Regents, *Annual Reports,* 1862–1863, pp. 4, 35–36; 1863–1864, p. 2.

university could not battle the strength of academic tradition. Men and women did not come to Madison just to obtain training as school teachers. They enrolled primarily in the preparatory and the academic classes which gave them a general liberal education and prepared them for professional careers. By 1865, the first six of the normal students who had enrolled during the war received their diplomas. All of them were women.[54]

Matters were different at the academies and high schools. There the normal training that had increased with the war continued unabated. In 1863 the superintendent of Grant County reported that 161 teachers had received instruction at the Platteville Academy, Lancaster Institute, and Tafton Seminary.[55] In the next year the superintendent of Adams County reported that teachers were being trained at Brunson Institute at Point Bluff.[56] From Trempealeau County came a report in 1865 that the "young and inexperienced teachers" were endeavoring "to qualify themselves for the work in which they are engaged by attending the best schools within their reach."[57] The normal school regents supported these activities by sponsoring teachers' institutes and by subsidizing normal classes at Lawrence University in Appleton and several academies and high schools.[58]

When the war came to an end and the need for teachers remained, the legislature in 1866 urged the normal school regents to establish and conduct state normal schools at various locations within the state. The legislators were prodded by State Superintendent Pickard, who, while acknowledging that colleges, academies, and high schools had done "much good," insisted that permanent state normal schools were needed "whose sole business shall be the training of teachers."[59] These schools were to familiarize both men and women

> in the theory and art of teaching, and in all the various branches that pertain to a good common school education; also to give instruction in agriculture, chemistry, in the arts of husbandry, the mechanic arts, the fundamental laws of the United States and of this state, and in what regards the rights and duties of citizens.

In addition the regents were authorized to encourage the presentation of lectures on "chemistry, anatomy, physiology, astronomy, the mechanic arts, agriculture, and on any other science or branch of literature. . . ."[60]

The legislation was an expression of legislative impatience with and lack of confidence in the state university. It showed a clear preference for local initiatives and instruction in practical fields. It had become evident that at the university neither students nor faculty were much interested in the pursuit of studies in teaching, agriculture, or mechanics. As far as normal work was concerned, students did not think it reasonable to attend a university in order to serve a few months or years as a schoolmaster or schoolmistress. The women who came to Madison wanted opportunities and studies comparable to those available to men. From a legislator's point of view the needs for common school teaching were local. They were not easily satisfied by one central institution that appeared more like a classical academy than a school responsive to the practical needs of the state's largely agricultural population.

At the same time the legislation clearly expressed the desire of Wisconsin's citizens to have access to educational institutions that would provide instruction in any field anyone might desire. The example of the Illinois State Normal University with its declared—though not realized—intent to offer instruction in agriculture and the mechanical arts underscored the Wisconsin legislators' demand for practical training in and information on agriculture and the trades as well as chemistry and household economy. Even lectures on university subjects such as astronomy and medicine and on any of the arts and sciences should ultimately be available at the state normal schools. These schools, so the sponsors of the legislation hoped, would become true people's universities, accessible to everyone in every corner of the state.

The results of the legislature's action were twofold. The university regents sought then and in the next decade to persuade the normal school regents to accept the university's normal work as one of the state's normal schools. When their entreaties were rejected, Chancellor Chadbourn transformed the normal department into a female college. He argued that he saw no reason why the university should concern itself with the training of elementary school teachers, an assignment that required work on a high or preparatory school level only.[61] Threatened by the suggestion which had been advanced as early as 1861 by the *Wisconsin Journal of Education* that the two boards of regents ought to be replaced by a state board of education, the normal and university regents subsequently came to agree on a division of labor.[62] The normal schools would take on the preparation of teachers for the common schools, and the university was to establish a chair of pedagogy. That step was taken in 1884 when the regents appointed Professor W. Stearns as the university's first professor of the science and art of teaching.[63]

The other response came from various localities in the state which sought to attract one of the new normal schools by offering a building or pledging tax revenues.[64] Thus for an initial local investment a community could assure itself of a state-supported school in its midst. This was all the more attractive because the legislature had in 1865 repealed the law of 1857 that had sent normal school fund money to private academies and colleges. Might it not now be possible to replace a financially insecure local academy with a state-supported normal school? The *Wisconsin Journal of Education* suggested just this in 1865: Let "the trustees of some of our ablest, largest, and most favorably situated Academies . . . boldly transform them into good Normal Schools without dependence upon the present precarious Normal Fund. . . ."[65] When a few weeks later the legislature repealed the 1857 law and ordered that the income from the normal school fund now go to state normal schools, several communities stood ready to seize the opportunity. In Wisconsin the time for the state normal schools had come.

The Normal School at Platteville

The citizens of Platteville in the state's southwestern corner were the first to respond. As a result on October 9, 1866, they witnessed the official dedication of the state's first normal school. As a local newspaper made it readily apparent, the importance of the new school lay not in its expected contribution to the common schools, but in its presence as an academic center for everyone's children regardless of their intended later occupations. Not only was it housed in the building of the old Platteville Academy, but it also inherited part of the academy's faculty. The community was thus assured of the continuation of secondary and, as we shall see, primary schooling. The *Grant County Witness* informed its readers:

> It will . . . be seen that a normal school combines all the advantages of a 1st class private academy with those of a state educational institution. Our youth, whether they design to become teachers or not, can thus have the advantages of the oldest teachers and the best educational facilities to be procured, at a trifling cost, compared with the expenses of a 1st class private institution of learning.[66]

After one year of operation the board of visitors of the Platteville State Normal School insisted strongly that the familiar academy program be continued. It would, they said, "elevate and dignify the school and widen the sphere of its influence." They must have felt that the prestige of the academy program outshone the as yet unknown powers of attraction of a normal school. The school, the board of visitors added, should qualify its students not only "for the more immediate duties of a teacher" but also "for the ordinary business avocations of life. . . ."[67]

That the visitors' observations accurately reflected the situation at the normal school became readily apparent during the school's first 14 years. As Table 5.5 shows, on the average no more than 45 percent of all attending students were enrolled in the normal classes. The remaining students took preparatory and general academic work or were part of the elementary model school. Those of the normal department were fairly evenly divided between men and women, though, as Table 5.6 indicates, in most years there were more women in attendance than men. But here, too, as in all the other normal schools we have studied, the number of graduates who attended the full three- or four-year normal course was small. Of the 1,300 women and 1,093 men who attended the normal course between 1868/69 and 1879/80, only 58 women (4.5 percent) and 65 men (6 percent) received their diplomas.[68]

A glance at Tables 5.7 and 5.8 shows that few of the graduating men and

Table 5.5. Departmental Distribution of Enrollments of Platteville State Normal School, 1866–1880

	Total Students in Attendance	Model School Students	Preparatory and Academic Students		Normal Students	
					Number	Percent
1866/67	210	70	41		99	47
1867/68	323	116	64		143	44
1868/69	364	49	165		150	41
1869/70	409	63	162		184	45
1870/71	391	55	163		173	44
1871/72	404	61	145		198	49
1872/73	408	65	161		182	45
1873/74	467	79	193		195	42
		Primary Department Students	Grammar Department Students	Intermediate Department Students	Normal Department Students	
1874/75	508	42	192	61	213	42
1875/76	479	40	179	56	204	43
1876/77	493	45	165	59	224	45
1877/78	492	44	180	44	224	46
1878/79	438	41	134	36	227	52
1879/80	469	48	160	42	219	47
Total, 1866–80	5,855	818	2,104	298	2,635	
Average percentage of normal students, 1866–80						45

Source: Annual catalogues of Platteville State Normal School.

Until 1874/1875 the normal course at Platteville took three years. In that year an elementary course of two years was distinguished from an advanced course of four years. The column headings for the data for 1874–1880 show the departmental name changes that occurred.

Table 5.6. Gender Distribution of All Normalites and of Graduates of the Advanced Class of Platteville State Normal School, 1860–1880

	Normal Students					Graduates of Advanced Class of Normal Program					Percent of Students Graduating from Advanced Class		
	Number			Percent		Number			Percent				
	Women	Men	Total	Women	Men	Women	Men	Total	Women	Men	Women	Men	Total
1866/67	61	38	99	62	38								
1867/68	79	64	143	55	45								
1868/69	81	69	150	54	46	2	6	8	25	75	7.4	26.1	16.0
1869/70	107	77	184	58	42	5	10	15	33	67	14.0	39.0	24.5
1870/71	92	81	173	53	47	8	4	12	67	33	26.1	14.8	20.8
1871/72	116	82	198	59	41	3	5	8	38	63	7.8	18.3	12.1
1872/73	92	90	182	51	49	11	15	26	42	58	35.9	50.0	42.9
1873/74	112	83	195	57	43	6	4	10	60	40	16.1	14.5	15.4
1874/75	109	104	213	51	49	6	3	9	67	33	22.0	11.5	16.9
1875/76	101	103	204	50	50	4	3	7	57	43	15.8	11.7	13.7
1876/77	125	99	224	56	44	4	3	7	57	43	12.8	12.1	12.5
1877/78	112	112	224	50	50	4	7	11	36	64	14.3	25.0	19.6
1878/79	123	104	227	54	46	5	4	9	56	44	16.3	15.4	15.9
1879/80	130	89	219	59	41	0	1	1	0	100	0	4.5	1.8
Average	103	85	188	55	45	5	5	10	45	55	15.7	20.2	17.7
Total	1,440	1,195	2,635			58	65	123					

Source: Annual catalogues of Platteville State Normal School.

Only the students in the advanced class of the normal program could graduate—that is, receive a diploma. From the school year 1866/1867 through 1873/1874, the normal course took three years to complete. Because it is unknown at what stage in the normal program each enrollee is in any given year, the percentage of graduating students has been calculated by dividing their number by a third of the total number of normal students for those years. In 1874/1875 the three-year course was replaced by a four-year course, so from that point on the percentage of graduates has been calculated by dividing the number of graduates by a fourth of the total number of enrollees.

women stayed for any length of time as teachers in the classroom. Over the course of the first eight years after graduation between 1869 and 1877, the percentages of the 49 women who engaged in teaching dropped from 88 percent after two years to 29 percent after eight years. Of the 53 men the corresponding drop occurred from 45 percent after two years to 13 percent after eight years.

What happened to the others? Two years after graduation 43 of the 49 women were still employed as classroom teachers, 3 were married and presumably not teaching, 1 was reported to have gone to college, and of 2 nothing is known (see Table 5.8). Six years later, the largest group of 25 was listed as married and presumably lost to the classroom, 14 were still teaching, of 6 nothing was reported, and 4 held other professional positions in education—

Table 5.7. Career Distribution of Platteville State Normal School Graduates, by Years since Graduation between 1869 and 1877

Year of Graduation					
	Total Graduates	After 2 Years	After 4 Years	After 6 Years	After 8 Years
1869					
Female	2	2 teachers	nothing listed, presumably married		
Male	6	5 teachers 1 not listed	2 high school principals 2 public school principals 1 lawyer 1 U.S. mail agent	3 high school principals 1 public school principal 1 lawyer 1 U.S. mail agent	2 high school principals 1 public school principal 1 lawyer 1 U.S. mail agent 1 not listed
1870					
Female	5	5 teachers	5 teachers	4 teachers 1 county super-intendent	3 teachers 1 county super-intendent 1 married
Male	10	9 teachers 1 not listed	2 teachers 2 principals 3 college students 1 clergyman 1 merchant 1 lawyer	2 teachers 2 county super-intendents 2 college students 1 clergyman 1 merchant 1 normal school professor 1 lawyer	2 teachers 1 county super-intendent 2 law students 1 clergyman 1 merchant 1 normal school professor 1 high school principal 1 lawyer
1871					
Female	8	7 teachers 1 married	7 teachers 1 married	6 teachers 1 normal school teacher 1 married	4 teachers 1 normal school teacher 3 married
Male	4	4 principals	1 principal 1 law student 1 lawyer 1 deceased	1 law student 2 lawyers 1 deceased	3 lawyers 1 deceased

(continued on the following page)

Table 5.7. Career Distribution of Platteville State Normal School Graduates, by Years since Graduation between 1869 and 1877 (*continued*)

Year of Graduation Total Graduates	After 2 Years	After 4 Years	After 6 Years	After 8 Years
1872				
Female 3	3 teachers	2 teachers	1 teacher	1 teacher
		1 married	1 married	1 married
			1 not listed	1 not listed
Male 5	2 teachers	1 teacher	1 teacher	1 teacher
	2 principals	1 principal	1 principal	1 principal
	1 high school	1 merchant	1 county	1 county
	principal	1 farmer	super-	super-
		1 not listed	intendent	intendent
			1 merchant	2 merchants
			1 not listed	
1873				
Female				
11	8 teachers	4 teachers	3 teachers	2 teachers
	1 college student	1 normal school	2 normal school	2 normal school
	2 not listed	faculty	faculty	faculty
		1 college student	5 married	5 married
		4 married	1 not listed	1 not listed
		1 not listed		1 deceased
Male 15	4 teachers	2 teachers	4 teachers	2 teachers
	8 principals	4 principals	1 principal	1 principal
	2 law students	2 law students	1 law student	1 high school
	1 farmer	1 medical	1 physician	assistant
		student	1 merchant	1 physician
		1 merchant	1 clerk of court	1 merchant
		1 clerk of court	1 farmer	1 clerk of court
		1 farmer	1 city editor	1 farmer
		1 city editor	4 lawyers	1 city editor
		1 lawyer		3 lawyers
		1 not listed		1 insurance
				agent
				1 banker
				1 industrial
				manager

(*continued on the following page*)

Table 5.7. Career Distribution of Platteville State Normal School Graduates, by Years since Graduation between 1869 and 1877 (*continued*)

Year of Graduation				
Total Graduates	After 2 Years	After 4 Years	After 6 Years	After 8 Years
1874				
Female 6	5 teachers 1 married	4 teachers 2 married	1 not listed 5 married	6 married
Male 3	2 principals 1 college student	1 principal 1 college student 1 not listed	1 teacher 1 principal 1 law student	1 teacher 2 lawyers
1875				
Female 6	6 teachers	2 teachers 1 college student 2 married	3 teachers 1 college student 2 married	3 teachers 2 married 1 deceased
Male 3	2 principals 1 college student	1 principal 1 college student 1 not listed	1 teacher 1 principal 1 law student	1 teacher 2 lawyers
1876				
Female 4	3 teachers 1 married	2 teachers 2 married	3 married 1 not listed	4 married
Male 3	1 teacher 2 principals	1 teacher 2 principals	1 principal 1 farmer 1 not listed	1 principal 1 farmer 1 not listed
1877				
Female 4	4 teachers	3 teachers 1 married	1 teacher 3 married	1 teacher 3 married
Male 3	2 teachers 1 college student	1 teacher 1 high school principal 1 college student	2 high school principals 1 farmer	1 high school principal 1 farmer 1 lawyer

Source: Annual catalogues of the Platteville State Normal School in Wisconsin.

Table 5.8. Distribution of Occupational Statuses of Platteville State Normal School Graduates from Two to Eight Years after Graduation in 1869, by Gender

	Teachers	Education Professionals	College and Professional School Students	Other Professionals	Married	Other Occupations	Unknown or Deceased	Total Number of Graduates
			NUMBERS					
Females								
After 2 years	43	0	1	0	3	0	2	49
After 4 years	29	1	2	0	13	0	4	49
After 6 years	18	4	1	0	20	0	6	49
After 8 years	14	4	0	0	25	0	6	49
Average	26	2	1	0	15	0	5	49
Males								
After 2 years	24	21	5	0	0	1	2	53
After 4 years	8	18	9	6	0	8	4	53
After 6 years	9	16	5	11	0	9	3	53
After 8 years	7	13	2	14	0	14	3	53
Average	12	17	5	8	0	8	3	53
			PERCENTAGES					
Females								
After 2 years	88	0	2	0	6	0	4	100
After 4 years	59	2	4	0	27	0	8	100
After 6 years	37	8	2	0	41	0	12	100
After 8 years	29	8	0	0	51	0	12	100
Average	53	5	2	0	31	0	9	100
Males								
After 2 years	45	40	9	0	0	2	4	100
After 4 years	15	34	17	11	0	15	8	100
After 6 years	17	30	9	21	0	17	6	100
After 8 years	13	25	4	26	0	26	6	100
Average	23	32	10	15	0	15	6	100

Source: Annual catalogues of Wisconsin State Normal School at Platteville.

1 was a county superintendent, and 3 were faculty members at normal schools. Put another way, eight years after graduating from normal school only 1 out of 3 of these women was still in the classroom and 1 in 11 was in a position of professional leadership. By far the largest group had married and disappeared from the workforce. Of another 12 percent we have no information. These, we must remember, were the elite of Platteville's women normal students. How many of the nongraduates played guest roles in the classroom we can only guess. If it had been the hope of the school reformers to create a professional corps of women teachers, they had not realized their goal here.

The career pattern of the 53 men gives us a different picture. Twenty-four of them, or 45 percent, were found teaching in the classroom two years after graduation, and 21, or 40 percent of the total, served as principals in their respective schools. Three were listed as college students, another two as students in law school, one as farmer, and of two others nothing was reported. Eight years after graduation the picture had changed rather drastically. Twenty-eight graduates, or 52 percent, were found in other professions or occupations. Lawyers led the group with 11, followed by farmers and merchants with 4 each, physicians with 2, and a smattering of other pursuits with 1 each. The next largest group consisted of professionals in education. Five of them were listed as high school principals, four as elementary school principals, three as county superintendents, and one as a normal school professor. This group of education professionals had shrunk from 21 two years after graduation to 13 after an additional six years. Even men in their elevated positions of professional leadership showed a notable lack of life-long commitment to service in education.

In its early years the Platteville State Normal School had furnished much-needed teachers and administrators for the public schools. But its graduates were not to remain in education. What the normal school accomplished far more impressively was giving a number of small-town and country boys a start as schoolteachers and administrators and then sending them on their way to professional and business careers. It did better with a few of its women graduates who became teachers in normal schools or rose to administrative positions in the public schools and stayed there. But the majority of the women graduates left teaching when they married. The Platteville State Normal School had not, as the education reformers had hoped, created a corps of professional teachers.

From Normal School to Teachers College in Iowa

The last of the midwestern state normal schools to be considered in this chapter is the Iowa State Normal School in Cedar Falls. It opened its doors in September 1876, a decade after the Platteville normal school in neighboring

Wisconsin had begun its work. Earlier attempts to create public normal schools in Iowa had been unsuccessful. By 1876 those Iowa elementary school teachers who received any training at all attended private normal schools and teacher institutes. For secondary school teachers and administrators the University of Iowa at Iowa City offered instruction.

From the start the sole mission of the Iowa State Normal School was to prepare teachers for the public schools. In clinging to that definition, the Iowa school differed from its sister institutions in Illinois, Kansas, and Wisconsin. As we know, not all of these early midwestern normal schools devoted themselves single-mindedly to teacher education. For its first 10 years the Illinois State Normal University had served as a state university. In Wisconsin the school in Platteville functioned more as a community college than as a normal school. Only the Kansas State Normal School in Emporia had restricted itself for awhile to educating elementary school teachers. It had done so reluctantly under pressure by the legislature, and it eventually concentrated on the continuing education of teachers and administrators already employed and seeking professional advancement.

In many ways the situations in Kansas and Iowa were similar. Each state provided separately for its university, its agricultural college, and its normal schools. Each would have to decide how these institutions would divide their responsibilities in teacher training. In Iowa the question would turn on the exact meaning of the phrase "to prepare teachers for the public schools." Some would argue that it meant for the normal school to lay a broad and thorough foundation for the work of the elementary teacher in the state's rural schools, while the university would train secondary school personnel.[69] Others would insist that the normal school was to provide educators for all levels and fields of public school work from elementary teacher to high school administrator.

Iowa State Normal's first principal, James Cleland Gilchrist, viewed his school's mission comprehensively. He thought of principals and superintendents in their original sense as principal and superintendent teachers. Everyone working in a school, whether administrator or specialist, being first and foremost a teacher, ought to have been trained as such. That meant he or she was to have been broadly educated and ready to take on many functions.[70] Thinking of teaching as a career with many different tasks, Gilchrist intended to offer college-level work at Cedar Falls. But because too many of his students entered with nothing more than an eighth-grade education, Gilchrist could not realize that goal at first.[71] It took 10 years, until the end of his presidency, before the school could offer a separate curriculum for high school graduates. These students, Gilchrist hoped, would then take college courses in foreign languages, laboratory work in science, and academic and professional graduate studies.

Even Gilchrist's initial 1876 program was ambitious. It consisted of a two-year course for elementary teaching, a three-year—so-called didactic—course for high school teaching, and a four-year—so-called scientific—course for principalships and superintendencies in high schools, academies, and normal schools. Work on kindergarten education and on school administration was included in all courses, making it evident that Gilchrist realized that in small rural schools, teachers had better be equally familiar with kindergarten as with administrative duties. These could become their lot at a moment's notice.

Gilchrist did not demand that all students who attended the Iowa State Normal School commit themselves forever to classroom teaching in an elementary school. At the same time, he did not appreciate the suggestion that some young men and women might want to use the school as a preparatory school for the university. He therefore demanded that his students take entrance examinations and that all students who expected "to assume responsibilities in the educational system should have actual practice in teaching before they became such public servants."[72]

This conviction led to Gilchrist's ceaseless agitation for the establishment of a model school. When the Iowa State Normal first opened, some advanced students taught classes in the preparatory department or in the elementary course. By 1883 the board of directors opened a separate "model school" for the observation of desirable teaching methods, organization, management, and discipline. Under the direction of a newly appointed teacher, normal school students observed classes at the model school and, at times, did some of the teaching. Board members, however, made it clear that practice teaching by normal students was to be an incidental part of the program. They were afraid that parents might accuse the normal school of using the model school as an experimental laboratory for the benefit of untrained teacher candidates.

Principal Gilchrist, however, was not entirely satisfied with the arrangements. Like the Westfield principals, he preferred a monitorial type of practice teaching whereby the normal school students taught their own classmates in the normal school and received feedback from their "students" as well as from the normal school instructor. This method permitted all of the normalites to gain practical experience in teaching advanced grades, though it did very little to accustom them to the ways of elementary school children. However satisfactory the monitorial approach was to Gilchrist and the normal school faculty, it did not please the teacher of the model school, who had not been accepted as a normal school faculty member. She resigned her position in 1886, pronouncing her assignment to be "a farce."[73]

Gilchrist's decade of leadership was followed by the 42-year rule of Homer Horatio Seerley. Seerley continued Gilchrist's policy of undivided attention to the education of teachers broadly defined. Save for senior high principals, most of whom were trained at the University of Iowa, the Iowa

State Normal School under Seerley became the foremost supplier of educators of the state's public schools.[74] Its curriculum gradually and steadily moved toward collegiate standards. Recognition from other academic institutions followed. By 1892 the Universities of Iowa and Michigan as well as Cornell and Grinnell colleges granted junior standing to the graduates of the four- and three-year courses. Five years later the University of Chicago accorded them senior standing.[75] The school at Cedar Falls expanded its academic and professional curriculum in the Westfield tradition and combined it with the Bridgewater tradition's emphasis on keeping the focus on the elementary classroom teacher.

Seerley did this by deliberately responding to what he recognized as the special needs of the Iowa schools. In 1893 he added a one-year course in primary school work and kindergartening. Four years later this became a two-year course. In that same year the normal school opened its first summer school with an emphasis on helping teachers of the ungraded rural schools.[76] By 1902 new courses were created to satisfy the special needs for "primary, music, drawing, reading, public speaking, and Latin teachers."[77] In 1903 the school introduced an advanced two-year course for high school graduates who intended to teach in secondary schools. This was the first college-level program offered by the school.[78]

Seerley also followed the Normal, Illinois, approach of offering continuing education to the state's teachers already at work. In 1899 he reported that over two-thirds of the 1,617 students enrolled in summer school were "practical experienced teachers," and that the school deliberately excluded "all except those who had been teachers or who expected to teach." For some years the Iowa State Normal School used the term "technical school" to distinguish itself from the colleges, the elementary, and the secondary schools and to emphasize its emerging character as a professional school.[79]

The logic of this development led in 1904 to Seerley's announcement to the trustees:

> There is good reason to believe that it is the intention of the state to have here a teachers school where the best of high school teachers and executive officers—principals and superintendents—may be trained. . . . For these reasons I recommend that another year's study be offered here and that a better degree and diploma be provided for the recognition of such additional study. . . .[80]

Thus began a standard four-year college curriculum whose graduates by 1908 were admitted to the Graduate College of the State University of Iowa. By 1912/13 the program enrolled 10 percent of all the students at Cedar Falls.[81]

The most significant of all the changes occurred on April 5, 1909, when the Iowa State Normal School became the Iowa State Teachers College. Within another three years, it was accredited as a college by the North Central Association.[82] It now offered 15 different programs. These ranged from the standard four-year course leading to the B.A. degree, the one-year professional course for college graduates, and other two- and three-year courses, to programs for various certificates.[83]

By 1909 the Iowa State Teachers College emerged as one of the nation's outstanding institutions specializing in the education of educators from the elementary school teacher to the public school administrator. President Seerley proudly reported that significantly larger numbers of students "enrolled in advanced courses." By remaining in school longer, he said, they laid the foundation for "a career in teaching rather than a temporary occupation."[84] The college, said Seerley, had developed the idea of training each student for some particular kind of teaching "more fully than any other teachers' school in the country." More than 20 different kinds of "special teacher preparation" were available at the teachers college—"more than half of them exclusively directed toward high school work."[85]

The unique role of the Iowa State Teachers College lay in its steadfast adherence to the combined Westfield and Bridgewater approaches. As recently as 1950 it received national recognition for having faithfully maintained its original mission. In that year the Strayer Commission stated: "The Iowa State Teachers College is one of the few higher institutions in the United States that devotes itself strictly to the professional preparation of teachers." The college catalogue underscored that policy. The college existed, it read, "to serve the public schools of the State of Iowa and the profession of teaching."[86]

Alas, that proud tradition came to an end 11 years later when the institution became the State College of Iowa. Its demise was reaffirmed in 1967 when the State College became the University of Northern Iowa. The single-minded commitment of administration and faculty to teacher education gave way to emphasizing the liberal arts and graduate work in educational and industrial technology. The old Iowa State Normal School had become a multipurpose regional university. It still trains teachers for Iowa's schools. But as in Illinois, Kansas, and Wisconsin, teacher training is no longer its sole mission.

6
The Professionalization of
Teacher Education

The Schoolmen vs. the People

American normal schools were created to turn the temporary occupation of schoolkeeping into a life-time career of schoolteaching. Schoolmen intended to use these schools as instruments of professionalization. With their help they wanted to replace the citizen-teachers with classroom professionals. But from the beginning the reluctance of rural school districts to recognize teachers as professionals and the related continuing refusal of teachers to regard their work as more than a temporary occupation defeated that aim.

In response normal educators began to redefine their meaning of professionalization. They projected a hierarchy of normal institutions. County training schools were to continue preparing young women for a few years' service in the classrooms of rural common schools, and state teachers colleges would educate male professionals as educational specialists, administrators, and normal school faculty members.

In the Midwest this amended version of the normal educators' strategy to professionalize by creating a hierarchy not only of institutions but also of their graduates was to arouse indignation and resistance. Parents, who as taxpayers were to pay the bills for the new state normal schools and teachers colleges, were not interested in subsidizing the training of professional educators. They wanted to send their daughters or sons to a normal school near home for a year or two of exposure to a program of general education. They were not interested, either, in the narrow, vocational orientation to classroom teaching that county normals were intended to supply. There, too, they preferred a program of general studies. Outside the circle of schoolmen and related professionals, the normal educators' program of professionalization, male-centered and without regard for the classroom teacher as it was, did not find many friends.

In Wisconsin the schoolmen and the people clashed most directly. Edu-

140

cation professionals—state, city, and county superintendents, editors of professional educational journals, promoters and friends of the public schools—did not like what they saw when the first state normal school opened in the building of an old academy, complete with its teachers and students. State Superintendent McMynn protested in 1867 that the normal school in Platteville was to train teachers for the common schools and not to become another academy or high school.[1]

He was supported by officials of the Wisconsin State Teachers Association and the editor of the *Wisconsin Journal of Education*. One member said at the association's 1871 meeting that the normal schools "shall embrace in their course of study only those branches taught in our district schools, with special training in methods and school management."[2] The *Journal* asked in 1879 that "the normal school not be required to give instruction in reading, writing, spelling, and arithmetic." It should admit only qualified students and "instruct them only in the science of teaching."[3] According to Wisconsin's educational officials neither elementary and remedial nor academic and preparatory instruction was any of the normal school's business.

At the same time legislators heard a different message from their constituents across the state. They spoke up for nonprofessional advanced educational opportunities that would leave their children free to choose any vocation they wanted or even permit them to transfer to a college or to the state university in Madison.

The Wisconsin normal school regents allowed their schools from the beginning to function as public high schools and community colleges. This had been true for the Platteville school and was to be true again for the Whitewater State Normal in 1868. The town of Whitewater for a long time sought to attract some educational institution beyond the common school level—an academy, a seminary, a military boarding school, a collegiate institute, a high school, a private normal school. All of these attempts failed. Then when the opportunity arose to bid for a state normal school, the town seized the moment. For the next 20 years the state normal school relieved Whitewater of the necessity of building a high school. The normal school took its place.[4]

Whether it was Platteville in 1866, Whitewater in 1868, Oshkosh in 1871, River Falls in 1875, and the remaining Wisconsin normal schools in subsequent years, the stories were to be similar. A substantial part of the student body enrolled to improve their general, post–common school education. As the Oshkosh board of visitors pointed out, the graduates of the rural common schools were not well enough prepared for professional work. "No matter what men say," they wrote, "the work in our Normal Schools, for a long time to come, will and must be academic. . . . They [the students] have no well defined knowledge, no power of expression, no power of reflection, and no good habits of study."[5] Many of the students, too, had no intention of preparing themselves for teaching. Platteville's *Grant County Witness* assured them that they need not worry about their pledge to teach in the common schools. The regents had promised, the paper said, to deal leniently with those who did not, and besides, the pledge could be honored by teaching in a one-student school. A Milwaukee newspaper asked plaintively in 1885: "Is there a normal school in Wisconsin?" Its answer was no—a state normal school could not be distinguished from a high school.[6]

The historical significance of this development lies in the fact that it was the normal schools rather than the land-grant colleges that really brought higher education to the people. If the latter permitted the working people of this country—the farmers and mechanics, as the contemporary phrase expressed it—to send their sons and daughters to their centrally located state university or college, the former took public colleges and universities out to where they were most needed—into the hinterlands and small towns where the people lived and worked. With the normal schools, true democracy began in higher education.[7]

The Redefinition of Normal Work: Wisconsin

Wisconsin normal educators chafed under the pressure of having to cope with ill-prepared students. They came to regard their task of training elementary school teachers as thankless, and they resented being asked to provide remedial and general academic education in their schools. Their goal was to follow the path indicated by the Westfield principals and to turn their schools into professional colleges and universities. To be able to offer professional training, they concluded, the state normal schools would have to appeal to career educators and eventually undertake educational research.

Normal educators were confirmed in that view in 1888 by James P. Wickersham at a meeting of the Department of Superintendence of the National Education Association. The former head of the first state normal school in Pennsylvania and superintendent of that state, Wickersham declared that the normal schools were able,

> from the numbers that attend them, to instruct, train, and inspire with professional zeal a body of teachers who, when scattered over a State, will, as principals of high schools, as superintendents of schools, as writers in educational journals, as instructors at teachers' institutes, as leaders in educational reform, become a powerful agency in uplifting and making more efficient the whole work of education. . . . The normal schools can become the fountain of professional *esprit de corps* among the teachers of a State.[8]

Reality, to be sure, did not always match the pronouncements. Students coming into the normal schools were often woefully deficient in academic preparation. The secretary of the Massachusetts State Board of Education, John Woodbridge Dickinson, admitted at the same meeting that he had "never known a candidate for admission to the normal classes to be fully provided with the elementary knowledge he is expected to be able to communicate when he takes up his work in the public schools."[9] Thus, he pleaded, the normal schools should not be criticized for offering remedial academic work.

But there were others, particularly university spokesmen, who replied that the normal schools had no business "filling the mind of those who attend them full of useful knowledge, nor even for training the mind of teachers to think for themselves."[10] Normal schools were not to stray outside their sphere of strictly professional training. Some critics even wished to hold them to the standards set in Prussia: a vocational institution for students who had attended neither high school nor university.

Confronted by conflicting advice, normal school educators found themselves in a quandary. Their desire to offer advanced professional work was checked by the inferior prior education of so many of their students and by the growing competition of universities. When they then proposed to offer remedial academic work and studies in the liberal arts, many of their critics charged them with deserting their primary responsibility to the elementary schools. And yet, their own ambitions made them loath to give up academic studies that would serve as a necessary preparation for advanced professional work.

In Massachusetts they redefined the meaning of "strictly professional" work. "A fair construction of the expression," wrote a member of the state board of education in 1896, was that it implied "that a broad and liberal education should be obtained in schools maintained for that very purpose before the student enters upon a professional course." This view led the normal schoolmen to demand graduation from high school of all of their entering students. While the high rate of secondary school attendance made such a demand feasible in Massachusetts, this was not necessarily true of other states.[11] In many states the normal schools therefore felt compelled to continue their policy of offering remedial academic work.

In Massachusetts, however, the normal schools taught academic work as a contribution to their students' general educational background. That was the purpose of the regular four-year course given at Framingham, Westfield, Salem, and Bridgewater.[12] Not all normal schoolmen agreed and, as a result, charged that offering the course tended to have the normal schools neglect the training of teachers in practical classroom skills. But that only brought out opponents who argued that the contrary policy of demanding high school graduation and dispensing with liberal education in the normal schools produced teachers who lacked a thorough grounding in academic subjects.[13] Normal schoolmen could not escape from that dilemma; they could only ignore it and opt for professional work however defined.[14]

In Wisconsin, normal educators took the program of their 1872 Boston convention as a directive to wrestle with the meaning of professionalization. They wanted to separate introductory or remedial work from the state normal schools, arguing that students entering this introductory work rarely had any intention of becoming professional teachers and simply looked for a chance to qualify quickly for a temporary or short-term teaching position.[15] The Whitewater board of visitors therefore recommended in 1884 that the school drop its introductory offerings and concentrate on the one-year elementary and two-year advanced course for teachers.[16]

This trend was supported by a flourishing program of teachers' institutes, which had been strongly encouraged by Henry Barnard during his short stay in the state. In 1883 it was further strengthened by the state-mandated practice of the public high schools offering courses in the "theory and art of teaching."[17] Spurred on by the institutes and given a platform by the high schools, Wisconsin normal educators began to plan for a system of county training or normal schools which were to become the effective source of teachers for the rural district schools.[18] By 1905 they had organized six and projected two. The *Wisconsin Journal of Education* welcomed the schools' appearance in the expectation that they would "in due time . . . do the professional work now performed by the elementary course of the regular normals."[19] They would leave the state normal schools free to professionalize and specialize and prepare teachers for the graded and city schools and high schools as well.[20]

A more protracted debate arose over the presence of academic and preparatory work in the normal school curriculum. The advocates of professional normal schools, such as Superintendent McMynn, disliked such work as much as, if not more than, the remedial and elementary efforts. Because it was indistinguishable from academic high school study, it deflected the schools from their proper task of preparing teachers. But others, such as President Stearns of the Whitewater State Normal School, saw academic work not necessarily as a liability. Studies in the history and philosophy of education were, in his opinion, an indispensable part of a solid professional education and an asset for well-prepared teachers. "Success in teaching," he wrote, "depends upon a clear perception of the ends to be attained, and an adaptation of means to secure them."[21] Good professional training demanded exposure to a liberal education as well.

As soon as more Wisconsin normal school leaders came to appreciate the role of academic work in professional education, they also recognized that it required a sustained effort over time. In 1891 and 1892 the *Wisconsin Journal of Education* argued that the normal schools should refrain from granting certificates at the middle of the full course and drop both elementary course and certificate.[22] The state normal schools could well afford to raise their demands and thereby more appropriately certify the competencies of the state's trained teachers. The abbreviated and remedial training for rural elementary schools would still be available in the county normals. By 1901 the Wisconsin State Teachers Association, much concerned with its own reputation, then added the last touch and asked that graduation from high school be made a minimum requirement for admission to a state normal school.[23] If that were achieved, academic work would no longer have to be required to make up deficiencies in the students' preparation. It could then be devoted to providing a solid and complete professional education.

Altogether, though, the normal schoolmen remained of two minds on the issue of providing academic and general education in the normal schools. They recognized it as a necessary preparation for their students but not necessarily as a responsibility of their own. In fact, they were wary about intruding on the responsibilities of high schools, colleges, and the university. In 1893 the *Wisconsin Journal of Education* pointed out that if professional education could so quickly be exchanged for academic studies, it would surely appear as having been in the past "in large measure a waste of energy." Nothing would hurt the prestige of the normal schools more than seeing "the ideal of scholarship in rivalry of the University held up as their more appropriate aim."[24]

The normal educators therefore preferred to ask for a good academic education as an entrance requirement so that they might be free to concentrate their own efforts on professional work in a college-level normal school. In that way they could achieve at the same time both the coveted professional school status and collegiate rank. In 1890 they were well on their way. By that year their graduates had already obtained permission to enter the University of Wisconsin as juniors. Six years later a conference committee of university and normal regents recommended the admission of normal graduates to the university's new two-year program for a bachelor of philosophy in pedagogy degree. For the regular university degree, normal graduates received only one year of transfer credit.[25] Beginning in 1907 and again in 1909 and 1913, unsuccessful attempts were made in the legislature to grant to the normal schools the right to give academic degrees. The time was not yet ripe.

Herbartianism in Illinois

While Wisconsin normal educators debated the kind of instruction they could best offer to their students, their colleagues in Illinois seized upon the cultivation of educational research and science as the way to professionalize. When John Williston Cook took over the reins from President Hewett at Illinois State Normal, the education of high school teachers came to overshadow the training of teachers for the elementary schools. Cook, like his successors Arnold Tompkins and David Felmley, no longer had any personal experience with the pioneering days of the Massachusetts normal schools. An Illinois

State Normal graduate and faculty member for 28 years, Cook left the school in 1899 for the presidency of a new Illinois normal school at DeKalb. Tompkins was a product of Indiana and Illinois colleges and universities and had taught in common schools, normal schools, and the University of Illinois. He left after only one year to take over the presidency of the Chicago Normal School. Felmley, too, was a product of the Midwest, and throughout his 30 years in office he was to lead Illinois State Normal University into the age of the teachers college.[26]

If Pestalozzianism and the idea of a normal school as an American version of a Prussian teacher seminary had constituted the first massive infusion of German pedagogy into the United States, then what became known during the 1890s as Herbartianism was the second. If Massachusetts had been the point of entry for Pestalozzianism, Illinois and its state normal university became gateways for Herbartianism. It was here that, under the guidance of the American Herbartians Charles DeGarmo, Frank McMurray, and Charles McMurray, the new pedagogy began to dominate the instruction in elementary education. Charles DeGarmo, a graduate of Illinois State Normal University, had taught at the model school from 1876 to 1883 and at the normal university from 1886 to 1890. Frank M. McMurray had graduated from the normal high school in 1879 and taught at the normal university from 1891 to 1892. His brother Charles, also a graduate of the normal university high school, taught at the normal model school from 1892 to 1899.[27]

The distinctive contributions of the Herbartians gave to the training of elementary teachers a decided theoretical-systematic bent. American Herbartianism was more comprehensive than the "object teaching" doctrine that had found a home during the 1860s at the Oswego State Normal School in New York. Its five-steps-of-instruction scheme provided a far more practical and easily understandable help to classroom teachers than William T. Harris' brand of pedagogical Hegelianism and G. Stanley Hall's child-study movement, two other then-current schools of thought in American pedagogy. The Herbartians introduced new concepts such as apperception—that new knowledge is learned and understood best when it can be related to what is already known and familiar to the child—and the culture epoch theory and the correlation of studies—that the subjects of the curriculum should be organized and integrated around historical periods. They placed great emphasis on the child's interest as a key factor to be considered in the learning process. Above all, they responded to the practical day-to-day questions of teachers in the classroom and placed renewed importance on the model school as their laboratory. Here, wrote Charles DeGarmo, "is the professional work that best fits for teaching."[28]

As the century drew to its close the systematic study of pedagogy in the classroom and the new importance of the model school were accompanied by a growing interest in the preparation of high school teachers. Illinois' governor John Peter Altgeld gave an unwitting assist in this matter when in 1895 he ordered the university high school to be closed. A state institution had no business, the governor argued, competing with local school boards. The high school students were absorbed into the model school and now provided training opportunities for the normal university's future high school teachers. At the same time normal graduates began to transfer with increasing frequency to a college or university where, within two years, they could earn a bachelor's degree.[29]

Professionalization vs. Feminization: Felmley at Illinois

Under David Felmley the university's push into professionalization continued. Flemley was a promoter of training for new fields and specialties. Teachers for kindergartens and of manual and household arts, agricultural and commercial subjects, drama and music all were going to be needed, and the Illinois State Normal University was going to provide them. In 1913 Felmley summed up his philosophy thus:

> The logic that justifies the normal school on the ground that the state must prepare its own teachers, carries with it irresistibly the inference that to perform its legitimate function, the normal school must make provision for the adequate training of teachers fitted to direct or to perform the work of every phase of the common school from the primary school to its culmination in the public high school.[30]

Felmley's view of professionalization implied that the normal school's approach was distinctive among all other educational institutions. "Only incidentally," Felmley insisted, should students acquire "a general education . . . in a normal school." Thus he expressed great unhappiness when north of Normal in neighboring Wisconsin that state's normal schools were recognized as junior colleges offering general education for students who intended to transfer to the state university in Madison. This was a false idea, Felmley maintained. The Wisconsin normal schools strayed from the professional path and that, he added, "must in the end prove harmful. . . . It means a divided aim, not merely a larger aim."[31]

Felmley's commitment to professionalization was spurred on by what he perceived as the steady progress of feminization throughout education. During the first decade of the twentieth century the share of women teachers rose from 71 percent to 81 percent in public elementary schools and from 75 percent to 85 percent in private elementary schools. In public high schools the increase was from 50 percent to 55 percent and in private high schools from 58 percent to 59.5 percent.[32] The causes of this feminization, according to a

1908 article in the *Educational Review* under the suggestive title "Why Teaching Repels Men," were that teaching was "a hireling occupation," that it was "looked down upon in the community" and "usually belittles a man" because "his daily dealing is with petty things, of interest only to his children and a few women assistants." Lastly, the article stated, "teaching tends to bad manners. . . . As a rule men teachers are uncouth, crude, ill at ease in company. . . . Men principals are often petty tyrants. . . ."[33]

Troubled by the profession's inability to bring men teachers into the classroom—even when, as the article pointed out, very attractive salaries were being paid—Felmley reacted by offering a professionalized normal school as a remedy. If only the normal school succeeded in making teaching a male profession, teaching might yet become an esteemed vocation. Men, wrote Felmley, "become village principals, principals of ward schools, county and city superintendents, teachers of agriculture, manual training, physics, biology, and other high school subjects." They added vigor to athletic, oratorical, musical, and dramatic contests. "To limit the activity of the normal schools of the Middle West to the preparation of elementary school teachers will cut off the attendance of men as completely as it has in New England."[34] Clearly, then, Felmley had given up on persuading women elementary school teachers to make teaching a life-long career. In Felmley's view women did not lend themselves to professionalization.

The logic of Felmley's view led inevitably to the demand that the new normal school be allowed to award professional degrees. Together with the other Illinois state normal schools at Carbondale, DeKalb, and Charleston, Felmley's normal university received the power to grant a bachelor of education degree in 1907. But only Illinois State Normal and Southern Illinois at Carbondale availed themselves immediately of the privilege. Northern and Eastern Illinois preferred to continue devoting their resources to the teaching of elementary teachers and to forego the growing competition with the University of Illinois over the training of secondary teachers.[35] Felmley, however, proudly reported six years later that of the Illinois State Normal University's 2,129 alumni, "608 have taught in high schools, 659 have served as principals and superintendents, 194 have been members of faculties of state normal schools, 101 of colleges and universities."[36]

Felmley's entire career demonstrates the commitment to educational professionalism. In 1902 he had organized the North Central Council of State Normal Schools, and in 1917 this organization expanded into a national association. In 1918 he was instrumental in planning the American Association of Teachers Colleges, which published its first yearbook in 1922. Fourteen years later the North Central Association joined the American Association of Teachers Colleges. In 1938 that organization replaced the Department of Normal Schools of the National Education Association and became known as the American Association of Colleges for Teacher Education. Graduate work was inaugurated at Illinois State Normal in the summer of 1944 and the first master of science degree was awarded in June 1945. The process of professionalization proved irresistible, and Felmley's legacy won the day.[37]

Normal Schools vs. Universities:

Illinois

Felmley's emphasis on professionalization and on the indivisibility of the pedagogical province not only extended the normal educators' claim to competency from the classroom to the administrative office, but it also brought them into direct conflict with the colleges and universities. These institutions were becoming increasingly interested in teacher training, especially in the education of teachers for the high schools. When in 1913 Felmley stated that "high school teachers should be trained in the same environment as elementary teachers," he did, in fact, directly challenge the universities. High school teachers, Felmley said, needed

> the same love of children [as the elementary teachers], the same knowledge of the problems of childhood. To train them in a separate school with different standards and ideals results in a serious break in spirit, in method, and in the character of the work as the child passes to the high school.[38]

Felmley was demanding and aggressive in his push to dispute the university's role in teacher education. In his view the colleges simply were outside their proper sphere when they proposed to educate high school teachers. Pedagogy, he claimed, was a newly emerging science whose insights had not been available in the past. Now its rising competence demanded change in traditional arrangements. Together with his presidential colleagues Homer Seerley of Iowa State Teachers College in Cedar Falls and John Kirk of Kirksville Normal School in Missouri, Felmley accused the universities and colleges of ignoring methods and psychology courses. The "Brahminical pundits of the traditional college and the arrogance of the university" blocked the path of educational progress.[39]

The tone of Felmley's pronouncements permits one to conclude that what provoked his outbursts was less a compelling insight into the nature of education as an indivisible province than exasperation at being ignored and brushed aside by the established powers of education in high school, college, and university. More than anything else Felmley felt the sting of class discrimination in the rebuffs he suffered. Separate training of high school teachers in colleges "begets an exclusive educational caste," he said. "Our schools are already suffering from this cleavage between the professional aristocracy of the high school and the commonality of the grades." College-trained teachers, he wrote, had transplanted the evils of the college into the high schools— "fraternities, club smokers, excessive devotion to athletics and to social functions. . . . Our great universities," he warned, "set a social pace not favorable to the plain living and high thinking, out of which grows the spirit of the consecrated teacher."[40]

Felmley's fusillade came after at least a decade of wrangling among normal school educators over the same issue. When the Chicago Normal School raised its entrance requirements to demand high school graduation, a Brooklyn contributor to the journal *Education* held this to be a signal that the normal school was "on the road to oblivion." To the writer that was timely indeed. Colleges and universities, he wrote in 1903, have entered upon the training of teachers and assumed their "appropriate functions of leadership." He cited Teachers College in New York as a splendid example. Other universities, he pointed out, had already introduced professorial chairs of education. "The fatuous faith in 'normal training,'" he wrote, "is giving way to a broader, more rational and more scrupulous conception of the proper preparation for teaching. . . . In the last few years pedagogy has become a part of the college curriculum."[41]

President Will Grant Chambers of the Minnesota State Normal School at Moorhead rejected that view as a "very short-sighted diagnosis, one that could not have been made by a person acquainted with educational conditions in rural communities." While improvements were necessary for normal schools that trained teachers for the cities, Chambers conceded, the training of rural teachers still required basic academic instruction for students who had not had a high school education. "To offer professional training alone to those who have had no instruction in the most necessary branches of knowledge would be like making razor blades out of pig iron." This was true, President Chambers wrote, because "the ranks of the profession are recruited largely from those families who are unable to educate the children beyond the scope of the local public school."[42]

Chambers stated that because universities were centrally located and not always easily accessible from every part of the country, they did not serve well the interests of a farming population. "Until the intelligence and ambition of the common people have been raised to a plane where they will go out in search for needed training, training must be brought to them, even though it be inferior to the best." That was the task the normal schools performed in the rural areas of the country. They served as true people's colleges, offering basic instruction as well as professional training. As for the universities, they aided in the normal schools' business by providing them with well-trained faculty members. According to Chambers the real task of the normal schools in 1900 had not changed much from what it had been half a century earlier. It bound these institutions to the common schools all across the country.[43]

Although the author of the offending article viewed the universities as knights on white chargers that came to the rescue of the faltering normal schools, Chambers and Felmley were suspicious of the universities when they intruded upon the work of the normal schools. Felmley, as I pointed out above, was quite disturbed at the progressing feminization of the teaching profession, and he intended to counter that trend by making the normal schools attractive to men. That meant that he wanted the normal schools to hold out the promise of professional careers in high school teaching and in administration. He neither wanted the universities to train the male education professionals and leave the women students to the normal schools, nor did he have patience with the state and county normals that continued to train women as temporary teachers for the country schools. He wanted the state normal school as a truly professional school to train future male educational leaders.[44]

Inevitably Felmley's campaign for the normal school as professional school would bring him and his like-minded colleagues into conflict with the universities. For Felmley this was all the more ironic because the University of Illinois, under the guidance of its first president, Regent John Milton Gregory, had deliberately avoided the field of teacher training. Gregory himself had been a champion of the normal schools as institutions for the general and practical training of teachers. But he had claimed the study of education as a proper task for universities: "Why should not the State University lend its aid and do *some part* of this work, thus linking itself more closely to the mighty machinery of public instruction, and stretching forth its helping hand to the grand task of the universal education of the people?" A knowledge about education, Gregory held, was to be part of every educated person's mental equipment. But it was to be only a part of educational knowledge, and that did not necessarily include professional training as a teacher.[45]

Gregory's views were not to survive the subsequent decades. Chiefly responsible for a growing university interest in training teachers was the rise of the high schools. In Illinois their number had jumped from 108 in 1870 to 208 at the beginning of the 1890s.[46] Their teachers needed education in advanced subject matter, and for that the number of the state's normal schools was clearly insufficient. Besides, the members of the Illinois State Teachers' Association realized that more than the usual normal training was needed. In 1885, prompted by earlier action in other midwestern states like Iowa, Michigan, and Wisconsin, they petitioned for a chair of pedagogy at the university.[47] During the 1890s, California, Minnesota, Nebraska, and Northwestern would make similar appointments.[48]

For awhile yet, interest in education remained in a minor key at Urbana. The curiously indecisive attempt late in 1890 to entice Charles DeGarmo away from his post as professor of modern languages at Illinois State Normal to take over the chair of psychology at Urbana illustrates the point. That appointment proved to be an embarrassment for the university. DeGarmo, one of the country's outstanding Herbartian educators, was interested in training teachers. The University of Illinois was not. Thus DeGarmo left one year later to take over the presidency of Swarthmore College.[49]

This hands-off attitude toward all things connected with education continued at Urbana throughout the 1890s. Professor Arnold Tompkins, the university's head of the education department and liaison with the state's high schools from 1895 to 1899, showed no interest in training beginning teachers. He believed in working with experienced educators who "have preparation and patient purpose to attain unto the higher phases of pedagogical thinking."[50] But there were few of them who were interested in these "higher phases," and those few had ample opportunity to seek such instruction in Urbana or Madison.

As far as the study of education was concerned, the University of Illinois continued to tread water. Tompkins' successor, Edwin Grant Dexter, exchanged the nineteenth-century philosophical outlook for a modern empirical approach and, like Tompkins, saw the university's task in training high school teachers. The normal schools, he held, were to train elementary school teachers and to carry out work below "university grade." The university's president, Thomas J. Burrill, emphasized again: "We do not want to duplicate or imitate the work of the State Normal School. We do not want to make a department which will be specially open to those preparing themselves for ordinary teaching and who take only pedagogical work in the university."[51] Too proud to bother itself with the training of elementary teachers and too contemptuous to devote itself to the scientific study of education, the University of Illinois seemed happy to leave these tasks to its sister institution in Normal.

But a change was to come with the appointment of Edmund Janes James in 1904 as president of the university. James agreed that elementary training was the proper business of the normal schools, but he thought a great university should have a school of education that pursued both the training of teachers and the advanced study of education. Dexter immediately repeated his insistence on a strengthened effort in the training of secondary teachers. He told his colleagues that, "inspired by our evident apathy," the normal schools of the state "[are] turning their attention to our problems, in a way that will in the end prove disastrous not only to the preparation of secondary but [also] of the primary force." Dexter could see the handwriting on the wall: Once the normal schools moved into the preparation of secondary school teachers, preparation of administrators would follow, and the training of primary teachers would suffer.[52]

Dexter, however, left the university in 1907 to become the U.S. state commissioner of education for Puerto Rico. It was thus left to his successor, William Chandler Bagley, to oversee the university's growing involvement in education. Bagley was convinced that, given the crying shortage of trained teachers in the United States, there was plenty of room for both normal schools and universities to engage in that activity without fighting each other in the process. Bagley, too, was realistic enough to accept the fact that normal school–trained teachers expected temporary employment before they married, went back to college, or engaged in another business. In phrases reminiscent of the citizen-teacher argument of the 1830s he urged that normal schools pay their students in exchange for their five-year commitment as teachers in the public schools, just as military cadets were paid and commissioned at West Point and Annapolis.[53] Those who wanted to continue teaching after their five-year stint could then avail themselves of further training at the university school of education.

Bagley's approach pleased the Eastern Illinois Teachers' Association as much as it disturbed Illinois State Normal University president David Felmley. Felmley could not but resent the relegation of his school to the training of temporary teachers, while at Urbana, Bagley campaigned for a school of education that would allow the training of teachers in special subjects such as agriculture, manual training, domestic science, mechanical arts, music, and drawing, as well as the education of teachers for "backward children" and of supervisory and administrative personnel. To accomplish all this, Bagley wanted a practice school which he described as "the most important part of the School of Education in so far as the professional training of candidates for high school teaching is concerned."[54] He also asked that principals and supervisors be able to take part of their work in summer sessions and write their dissertation while away from campus.[55]

Bagley's campaign climaxed in 1910 with a petition to the legislature for authorization and funding to construct a school of education. The school was to admit as juniors the graduates of normal schools who had also attended a university-approved high school.[56] It was to engage in all the far-flung activities from teacher training to educational research and the continuing professional training of experienced teachers and administrators. Its inauguration, however, shifted attention away from teacher training to empirical research. For the instructional program this brought a vast proliferation of courses, particularly at the advanced level. The new empirical science of education took command.

> The faculty did not lose sight of the public schools, [the school's historians wrote,] but the scope of its sight increased to include national as well as state and local problems and issues. As it dealt with the issues, it reduced them to their constituent parts. And, in the process, the classroom where the teaching-learning process actually occurs fell from the center of focus.[57]

Concern with teacher training became faintly old-fashioned.

At Illinois State Normal, President Felmley was bitterly resentful. By undercutting the work of his school the university had made it very difficult for normal graduates to get high school positions in the state. "Do you believe," Felmley asked Urbana president James, "that the educational and intellectual interests of a state as large as Illinois are best served by such concentration? Does it not mean a sort of educational trust?"[58] The question remained unanswered.

Kansas and Iowa

Felmley's troubles were familiar to normal school educators everywhere. Urbana's rise was repeated, albeit with local variations, in Lawrence, Iowa City, Madison, and other university centers. At Emporia, for example, the failure of the Kansas State Normal School to become an effective force in training the state's rural elementary teachers and its single-minded concentration on training professional leaders provoked the resentment of the university at Lawrence. Taking the university's side, the Kansas legislature in 1899 authorized university graduates who had earned a teacher's diploma to be awarded a teaching certificate without examination. This was a privilege that had previously been granted only to Emporia students. Ten years later, at about the same time as in Illinois, the university opened its school of education to train high school and college teachers and administrators. Here as in Illinois the university was not willing to let the state normal school move unchallenged into the training of secondary teachers and school administrators.[59]

In Iowa, President Seerley's elevation of the Iowa State Normal School to the Iowa State Teachers College soon aroused resentment and recriminations. Many Iowans thought that Seerley wanted to monopolize all teacher education in the state in his hands.[60] Already in 1906 a committee of the legislature had charged that the school had exceeded its franchise by attempting to train teachers for high schools and in subjects unnecessary for common school teachers. It duplicated the work of other state institutions, the committee charged, employed too many teachers, and paid them too much.[61]

The unfriendly voices grew more insistent when charges of neglect of the original mission were added. Seerley and the Iowa State Teachers College, it was held, had failed to pay undivided attention to the need for training teachers for the one-room rural schools. These needs, many felt, were shunted aside in the enthusiasm for psychology and methodology, for preparing high school teachers in such specialities as manual and domestic arts, commercial studies, and agriculture.[62] But when James H. Trewin, president of the state board of education, pushed Seerley in 1912 on the need for training teachers for the rural schools, Seerley complained abut the injustice of such reflections. He pointed to the summer courses provided for rural teachers at Cedar Falls and recommended the establishment of Departments of Rural Education and Extension Services. Characteristically, he urged the board to push the legislature for statutes that would raise the certification requirements for rural school teachers beyond those specifying normal training in high schools.

But accusations also came from outside the state. Henry S. Pritchett, president of the Carnegie Foundation, questioned the inclusion of superintendents, principals, and high school teachers in Seerley's definition of common school teachers. He wanted the teachers college to cease issuing degrees and offering art courses. Instead it should concentrate on training teachers for the elementary schools. He advised the Iowa State Board of Education and—presumably through his secretary, John G. Bowman, who later was to become the president of the University of Iowa—persuaded the board to resolve on October 8–9, 1912, that all professional education and liberal arts courses beyond the sophomore year be discontinued at Cedar Falls.

Thus Seerley found himself embattled on several sides. With the change from normal school to teachers college in 1909 had come a transfer of administrative control from the board of trustees and fiscal supervision from the board of control to the new Iowa State Board of Education. As the new board directed the affairs of all three state institutions—the University of Iowa in Iowa City, Iowa State University in Ames, and Iowa State Teachers College in Cedar Falls—Seerley's recommendations for his school were bound to compete directly with those of his colleagues and competitors in Iowa City and Ames.

The point at issue was the nature of professional education needed or desired for public school teachers. For Seerley and his predecessor, Gilchrist, that had always included—as goal if not always as reality—a complete undergraduate education in the liberal arts, the preparation of teachers for the high schools, and training for administrative and other professional positions. Like his Illinois colleague David Felmley, Seerley doubted that private colleges and state universities were in a position to prepare secondary school teachers well. He thought little of proliferating small normal schools across the state which could offer little else but meager and general courses.

Instead, he stressed the superiority of having one central state normal school train for many specialities. "Personality, adaptability, spirituality, mental balance, comprehension of all the peculiarities of human development from infancy to maturity, insight into method and practice are all of equal importance to scholarship," Seerley wrote to Henry S. Pritchett on July 22, 1911. "Since state normal schools gave notable attention to all of these characteristics and need not be lacking in culture and high scholarly teaching and do exhibit in actual practice these fundamentals," he continued, "they are admirably organized to train superior high school teachers."[63]

For Seerley the profession of teaching required a technical or professional education that could be offered only in an institution especially and exclusively devoted to such instruction. As he wrote to the state board of education on August 1, 1912: "All subjects taught in a teacher's school should be developed and mastered from the standpoint that a teacher needs to consider. . . ." In Seerley's view, a liberal arts education at Cedar Falls was to be technical, not general or preparatory. It had to incorporate the "point of view and spirit of training" that was "absolutely essential to the making of a thoroughly competent, self-sacrificing teacher."[64]

Various explanations have been offered to account for the 1912 resolution of the Iowa State Board of Education to discontinue all professional education and liberal arts courses beyond the sophomore year at Cedar Falls. According to a contemporary, "a conspiracy of university people" supported the idea.[65] Another motive is said to have been jealousy of those in Iowa who disliked Cedar Fall's monopoly. They wanted the college to be reduced to a two-year school, and other normal schools to be opened across the state. However, as it turned out, upon pressure from the legislature, which had in turn been besieged by friends of the teachers college, the board withdrew its decision on April 3, 1913. Thus, wrote one observer, "ended [a] major campaign. . . . And so, too, the teachers college idea was successfully defended in Iowa, and the State was definitely committed to the maintenance of a standard four-year college program at Cedar Falls."[66] The emphasis on professionalization persisted. At Cedar Falls it meant single-minded concentration on preparing candidates for all positions in public education.

Wisconsin

To educators in Wisconsin the strife between partisans of the university at Madison and the state normal schools had been a familiar story as well. From the state's very beginning teacher education was claimed as university duty, though when it finally started during the Civil War it was seen as a distinctly minor, unimportant activity for the benefit of women students. In 1868, after the first two state normal schools had been opened, the university then closed its normal department and remained reluctant to encourage its faculty to engage in teacher training. "It was as if there were something slightly improper in a university's open espousal of the training of either high school or elementary teachers, and the professors were vaguely embarrassed about it," remarked the university's historians.[67]

The opening of state normal schools after the war made it unnecessary for the university to concern itself with teacher education. Both the legislature and state superintendent confirmed that sentiment and made it difficult for university graduates to be certified properly. They could obtain a teaching license only after they had taught for 16 months following graduation. The old suspicions about academics removed from the real world of common schools and school politics persisted.

Yet matters differed when it came to the education of school leaders, spokesmen, administrators, and high school teachers. Already five years before the arrival in 1884 of John W. Stearns as professor of pedagogy in Madison, a university or college diploma had become the prerequisite for principals of public high schools, and in 1888 the regents established a chair of psychology.[68] Apparently these new developments in pedagogy met with the approval of both normal and university regents and the Wisconsin State Teachers Association. In 1887 and 1888 the association sponsored four-week summer sessions for teachers on the Madison campus. In subsequent years Professor Stearns served as director, and the legislature gave financial support.[69] The university obviously was seen as the proper place to provide in-service and continuing professional education.

Matters did not change much during the 1890s. The normal schools trained teachers and the university offered instruction in pedagogy and psychology as advanced and professional training. Professor Stearns repeatedly urged that the university respond more vigorously to the state's needs for high school teachers. University students who intended to teach in the public schools, Stearns held, were to receive special diplomas only when they had completed a course for teachers, had taken specialized work in pedagogy and psychology, and had demonstrated proficiency in one high school subject.[70] As the century drew to its close it became clear that disputes would inevitably arise over whether, without the addition of scholarly work in pedagogy, the normal schools could compete with the university in the preparation of high school teachers and administrators.

For the normal schools the growing competition with the university raised the question of how they could survive in this struggle without having the facilities and the power to grant academic degrees. University faculty members on their part became aware of the normal schools' desire and tried to forestall it. They sought an agreement with State Superintendent Cary to assign the training of high school teachers to the university and leave the normal schools to offer a two-year course for the training of rural and urban elementary teachers.[71] The scheme failed because the normal educators did not relish being barred from training teachers for the high schools. In subsequent years, President Van Hise repeatedly urged the legislature to take up the proposal, "not because it is advantageous to the University, but because it is fundamentally right—because it is for the best educational interests of the State."[72]

For awhile it appeared as though Van Hise's views would prevail with the legislators. In 1911 they decreed that the normal schools, unless especially authorized by them, were not to offer more than two years of instruction. Yet their law also did not settle the matter. University–normal school relations remained strained, and the university continued to suspect that the normal schools were bent upon obtaining the authority to grant degrees.[73]

The *Wisconsin Journal of Education,* whose editors represented the views of the state's public education establishment, supported the university in its resistance to giving degree-granting power to the normal schools. Wisconsin's public schoolmen had always bemoaned the absence of any institution that would devote itself single-mindedly to professional teacher training. They therefore did not cherish the ideal that the Wisconsin normal schools would follow the path of professionalization and desert the training of classroom teachers for the more prestigious labors of training educational leaders. In 1915 the *Journal* attacked the normal schools for having nurtured false ambitions of becoming like high schools and colleges. The normal schools, the *Journal* editorialized, "have not been convinced that it was as dignified and meritorious to train teachers as to give instruction in geometry, Latin, and physics." One year later the tone was even sharper: "This will be as good a place as any to say that just to the extent that the normal school aspires to academic distinction, just to the extent that it tries to become a college, just to that extent it is bluffing."[74]

By the end of the First World War, university spokesmen and public schoolmen seemed ready to compromise and settle their dispute. Professor Michael Vincent O'Shea of the Madison faculty repeated in 1918 a proposal for an "educational economy" in which the county normal schools would train rural teachers, the state normal schools would provide primary school teachers for graded and city schools, and the colleges and university would be responsible for the education of high school teachers.[75] The scheme sounded logical and simple. All that was needed was everyone's willingness to cooperate.

The prospects for agreement were brighter yet when even the normal regents joined in. Once the war had ended they were ready to devote their institutions single-mindedly to professional work in education. They had come to realize that there was not one school in the state that pursued that purpose alone. The county training, or normal, schools gave remedial and elementary instruction to prospective teachers in the rural schools; private colleges, academies, and public high schools offered normal training as a secondary concern; and for the university the effort to educate administrators and teachers for the secondary schools was only one of many pursuits.[76] Thus the normal regents decided to cut through the tangled complications by discontinuing all subjects not primarily, definitely, and exclusively part of teacher education. They also rescinded their efforts to offer technical and vocational education to returning veterans.

For the normal regents these decisions did not mean a capitulation before the university. They did not thereby give up their claims to a four-year college course and degree-granting powers. They hoped, rather, to offer their retreat from a two-year program of general, academic, and vocational education as a trade-off for legislative authorization to engage in a full four-year program of professional education for high school teachers and teachers of special subjects. What may have appeared to some as a concession was in reality another way to gain both the power to grant degrees and the status of a professional school.

As plausible as this scheme appeared, it had not, however, taken into account the desires and needs of Wisconsin's taxpayers. For them the dispute between the university and the normal schools was of little account; they saw it as a battle over "turf," over who was to teach which subjects to what audience. They cared, however, about the opportunities they desired for their children to receive both a general and a professional education close to their homes. Thus they resented the normal regents' decision to scuttle academic and vocational education in favor of a single-minded emphasis on teacher training. There were other careers and other interests for which their children needed to be educated.

The normal regents soon were to hear the angry reaction. The *Wisconsin News* argued that their policy would "unload over a thousand students on the university, deprive hundreds of others of the opportunity for a higher education, and necessitate an immediate and heavy increase of appropriations for the university."[77] In Milwaukee, normal school students and supporters rallied to preserve the junior college and commercial arts classes.[78] Petitions to keep the college courses flooded the Wisconsin State Assembly. In 1923 Governor Blaine vetoed a bill that would have barred the normal schools from offering academic work. "I see no reason," said the governor, "why young men and women might not take additional work at the several normal schools, and I am not concerned whether such work is called college work or teacher training or whatsoever other name might be applied to it."[79]

In May of 1925 the legislature, responding to the uproar in the press and the complaints of the people, reversed itself and permitted the regents to change their normal schools into four-year teachers colleges which could award bachelor of education degrees to their graduates. The Wisconsin state normal schools had finally attained the long-hoped-for collegiate status. At the same time the regents were authorized to award one-year certificates for teachers in rural schools on the same terms as such certificates had been awarded by the state superintendent to the graduates of county normal schools.[80] To avoid duplication of efforts and to strengthen further the position of the state normal schools, the legislature in 1929 cut off state aid to county normal schools located in counties that were also home to state normal schools.[81]

The events of 1925 made it abundantly clear that no matter what the normal regents thought or what the state's educational establishment or the university considered to be efficient and professional, the people looked upon the normal schools and now the teachers colleges as their preferred institutions of advanced education. They wanted them as colleges close to their homes and capable of offering academic and vocational education at low cost. By 1930, after the onset of the Great Depression, they ratified their conviction by their attendance. In the fall of that year, the Interim Legislative Committee on Education reported, the teachers colleges had experienced a 15 percent increase in attendance, and the county normals an increase of 10 percent. It was clear to the committee, that many students—too many, the committee thought—entered "with neither the desire nor the intention of teaching, but with the object of transferring to the university or to other private colleges."[82]

In Wisconsin the battle between the normal schools and the university would ultimately be ended by the intervention of the state's governor and legislature. In 1951 the state teachers' colleges were transformed into liberal arts colleges, and in 1964 they became state universities. In 1971 they were incorporated into the University of Wisconsin System. The battle of the normal schools with the university had ended in merger. Here as elsewhere the university had not succeeded in holding the normal schools strictly to the task of training elementary teachers. It had not been able to prevent the normal schools from venturing into professional education. Instead the merged institutions now carried out all these tasks jointly.

In their dispute with the tax-paying citizens, the schoolmen fared less well. Their vision of normal schools and teachers colleges as professional schools could not prevail against the popular commitment to public universities as multipurpose institutions. When the teachers and state colleges in Wisconsin became part of a system of state universities, they could no longer see themselves either actually or potentially as single-purpose professional schools. In Illinois, Kansas, and Iowa, where the old state normal schools retained their institutional identities, they did not become professional schools either. They emerged as twentieth-century people's colleges.

7
Professionalization
The Betrayal of the Teacher

The Case of Kansas

By the mid-1920s single-purpose normal schools and teachers colleges were beginning to disappear. A gradual metamorphosis had set in that saw their transformation into state colleges and universities. The education of classroom teachers was not going to remain their only or even their central task. As we have seen in the case of Wisconsin and as one can observe in other states as well, normal educators were ambivalent in their reactions. They resisted this trend if it meant yielding institutional influence to colleagues in other parts of their college or university. They welcomed it if they could now devote their energies to educational research, in-service training, and consultancies, and to the training of curricular and professional specialists, administrators, and faculty members of schools and colleges of education. For the majority of teacher educators the professional prestige to be gained by exchanging the education of classroom teachers for the opportunity to move into graduate and professional instruction was irresistible. For them professionalization came to mean the relegation of teacher education to the least-valued assignment in departments and colleges of education.

In Kansas the desertion of the elementary teacher had begun at Emporia under President Albert R. Taylor in the 1880s. Taylor had committed his school to the training of educational leaders. In 1899 he reported proudly:

> A glance at the alumni register shows that four of them are professors in state colleges; thirteen professors in state normal schools in six different states and territories, one of them being the principal; one is professor of pedagogy in a college of good standing; and several others are professors in good colleges in this and other states, one of them being at the head of the Mennonite college in this state, and one at the head of the Mennonite mission school of Manitoba. Graduates and undergraduates are superintendents of four Indian schools. . . . Twelve of the graduates are

assistant teachers in the State Normal School of Kansas; twenty-six of them occupy important city superintendencies, including three of the six really first-class cities of the state—Topeka, Leavenworth, and Pittsburg. . . . About 100 are principals of third-class-city schools, and about a dozen of ward schools; twenty are principals of high schools, and forty-two assistant principals and teachers in high schools. The principalships of two of the six county high schools are filled by its students, and graduates are teaching in the remaining four. Two hundred of its graduates are teaching in the grades in the city schools, and fourteen former students were elected to county superintendencies. . . .[1]

As for classroom teachers, a 1914 survey of Kansas high schools showed that 87 percent of normal school–trained teachers in the state's urban high schools had attended the Emporia school.[2] But in the rural elementary schools, reports from 1889 and 1899 showed that here were to be found the women who had accounted for more than 60 percent of the Emporia normal school students (see Table 7.1). On the average they taught less than six years in the rural common schools of Kansas (see Table 7.2). Of them President Taylor wrote that, "in the natural order of things, most of them become home-keepers after a few years of service, and what fine mistresses of the manse does this education make of them!"[3] Fewer than a quarter (22.5 percent) did not turn to "the manse" but devoted 10 or more years of their lives to teaching. Fewer yet (11 percent) reached administrative or professional appointments. It is clear, then, that, though more women than men chose to be trained for teaching, they followed that occupation as a short-term pursuit, and those few who stayed with it for longer lagged behind their male colleagues in achieving advanced positions in either teaching or administration.

The 1870 statement of the Leavenworth superintendent that the Kansas State Normal School in Emporia did not provide classroom teachers for the common schools could have been reaffirmed 30 years later. Not the school in Emporia but local high schools with a normal department supplied the demand:

> You established a Normal Department in connection with your [high] school. You solicited some of the most intelligent young ladies of your city and encouraged them to enter and prepare themselves for teachers. The Superintendent took charge of this class, and the result has been that the large proportion of those who entered that class are now teaching your schools in the most satisfactory manner, under the charge of competent Principals who give direction to their work.[4]

At Emporia and at the other state normal schools at Fort Hays and Pittsburg, only their training high schools offered instruction to future elementary

Table 7.1. Distribution of Alumni of the Kansas State Normal School in Emporia, by Program and Gender, 1865–1899

	Model School	Normal School	
		Number	Percent
1865–89			
Men	1,047	1,654	38.55
Women	1,429	2,636	61.45
Total	2,476	4,290	
	(2,865)	(4,879)	
Graduates		382	8.90
1865–99			
Men	1,838	6,680	36.51
Women	2,615	11,616	63.49
Total	4,453	18,296	
	(4,842)	(18,885)	

Sources: Based on Everett D. Fish and Kathryn E. Kayser, "An Outline of the History of the Kansas State Teachers College of Emporia 1865–1934," M.S. thesis, Kansas State Teachers College, n.d.; number of graduates taken from *A History of the State Normal School of Kansas for the First Twenty-five years* (Emporia, 1889), p. 144.

Note: Figures in parentheses indicate discrepancies due to lack of information and inconsistencies in the sources.

Table 7.2. Gender Distribution of Graduates of the Kansas State Normal School, by Various Categories of Service in Education, 1867–1880

Graduates Who Became Educators	Men	Women
Total number	38	62
Total number of years taught	232	322
Average number of years taught	6.11	5.19
Percentage teaching 10 or more years	26.32	22.50
Listed as administrators, principals, and professors		
Number	17	7
Percentage	44.74	11.29

Source: Based on *A History of the State Normal School of Kansas for the First Twenty-five Years* (Emporia, 1889), pp. 63–70.

teachers. The teachers attended these training schools for up to a year and received either a one-year or three-year normal school certificate. They could also enroll for an 8½-week spring or summer term at one of the state's normal schools. They then usually taught for a few years in the state's rural common schools. But whether they were in possession of a one- or a three-year certificate, their preparation was modest, to say the least.

As Table 7.3 shows, at Emporia three out of five students earned a one-year certificate. But even that number, large in relation to the school's total effort, did not fill the state's needs. The Zook Commission of the United States Bureau of Education, which surveyed the institutions of higher education in Kansas, remarked in 1923:

> The [Kansas] normal schools, which ought to be training thousands of young people annually for the rural schools, have through the summer and spring terms and in the one-year curriculum only a moderate influence on either the schools or teachers. This work is good so far as it goes, but it is a very inefficient and unsatisfactory way of building up the preparation of rural school teachers.[5]

The educators at the Kansas State Normal School in Emporia were eager to keep their students for a longer period, but to justify this they felt that they had to go beyond the preparation for elementary school teaching. They introduced courses for specialized subjects and administrative careers and shifted their attention from the rural schools to graded and city schools as well as to high schools. In that endeavor they were encouraged by the demands of urban school boards for better-prepared teachers and by the 1905 decision of the legis-

Table 7.3. Distribution of Degrees and Certificates Awarded by the Kansas State Normal School in Emporia, by Type and Year, 1921–1922

	Years of Study Required	Number of Degrees and Certificates Awarded		Percentage of Students Receiving Degrees or Certificates	
		1921	1922	1921	1922
B.S. in education	4	58	71	4.33	5.03
B.S. in commerce	4	2	12	0.15	0.85
B.S. in music	4	3	3	0.22	0.21
Life Certificate	2	166	169	12.40	11.98
Special Certificate	2	88	88	6.57	6.24
3-Year certificate	1	142	202	10.60	14.32
1-Year certificate	< 1	880	866	65.72	61.37
Total		1,339	1,411	100.00	100.00

Source: George F. Zook, *Report of a Survey of the State Institutions of Higher Learning in Kansas*, U.S. Bureau of Education, Bulletin # 40 (Washington, DC: Government Printing Office, 1923), p. 70.

Note: Columns may not add to totals shown because of rounding.

lature to permit the state normal schools to grant degrees. This was soon followed by the development of four-year courses for the education of high school teachers. By 1922 one out of four of the school's students remained longer than one year. Those who attended two years were given a life certificate that allowed them to teach in both elementary and high schools. A special three-year certificate for teaching vocational subjects in either high or elementary school was also obtainable after a two-year course. By 1922 the catalogue stated that, for an extra fee, students could take work also in preparation for civil service employment and for office work as stenographers, secretaries, and bookkeepers. Kansas educators had quietly given up any claim of their normal school being exclusively devoted to the education of classroom teachers.

The Zook Commission did not fail to note that decision. In the light of the persistent weaknesses in the preparation of rural elementary school teachers, it charged that without having accomplished their original goal the Kansas normal schools had given in to pressures and temptations and had begun training high school teachers and teachers of vocational schools. They were engaging in unwarranted competition for students with the universities and colleges, had committed themselves to considerable expenses in the creation of laboratory and shop facilities, and had given in to local demands and now offered trade and vocational education apart from the preparation of teachers.

All this, the commission thought, added up to a betrayal of a past obligation and disregard for a present need:

> . . . there can be little doubt that to a certain extent the attention of the administration and the faculty at the normal schools has been drawn away from the curriculum and the subjects necessary for the preparation of elementary-school teachers. . . . The normal schools have entered a field of work some of which is not being performed on a high collegiate plane, and yet which to a considerable extent has claimed the attention of the normal schools sufficiently to reflect unfavorably on the superior quality of work otherwise possible in the preparation of elementary and rural school teachers. . . .

By permitting the granting of degrees and certificates to vocational teachers, "the State legislature deliberately invited the normal schools to . . . [divert] their attention from their primary function, the training of elementary-school teachers."[6] It seemed that the teacher educators went along only too willingly.

The Missouri Report

The complaint of the Zook Commission regarding the neglect of the needs of Kansas elementary schools for well-prepared teachers echoed an earlier similar indictment of the normal school establishment in Missouri. In that state the train of events had been set in motion in 1914 when Governor Elliott W. Major requested the Carnegie Foundation for the Advancement of Teaching to survey the state's institutions and programs for teacher education. "We have a great university and five splendid normal schools, and teachers' training courses in about 75 high schools," the governor wrote. "The question, however, is ever open as to what is the best preparation and what is the duty of the State in meeting it. . . ."[7] The governor, legislators, and citizens raised the legitimate question of how, given the imperative to expend public funds wisely, the task of teacher training could best be carried out among various institutions.

The Carnegie Foundation accepted the assignment, but turned away from the question as posed. It refused to tackle the vexing problems of duplication and turf battles among the many institutions involved in teacher training and addressed itself instead to issues important to professional educators. It limited its inquiry to Missouri's state and city normal schools and stated as its sole objective the determination of "good practice in the largest field of professional training for public service in our country. . . ." It commissioned a selected group of education professionals to investigate one particular kind of professional practice and one particular type of professional institution. It asked this commission to address itself to "men and women who are working in a distinct professional field, namely, that of teaching. . . ."[8] In doing this the foundation allowed itself to be guided by professional considerations to the exclusion of the wider political issues. In effect, it ignored, even repudiated, the interests of legislators and lay public. It undertook its task as a purely professional matter.

The report, a massive volume of 400 pages of text and 50 pages of statistics, did not pull any punches. It severely criticized the Missouri normal schools for undermining the professional status of the state's elementary school teachers. It cited as example the Missouri State Normal School in Kirksville whose president, John Kirk, together with Iowa State Normal president, Homer Seerley, had been one of the most outspoken foes of the colleges and universities.[9] The report pointed out that the school's 1876 catalogue had assigned the four years of instruction to different levels of accomplishment. The first-year course, which was attended by the large majority of the school's students, was to train teachers of ungraded rural schools for what was described as "the grandest work of the age" but which represented, at the same time, the lowliest level of professional achievement and prestige. The second-year course was to fit graduates "to take charge of primary and grammar school departments of graded schools and of the best country schools," and the third-year course was to prepare teachers for graded and high schools. The fourth-year curriculum, then, fitted teachers "for the best positions, such as principals, assistants, professors, and county superintendents."[10]

The commission recognized that such an approach to teacher training was built around the incentive of promotion to climb "the educational ladder from the rural school to the graded town school, thence to the high school and superintendency, to be followed by 'institute' or normal school work." Many normal school courses, the commission wrote, "were frankly makeshifts to help a teacher climb, say, from the seventh grade to a high school position." This deliberate encouragement of students to make elementary teaching a stepping stone toward high school teaching, teaching and supervision of special subjects, and school administration, the commissioners emphasized, "constitutes the most serious charge against them [the normal schools]."[11]

The commissioners drove home their point: "The thought of each kind of work as a goal in itself, worthy of extended and special preparation and of equal dignity with any other, does not occur. For the rural teacher the time when he shall become a 'principal, professor, or county superintendent' is the zenith of desire. . . ." With their characteristic bland outlook the commissioners then softened their indictment by adding that, thankfully, times were changing. It would soon become true that a teacher might "look forward to recognition and promotion within the field of service where he did his first teaching." They did not indicate, however, on what evidence this expectation was based.[12]

On another subject, the Carnegie Foundation's commission chided the normal schools' unseemly desire to compete with the university and the colleges for students by offering them work of a nonprofessional nature. Operating on the assumption "that it is the duty of the normal school to train teachers," the commission found that, though this assumption received lip-service from the state's normal schools, it was not everywhere carried out with single-minded devotion. All Missouri normal schools, the commissioners noted, had begun their work by stressing the professional preparation of teachers and regarding academic instruction as supplementary and remedial. After 30 years, however, the schools at Kirksville and Cape Girardeau had branched out to become people's colleges. After one year the Kirksville school, to be sure, abandoned the attempt to diversify because it could not attract sufficiently prepared students. The school at Cape Girardeau, however, continued to offer courses in academic subjects, agricultural and manual training, domestic science, domestic art, music, and business. While the schools at Warrensburg, Springfield, and Maryville adhered to their legal purpose, by 1916 the Maryville normal simply called itself an educational institution and no longer listed the requirement of a declared intention to teach.[13]

The commissioners enumerated three reasons why the normal schools had allowed themselves to deviate from a strictly professional task and to offer general academic work. The first was their students' prior education, which had been exceedingly defective and required remedial academic work. The second stemmed from their students' reliance on teaching as "a most obvious resource for temporary support." This led students to accept the professional studies as but "a necessary incident" and to place greater value on "the academic work that would be accepted for credit in another and higher institution." The normal schools, in turn, wanted to be accommodating to their students "who were using the teaching profession merely as a ladder. . . ." Third, and finally, the normal schools, being largely under the influence and control of local boards, responded directly to the wishes and needs of local taxpayers. "The fundamental theory of a school to train public servants for the benefit of the state," wrote the commission, "is largely obscured by the more attractive idea of a place where local youth may prepare for college, or even pursue collegiate studies and acquire degrees." [14]

To the commission the introduction of academic studies at the normal schools had been "positively disastrous." Its worst effects, the members felt, had been on the teaching staff. Faculty members became divided between highly reputed academics and lowly regarded teachers of educational subjects. The commission did not hide its displeasure with, nay, scorn of, the developments at Cape Girardeau. That school, they wrote, could not be "a good normal school and a 'great college' on the same appropriation." It and all the other Missouri normals should make the preparation of teachers "their sole purpose and concern." This was no longer such a difficult task, because high schools appeared in larger numbers and normal school graduates were allowed to transfer credits to the school of education of the university. [15]

As for the normal schools' desire to become colleges, the commissioners countered that they viewed "with increasing suspicion individuals and institutions that multiply their avowed aims while their resources remain the same. . . ." [16] Normal schools might be excused for having taken up college work when the universities at first refused to prepare high school teachers and administrators. But they could no longer be found blameless when they but sought heightened prestige, regarded college work as their right, or responded to competition from other normal schools. [17]

The rural problem, the commissioners found, did not lie with ambitious faculty members or administrators but with students who had no intention of teaching and who attended a normal school only as a substitute for a community college. Here the commission was prepared to be radical: Such students, they advised,

> should be dealt with drastically, as the institution values its professional integrity. If elementary and high school instruction in this country is ever to be cleared of its traditionally random and trivial reputation, training agencies must insist on a curriculum so specific in character as

to make its choice a fateful step in an individual's career. There will doubtless always be quondam teachers who fail and practice law, just as there are quondam physicians who fail and sell insurance, but it is intolerable for an honest training school so to relax its administration and enfeeble its courses as to put the transient at ease. Every normal school student should feel behind him a full tide of pressure from every quarter urging him to teach and to do nothing else, and he should contribute the impetus of his own clear decision to the general impulse. [18]

The influence and control exercised by local boards gave undue weight, the commissioners felt, to the wishes of local taxpayers who wanted educational institutions in their community that might prepare their children for college or allow them to earn academic degrees. Such "democratic" governance, the commissioners complained, only gratified "the popular local fancy." They compared it unfavorably to the modern notion of professionalization, which held that "an intelligent society has learned not to interfere with competent professional service. . . ." [19]

The Cul-de-Sac of Professionalization

The Carnegie Foundation's commission, it must have become obvious by now, was inextricably committed to the idea of professionalization. The professionals and their interests were given priority. The wishes of students and local boards were seen as "democratic" interference with "professional" requirements. Implied in this notion of professionalization were efficiency in administration, rationality in the distribution of functions, and strict adherance to a program of teacher training. On the conflict between normal schools and universities, referred to in the governor's initial question, the commissioners held that all state normal schools should become colleges of education of the state university. [20] That, Henry S. Pritchett, the Carnegie Foundation's president, remarked with great rhetorical flourish, would go a long way toward establishing in Missouri "an enlightened administration of the state's entire teacher-training function exercised from a single directing body equipped to prepare teachers for all schools as thoroughly as possible." [21] Anyone who remembered Pritchett's advice to the Iowa State Board of Education in 1912 to streamline the administration of teacher training in the state could have predicted his message to the governor of Missouri. [22]

The commissioners' commitment to professionalization also showed in their reliance on educational administrators for raising the competencies of and promoting the rewards for meritorious teachers. It was the foremost duty of municipal and state school executives, they wrote, to protect and promote "a community's most precious asset"—the classroom teachers. It is significant that the commission did not see the teachers themselves as professionals who could be expected to take their destinies into their own hands. To the contrary, in the commission's view it was not "proper . . . that teachers themselves should agitate, unionize, and strike. . . ." Apparently, the commissioners equated teacher professionalism with unionization, agitation, and strikes. It seems not to have occurred to them that teacher professionalism in its concerns and methods of operation might equal that of school administrators and of the commissioners themselves.[23]

Not only was the commissioners' idea of professionalism and professionalization restricted within the bounds of an administrative leadership, it was also silently assumed to be appropriate only for male members of the educational hierarchy. Despite the large percentage of women in the normal student population—the Missouri statistics for 1913/1914 showed 7,134 students in all of the state's normal schools; of these 5,154, or 72 percent, were women[24]—all the references to teachers in the quotations cited above are to men. *He,* not *she,* would someday become a normal school professor or superintendent or would be professionally recognized as an elementary teacher. Though Pritchett paid complimentary lip-service to "the brave womanly figure that carries on its slender shoulders so heavy a responsibility" and who labors under the handicaps of "the restricted preparation, the lack of sympathetic counsel, and the scant pay that are the characteristics of elementary school teaching today . . . ," he did not see the "profession" implicated in this situation. He laid the blame at the doorstep of "the almost universal superficiality of our people" which was reflected in the schools.[25]

The commission pointed to the same superficiality as villain when it wrote of the normal schools' desire to compete with the colleges and the state university. This unseemly and arrogant ambition was the product of democratic striving. It had to be opposed through an appeal to the professionalism of educators who would recognize that their only means to achieve greater effectiveness was cooperation, not competition, among educational institutions and central administration of the state's teacher training schools. Such cooperative, comprehensive efforts, Pritchett wrote, would not fail to evoke the support of the public. There was need, he lectured, for "an aroused public opinion that will demand sincere teaching and a body of teachers who will educate the children of the nation to the ideals of simplicity, sincerity, and thoroughness. An honest system of education and a clear-thinking public opinion must be developed together." To initiate such an effort would be the responsibility of the state's educators, who have "the spirit which rises out of professional training. . . ." With these grandiose pronouncements of largely self-serving propositions the Carnegie commission returned to its main point: The final answer to the problems of teacher training lay in an increased professionalization.[26]

The Carnegie report had correctly identified the normal schoolmen's neglect of the elementary school teacher and her training as the basic fault of American public education. The irony of the report's recommendations lay in the fact that it called upon the very same factor—the normal schoolmen's commitment to professionalization—as the remedy for the problem. It brought to the surface the commissioners' own contempt for democratic institutions and the low opinion they held of the capabilities of the country's elementary school teachers. The desire for professional prestige and status had led the normal educators to relegate the education of elementary school teachers to county and city training schools. Now they heard from the commission that their very commitment to professionalization, combined with a severe check on their democratic impulses, should yield the desired results of a return to a commitment to the education of the classroom teacher. The cause of the malaise was to be its cure.

Professionalization and the High School Teacher

Teacher educators were only too willing to adopt the gospel of professionalization. They assumed, for the most part, that elementary school teachers would avail themselves gladly of the training offered in city and county normal schools and accept the marginal status they were assigned in the state normal schools and teachers colleges. The case was different with the country's high school teachers. In urbanized areas of the East and the Midwest, high school teachers found valuable allies in the presidents, faculties, and trustees of universities, who—as we shall see below—had been largely responsible for the education of these teachers. Thus high school teachers were not, at the outset, disposed to accept the normal schools and teachers colleges as proper institutions for their own and their colleagues' education.

American high school teachers looked back on a proud tradition of community leadership. They traced it to colonial days. The schoolmaster of the Latin grammar school had been, of necessity, a college-educated Latinist.[27] Men like Ezekiel Cheever of the Massachusetts Bay Colony had become famed for their scholarship and had enjoyed a reputation on a par with that of ministers or lawyers. Many of them had in fact taken over professional positions as minister, lawyer, physician, or magistrate.[28] Even while they taught school they had enjoyed a reputation of learned scholars who were destined for rewarding careers. And, what is more to the point, they had served as role models for America's grammar and high school teachers of the nineteenth century.

The tradition of the schoolmasters of the municipal grammar and college preparatory Latin schools of the eighteenth and nineteenth centuries was kept alive by the Boston schoolmasters, who, in the 1830s and 1840s, had been bitter enemies of Horace Mann and his promotion of the normal schools. These schools, the masters had protested, "may be made highly useful in the great work of enlightening the community, but the friends and advocates of such institutions never can exclusively claim the title of educators in free America." Their graduates, the masters insisted, could not compare with themselves, "many of [whom] . . . have enjoyed all the literary advantages of the college or the university . . . [or] have had opportunities, perhaps no less valuable, and . . . have had much experience."[29]

To be sure, the Boston masters of the 1830s and 1840s were few in number, but the proportion of college-educated high school teachers did begin to increase towards the end of the century. In New Jersey their share reached about 15–20 percent between 1871 and 1895. By 1906, 65 percent had obtained college degrees, and 25 percent were graduates of normal schools.[30] Sizer reports for 1893 that roughly half of the secondary school teachers in the United States held bachelor's degrees.[31] Statistics gathered during 1891–1893 in the New England states corroborate that figure. There, 56 percent of the high school teachers were college graduates, 21 percent had graduated from high or normal school, and only 23 percent had never completed a secondary course of instruction.[32] Edward Krug wrote that half of the high school teachers in Wisconsin and Maine during the 1890s were college graduates; in Minnesota and New Hampshire he believed that figure to have gone up to two-thirds.[33] From a study conducted in 1904 in 19 states, the District of Columbia, and the Indian Territory we learn that 70.3 percent of the male teachers employed in high schools and 53.3 percent of the female teachers were college graduates, and another 15.2 percent and 11.7 percent, respectively, had graduated from normal schools.[34] As sketchy as they are, these figures nonetheless indicate that toward the century's end the high schools had begun to increase their reliance on college-educated teachers.

The college-educated high school teachers took pride in their education, seldom failed to promote the cause of academic training, and looked askance upon teacher training in the normal schools. In his reminiscences James H. Baker—who during the 1880s was a high school master in Colorado and during the 1890s served as the only high school principal on the National Education Association's Committee of Ten for the standardization of the high school curriculum[35]—wrote that high school teachers then held teacher training as conducted in the normal schools "to be something of a fad," and only few of the masters could be found in the National Education Association. "A schoolmaster may be forgiven," Baker added, "if he has never been greatly influenced by 'fads' and has not placed overemphasis on study of nerve cells, sense perception, special abilities, culture epochs, apperception, or other proposed ways of universal truth."[36] The "old-school" high school masters believed in academic education for themselves, the "birch and the ruler" for their students—both the Boston masters and Baker agreed on this—and, above all, in the importance of a lifetime's experience a teacher had gathered inside and outside the schoolroom.

Sentiments such as these prompted Massachusetts high school masters at a conference in Boston in January of 1890 to consider founding a training school for high school teachers which would accept only college graduates. They argued that it was "the high school teacher's task to prepare his pupils for a liberal course of training, and therefore he should himself have passed through that training."[37] In the Midwest, high school teachers gathered in the Michigan Schoolmasters' Club and discussed similar issues. They stressed matters "that pertain to our common work, with particular reference to high school and collegiate training. . . ." At the club's first regular meeting on May 1, 1886, a speaker made clear the members' contempt for the normal approach to teacher education. "Quite a large portion of the teaching fraternity," he said, "are making of method, if not a fetish to worship, at least a hobby to ride—and that to the detriment of the country's highest pedagogical interests." In a veiled slap at the National Education Association another declared the club's intention to debate subjects that were "left untouched by associations that now exist." Reflecting the gender distribution of the Latin-trained teachers, the club initially limited its membership to male college graduates. After three years, however, it opened its doors to women.[38]

By the time the Committee of Ten had begun its work in 1890 under the leadership of Harvard's president Charles William Eliot, teachers in the academic high schools were an articulate group and were recognized as such by the committee. They and their schools served an elite. As the committee put it, they educated

> that small proportion of all the children in the country—a proportion small in number, but very important for the welfare of the nation—who show themselves able to profit by an education prolonged to the eighteenth year, and whose parents are able to support them while they remain so long at school.[39]

If high school students were deemed so important "for the welfare of the nation," could less be said for their teachers?

To insure their elite status and fortify their relationship to the colleges, the academically trained Latin grammar and secondary masters of the upper Midwest supported the North Central Association of Colleges and Secondary Schools, which had been founded upon the initiative of the Michigan School-masters' Club on March 29, 1895. The association brought college and normal presidents together with high school principals and superintendents from Ohio, Michigan, Indiana, Illinois, Wisconsin, Iowa, and Missouri. Like the already existing similar associations in New England and the Middle Atlantic

States, the North Central Association was to promote greater uniformity in secondary curricula and in the requirements for admission to college. The secondary masters embraced it because they had come to resent the growing practice of recruiting high school teachers from the ranks of normal school–trained elementary teachers. They viewed this upgrading of common school teachers as an abomination and a threat. They held no brief for normal president Felmley of Illinois, who, as we know, had asked that elementary and secondary school teachers be trained together in his school. They feared that if they failed to act they would soon be overcome, as it were, by the advancing tide of academically ill-prepared elementary teachers.

At the 1896 meeting of the North Central Association, President James Burrill Angell of the University of Michigan came to the support of the secondary masters. Angell pointed out that though New England high schools had not been founded initially to serve as college preparatory schools, they had now become just that. In the Midwest, by contrast, high schools created to give "a somewhat generous education" had always served as preparatory schools. "They bid fair," Angell added, "to be the preparatory schools from which our colleges must draw the great majority of their students."[40] Therefore it was clear that high school teachers and administrators ought to recognize their special college preparatory function and protect themselves against being diluted from below with teachers who had been trained to concern themselves with general and vocational education. High school teachers quite properly were to be on guard against being treated like elementary teachers.

Common School Party vs. College Party

The battle lines were being drawn, and the academic high school teachers distanced themselves from their colleagues in the elementary schools. It did not take long for two distinct parties to appear on the scene. The academic high school teachers with a supporting cast of university presidents and professors made up the college party, while public school administrators, teacher trainers, and educational journalists emerged as spokesmen for their opponents, the common school party. Its members charged that a college-dominated high school constituted a threat to the public school's real mission and a perversion of its purpose. They cited Mr. Mayo's charge that the high school teacher who had graduated from college understood neither the common school student nor the common school teacher. For the first task, he lacked the requisite pedagogical and psychological training presumably dispensed in the normal schools; for the second, his arrogance prevented him from appreciating the qualities of his colleagues.[41] The partisans of the common school thus set out to battle with their rivals in the college party.

What stands out as noteworthy about this conflict is that for a long while and with few exceptions elementary school teachers stayed away from the battle and remained silent. They did not speak for themselves. They did not in any visible or audible form enlist in the common school party, to which, had they chosen sides, they would have belonged. Perhaps this was because, as women, they had been trained as dutiful and compliant teachers to bow to the directives of their male superiors. Perhaps it was a result of their self-perception that they were but temporary employees who would ultimately give up their work for marriage and motherhood and thus had no stake in the outcome. Perhaps it was also because some of them hoped to be called some day to teach in the secondary grades and thus were anxious not to offend spokesmen of either of the two parties. At any rate, they remained on the sidelines while the spokesmen of the common school party, almost uniformly male, went to battle with the college party, without being advised or informed about the desires of the teachers.

In Massachusetts one of the early leaders of the common school party was John W. Dickinson, secretary of the state board of education during the 1880s and 1890s. Dickinson spoke for the cause David Felmley had promoted in Illinois. Because the principles of teaching were identical at every level, both Dickinson and Felmley argued, they had to be taught in the same fashion to teachers of all grades. Elementary and secondary school teachers were to be trained together in normal schools.[42] That doctrine became permanently enshrined as part of the common school party's credo. It was heard decades later when, for example, Edgar B. Wesley repeated it in his book on the National Education Association. Wesley blasted the veterans of the college party for having been willing to sacrifice "the welfare of nine-tenths of the [high school] students . . . in order to concentrate upon the college prospects of the one-tenth. College men," asserted Wesley, "were not interested in secondary education; they were interested only in college-preparatory training. In truth," he added, "many high school teachers had the same attitudes."[43]

When the dust finally settled in the late 1940s and early 1950s on the common school party's largely successful campaign, it became apparent that the party's anger had been directed primarily against academically inclined high school teachers and principals who had resisted the relentless drive of the education professionals to overrun them with upgraded elementary teachers and to extend administrative oversight to them. To the spokesmen of the common school party, that resistance had been all the more maddening because the party had been successful in other areas of its campaign. The common school party could, after all, count in its camp the schoolmen in normal schools, teachers colleges, and university departments of education.

Harvard and the Classroom Teacher

The common school party's greatest triumph, however, was to come shortly before the turn of the century when it successfully invaded Harvard University and determined the direction of the university's work in education. At Harvard the relationship between college and the public schools and their teachers had begun under the presidency of Charles William Eliot.[44] In 1890 Eliot asked the college faculty to consider the introduction of "a possible normal course of one year." The course was to offer no credits but expose its students to a study of methods deemed suitable by the instructor for high school teaching.

The faculty agreed and Eliot appointed Paul Henry Hanus to teach education at the college. This was followed in 1892 with Eliot's establishment of the Schools Examination Board to assess the programs of Massachusetts high schools which had asked for its services. Harvard's and Eliot's impact was to culminate in 1893 with the publication of the National Education Association's Committee of Ten Report on the curriculum of the nation's secondary schools. Eliot had been the committee's chairman and the author of the report.[45]

Eliot quickly achieved the aims he had pursued through his involvement with the Schools Examination Board and the Committee of Ten. He impressed his views on the necessity for academic work of high quality on the nation's high schools. Yet he also came to depend, willy-nilly, on the initiatives pursued by Professor Hanus. And here we encounter a familiar story. Hanus shifted the emphasis from the preparation of classroom teachers to the training of administrators. "Successful and ambitious teachers," Hanus wrote in 1899, "are naturally turning to the university for the training which they need to enable them to compete successfully for all the higher positions in the profession."[46] These higher positions were neither to be found in the classroom nor were they to be reserved for men or women who excelled as teachers. Hanus wanted to dissociate the teacher from the administrator as much and as clearly as possible. He wanted to make it impossible that superintendents could ever again be called—as Charles Francis Adams had done in 1889— "grammar school teachers gone to seed or ministers and politicians out of a job."[47] Administrators were to be trained experts in the science of school management. This new calling was to be a career worthy of a man's life-long professional commitment. Teaching was but a preliminary, alas necessary, step on the way. Only women and men without ambition, Hanus implied, would remain classroom teachers throughout their careers. No particular heed had to be paid to them and their concerns.

Hanus' directions at Harvard brought specialization and the dominance of educational administration over the curriculum. As Arthur Powell, the historian of the Harvard Graduate School of Education, put it:

> The most dramatic change was the emphasis he [Hanus] gave to training experienced administrators at the graduate level rather than prospective

teachers in Harvard College. Administrative training expanded his own political influence and self-esteem at the same time that it caused far less collegial friction than had teacher education. Significantly, school administrators seemed more important than teachers because their role was to direct education conceived of as a "social force."[48]

Eliot, however, was not entirely convinced. He had to take into consideration the jaundiced view taken by most of his faculty at the college toward the new work in education. Eschewing any title like education or administration, he promoted Hanus to a full professorship in "the history and art of teaching," and in 1905 held Hanus' instructional budget down to a modest $5,000. At Teachers College in New York, where, as we shall see, professional work in education had also begun, the instructional budget was listed as $282,000.[49] Clearly, Eliot moved with caution.

Under Eliot's successor, Abbott Lawrence Lowell, the emphasis on research and the unwillingness to provide teacher training for undergraduates grew more pronounced. Hanus' colleague, Henry W. Holmes, who was to become dean of education in 1920, remained suspicious of the emphasis on research and the "science of education" and continued to speak up for teacher education. Experimental psychology and quantitative measurements lent themselves badly, Holmes thought, to the study of human beings and to educational reform. They could tell what existed, but they could not say what ought to exist. They might bring renown to the educational researcher, but they would be of little help to the teacher in the classroom. After 1914 Holmes was instrumental in decreasing the importance of research at Harvard and assigning greater concern to educational reform.

That preoccupation with educational reform, however, was far removed from teacher training. As Powell describes it, it sought to socialize education, which meant "to extend adult supervision over an increasing fraction of the life experiences of young people." The junior high school, supervised recreation, vocational guidance, the Boy Scouts, commercial, agricultural, industrial, and religious education became its achieved and desired concerns; the opening of new careers its goal. Wrote Powell: "The faculty no longer wished merely to train teachers, principals, and superintendents; they wished to create new specialized jobs. . . . The Division of Education soon became more entrepreneurial and propagandistic."[50]

The next step in the fortunes of the study of education at Harvard came in 1920 with the creation of the graduate school of education. Dean Holmes's aim was to take high school teachers and turn them into educational specialists or administrators. Though Holmes continued to pay lip-service to the preparation of undergraduates and graduates for classroom teaching, the realities of supply and demand effectively subverted any such hopes. The part-time study of experienced educators now became the rule at the graduate school of education.

Four years later Holmes sought to attract young students inexperienced in teaching to a two-year program of graduate instruction. He meant to model the conveyance of professional knowledge on the training provided in law and medical schools. He hoped to send out effective educators who had all been socialized in a one-year common course and a second-year program of advanced specialization. The keystone in Holmes's arch of professional training was the one-year common course. It was to restore professional respectability to the classroom teacher by creating an esprit de corps among all its graduates.

Holmes's central idea was appealing enough and addressed itself to one of the key factors in the problematic situation of the American classroom teacher: his or her lack of professional standing. Holmes maintained that when future superintendents and future classroom teachers were taught in the same classroom and trained in the same principles of education, they were both presumed to be equally competent in the grasp of their professional fundamentals. Both would then move with equal confidence and proficiency in the execution of their professional duties. The gulf that yawned between the lowly classroom teacher and the superior administrators would thus disappear, and teachers would become colleagues of equal standing and responsibilities in the day-to-day running of their schools.[51]

Holmes's proposal did not fare very well at the hands of his colleagues. Not only did he have to endure the ridicule of his Chicago colleague Charles Judd and the opposition of Dean James Russell at Teachers College in New York, but he also had to face dissension and opposition within his own school. Judd urged Holmes to be done with teacher training and to develop research, and Russell promoted the separation of research training from preparation for professional tasks. For Holmes the end came in 1939 when the new president, James B. Conant, asked for his resignation as the price for continued financial support of the school by the university.[52]

With Conant the debates over the fate of the school of education took an entirely different turn. Conant was committed to science and academic scholarship and suspicious of education as a scholarly field. He was, however, deeply concerned over the role the university should play in the education of secondary school teachers. The first result of his initiative was the introduction in 1936 of the master of arts in teaching (M.A.T.) degree, jointly sponsored by the academic departments of the college and the graduate school of education. Gone now was Holmes's ideal of a common advanced degree for all educational professionals. As Powell described it: "Prospective educators would first prepare just for teaching, through either undergraduate study in institutions that offered it or through the graduate M.A.T. Then, following successful teaching experience, they would return to pursue a specialized Ed.M."[53] The hierarchy was back in the saddle.

Under Conant's guidance the Harvard School of Education came to place greater reliance on social science research and teacher training. In both instances the specifically education-directed emphasis on psychology, statistics, tests, and measurements was replaced with utilization of social scientists who were urged to bring their research to bear on the nation's educational problems. Earlier endeavors to build a "science of education" or to produce educational practitioners were played down.

But this, too, did not last. After 1951 Dean Francis Keppel recognized the nation's growing need for well-trained teachers and administrators, and hoped to attract the academically talented graduates of liberal arts colleges into the teaching profession. In that he received the support of the Ford Foundation's Fund for the Advancement of Education, which sought to make a public school teaching career more attractive to able students by favoring academic work in subject matter over courses in education. Career recruitment became the new gospel.

The program encountered the familiar dilemma that, short of leaving the classroom for the administrative office, there was no such thing as a career for classroom teachers. There was talk of promoting the idea of team teaching as a way of functionally differentiating degrees of mastery among teachers. There were also attempts to establish career ladders for master teachers by providing for M.A.T.'s the opportunity for doctoral study in teaching. But what started out as a concern for the classroom teacher and his or her career ended in discussions over the school of education's relations to the public schools. Could these be put on the same basis as medical school and hospital? The final result came in 1959 with a $2.8 million Ford Foundation grant that, as Powell put it, celebrated "a career progression that ideally included the M.A.T. program, a period of teaching experience, and then doctoral study. . . ."[54] Again, the gifted and ambitious classroom teacher would have to leave both classroom and teaching.

Powell concludes his book on the Harvard Graduate School with these observations on the place of teachers and teacher education at Harvard:

> The role of the classroom teacher was rarely regarded as important in itself. Harvard's main intention was to recruit and advance a heretofore missing elite; the traditional teaching job was an obstacle to this recruitment and so had to be changed. As long as the national teacher shortage existed, the strategy worked well. But when that crisis receded by the end of the sixties and external support for the M.A.T. ended as well, no deeper commitment to teaching careers as self-evident priority remained. An emphasis on educational jobs distant from children re-

emerged. Unlike earlier times, many of these jobs were located outside school systems or schools of education.[55]

The classroom teachers had lost out again.

Teachers College Follows Suit

What had taken place on the Charles River in Cambridge was to repeat itself at the academic colossus on the Hudson in New York. What eventually became Teachers College of Columbia University began as the Kitchen Garden Association, subsequently renamed the Industrial Education Association, a philanthropic organization in New York City devoted to the manual or industrial education of immigrant children. Early during its existence in the 1880s the association recognized the need for teacher training and educational reform. This led in 1887 to the founding of the New York College for the Training of Teachers. Its purpose, so its charter stated, was "to give instruction in the history, philosophy and science of education, psychology, in the science and art of teaching, and also in manual training and the methods of teaching the various subjects included under that head."[56]

Teachers College, as it was formally named in its charter of 1892, was conceived as a two-year professional school for both men and women with the right to confer the degrees of bachelor, master, and doctor of pedagogy. It deliberately sought to avoid competition with the existing normal schools by requiring its students to have completed their secondary education in either high or normal school before they enrolled.

Nicholas Murray Butler, the first president of Teachers College, viewed his school's program as continuing the professional preparation of teachers where the normal schools had left off. The college was to merge a general academic with a pointedly professional education. Being an institution of collegiate rank and taking for granted a completed secondary education of its students, Teachers College expected to avoid the dilemma of the normal schools. It intended to be able to concentrate on professional studies without having to fear the charge that its graduates were not prepared as classroom teachers. To accomplish this fusion of professional and general advanced academic work the college sought an association with Columbia University, its faculty, and its library.

This association began in 1893, was strengthened five years later when Teachers College became an integral part of Columbia, and completed in 1915 when it was recognized as a faculty of the university. It brought with it a steady rise in both the standards expected of students and those demanded in the instructional work. Only applicants with at least a two-year college or technical school education or with experience as classroom teachers were permitted to enroll. The course offerings expanded in several new academic and professional departments. The measure of innovation is best illustrated when one realizes that education work in other universities was usually conducted in one department. By 1906 there were 72 advanced courses in about a dozen departments available to the Teachers College student.[57]

Teachers College stressed high academic and professional standards. By 1905 the college abandoned its two-year course for teachers, and in 1914 the school of education was recognized as a graduate school. But this very advance also meant that, steadily and irresistibly, Teachers College moved away from its original function of teacher training. As its graduate work expanded and as it attracted more and more students from across the nation and other countries its appeal and its policy changed accordingly. In 1913 Dean Russell announced: "The obvious policy . . . [is] to keep on doing what it [Teachers College] has been doing so successfully for a decade, *viz.,* train the teachers of education for other professional schools and equip men and women for positions of leadership in every department of educational service."[58] As a training ground for faculty members of professional schools and for educational leaders, Teachers College had moved a long way from the concerns that once determined the work of teacher educators.

Eight years later Dean Russell was ready to abandon the undergraduate teacher training function altogether and concentrate on graduate professional work. In 1926 all undergraduate work ceased at Teachers College and all subject-matter instruction was to take account of its application to school problems. As the historians of Teachers College put it, there was now only one type of student to be enrolled in the institution—the "Teachers College professional student."

To aid their progress a reorganization in 1934 created the five divisions of foundations, administration, guidance, instruction, and measurement and research. The college now recognized function rather than type of school or level of instruction, and by 1935 added the advanced school of education "for the development of an educational elite" and established a new professional degree, the doctorate in education (Ed.D.).[59] The new degree program would allow its students to pursue practice-directed professional tasks, while the old Ph.D. would continue the emphasis on research. At Teachers College, as elsewhere, the triumph of research and the scientific study of education meant, as Dean Russell put it, that the institution's resources were now fully devoted to serve the new students, the "experienced teachers, administrators, supervisors."[60] There was no more room in the house for the beginning classroom teacher.

Chicago: The Science of Education

What Harvard and Teachers College had demonstrated in the East, the University of Chicago would carry out in the Midwest—professionalization everywhere meant the neglect and banishment of the classroom teacher. For the professionalizers in the Midwest, a science of education as the embodiment of rationality and efficiency became the new battle cry. And, as Michael Katz pointed out, the new science of education based itself on suppositions and emphases that had been unknown to nineteenth-century normal educators.

In looking at that transformation at the University of Chicago, Katz juxtaposed a 1902 statement of John Dewey's with a 1923 pronouncement of Charles Judd's. Dewey had urged students of education to familiarize themselves with psychological principles, the methods and results of the study of intelligence, ethics, and history before they turned to the study of education itself. Judd instead demanded that his students embark on "a complete survey of education" that included school administration, educational measurements, history of school practices, methods of instruction, and educational psychology. This would insure, he wrote, that their study of education was based on fact rather than tradition or opinion.[61]

The change involved a departure from philosophy and theory and from a concern for seeing education in its total social and historical context. It involved likewise a turn away from normative ethical concerns. Instead, Katz wrote, "university educationists hoped to create a discipline through surveying the field of education as it existed in the real world and then breaking down its subdivisions as minutely as possible."[62] Scientists dealt with "the real world" and had no patience with idealistic projections of what ought to be. To be scientific meant to deal accurately with the minutiae of everything, since every large thing was composed of many little things and could be understood only as an aggregation of these little things. Thus counting or quantitative measurement became a key skill of the educational scientist.

As far as the curricula of schools of education and teacher training programs were concerned, "diffused, sprawling, and specialized patterns of course offerings replaced general and theoretical programs." At Chicago a 1922 announcement read that "in place of general courses in public school administration, courses are now given in school finance, the administrative management of pupils, and the organization and supervision of the teaching staff." All courses in philosophy were dropped from the program. The science of education, wrote Katz, "was to be a science with no theory, no distinctive way of looking at the world, and no methodology other than the survey."[63]

This splintering of educational scholarship into small specialties was a result of professionalization among teacher educators rather than a response to the needs of the public schools and their teachers. At Chicago, John Dewey had based his work in education on a unified theory that was then tested by experiment in real classroom situations of his laboratory school and evaluated in discussions in his seminar. The needs of the classroom stood at the center of Dewey's approach. He used his school as an experimental base for the collaboration of scholars from many disciplines, and the reaction of the children served as the test. The classroom brought together scholarship and life.

But Dewey left in 1904, and his successor, Charles Judd, the elected president of the American Psychological Association, did not share Dewey's concerns. As Woody White noted, Judd wanted to transform the study of education into "a legitimate university discipline" and into "a respectable profession for white men. . . . Under Dewey," White wrote, "the study of education was broad and encompassing; under Judd it would be narrow and vocational."[64] If for Dewey the classroom with its children and teachers had stood at the center of attention, for Judd it was of secondary importance. Children learned primarily through imitation, he believed, and the laboratory school exchanged experiment and innovation for traditional learning and emphasis on talent and scholarship. Dewey's classroom teachers had been expected to report and analyze their classroom experience. Judd, wrote White,

> was more concerned with the construction of laboratories that resembled the isolated experiment stations common to the physical and biological sciences. For Judd measurement by the use of special machinery was necessary because it gave educational research the quality of precision absent from Dewey's work.[65]

The science of education was to be based on survey and research.

Because in Judd's view such a science required an independent body of information, undergraduates to be trained as teachers and graduate students to be trained as educational researchers or administrators should not be required to study other subjects. For them a new array of education courses was to be developed. This meant, for example, that the curriculum of future secondary school teachers could not be organized around subject matter courses, but was to be based on Judd's "Psychology of High School Subjects" course. As one might expect, this approach encountered serious difficulties and aided Judd's movement away from teacher education to administration. His educational psychology course became the initial offering for students in educational administration.[66]

The development of educational administration as a specialized field with its own body of principles and knowledge then was the crowning achievement of the science of education. It now made clear that administrators were not, as Dewey once held, teachers with added responsibilities, but specialists of high standing. John Franklin Bobbitt, a junior Chicago colleague of Judd's, put it well: "The supervisor is no longer just the best teacher but a professional armed with different skills and information."[67] Among these skills belonged the construction of a school's curricula—a task once assumed by the teacher.

By the 1920s teacher training thus was gradually replaced at Chicago by the science of education and the professional preparation of school administrators, college instructors of education, and educational researchers. As early as 1914 Judd had editorialized in the *Elementary School Journal* that "in view of the importance of problems of organization it seems wise to allow the individual classroom to sink into the background for the time being in the effort to develop a general science of elementary school administration."[68] As far as the curriculum was concerned, Judd's greatest moment came when he could report that "a number of sharply differentiated courses in particular phases of school organization have been worked out resulting in a professional curriculum comparable to the best medical schools."[69]

White also made it very clear that Judd's move away from training teachers to preparing administrators involved a very deliberate attempt to attract men rather than women to the study of education. As it had been with Felmley at the Illinois State Normal University, so was the strategy very successful in Chicago. The University of Chicago Survey reported that between 1911 and 1929 the percentage of male Ph.D.'s in art and literature was 81, whereas in education it reached 99. Of 83 recipients of the doctorate in education during this period, only one was listed as a high school teacher upon graduation. One year later, even that one was no longer teaching school. Eighty-five percent of the group then served in higher education, and 11 percent in public school administration.[70] Because Chicago concentrated on specialized graduate training, it was inevitable that under the then-existing social philosophy neither women nor black students were welcome for entry into the educational profession.

By 1933, White reports, Judd had succeeded in ending the Chicago School of Education's responsibility for the training of classroom teachers. That was given to the university's new Committee on the Preparation of Teachers. What happened at Chicago, we know, happened in different ways and under different circumstances at Columbia and Harvard as well. The professional educators turned their backs on what one might well describe as the education profession's most important and most basic responsibility. They no longer prepared beginning teachers for the classroom. They groomed experienced teachers for supervisory and administrative positions, they prepared instructors for professional schools, colleges, and universities, and they trained educational journalists, researchers, and professionals. Research, consulting, and career development had become their primary tasks; school teaching an undesirable activity, "unworthy," as White wrote, "of a white man's life work."[71] Pity the poor teacher. The profession's top schools were not for her.

8
What of the Teacher?

The Nineteenth–Century Record

The normal school educators did not succeed in making their institutions the reliable source of classroom teachers for the country's public elementary schools. Their original intent to give internal strength and staying power to the common school movement by creating a professional corps of teachers was never realized. Neither with men nor with women did Horace Mann and his friends succeed in moving rural New England elementary school teachers beyond the citizen-teacher status. Mann's successors in the East and the Midwest were soon persuaded to shift their attention to the more prestigious task of training education professionals.

The reasons for their failure were several. Unlike their models in Prussia, American teachers had not grown up in a class-based society. They did not accept a lifetime schoolteaching position as a privilege or reward. They were not grateful for having thereby been raised above the social level into which they had been born. Americans, and particularly so midwesterners, did not accept as given and fixed a system of inflexible social classes. They were forever on the move, geographically and socially, and they were to continue to view schoolteaching as a temporary occupation. For them it was but a step on the ladder to economic advance or to matrimony.

The hopes of Mann and his supporters and all the other public schoolmen thereafter foundered on the shoals of local and district control. The schoolmen had never been able to challenge the power of local boards and county superintendents over the common schools and the pay of their teachers. Elected school board members rarely paid more than minimal wages to their teachers and, for the most part, were unwilling to grant professional recognition to the men and women who taught their children. They habitually looked upon women teachers as the daughters of their neighbors. They expected them to teach as a way of repaying familial debts they owed to their

communities and as part of their own education for future woman- and motherhood. Besides, school board members often argued, an unmarried woman
had no family obligations and could get along on less money than a man.
Men teachers were expected either to be incapable of other work or to be
students earning their way through college.

Under these conditions it was unrealistic to develop normal schools that
could imitate the Prussian teacher seminaries and produce trained professional
teachers in sufficient numbers. The Prussian noncollegiate, vocationally
trained schoolmaster who committed himself to a lifetime of classroom teaching
in an elementary school would never be welcomed by Americans. The Prussian
seminaries, their instructors and students, whom Cousin had described with
such admiration, could not possibly find a home in the United States. George
B. Emerson put his finger on perhaps the most crucial point when he said in
1859: "There is no class of free people in this country so low as those for whom
the Normal Schools of Prussia are designed."[1]

New England normal school principals and instructors drew the consequences. They saw their students move to city schools or leave teaching altogether. They noted an older student group attending their institutions as
stepping stones to further college and professional education or employment.
Seeking to make the best of that situation and falling back on their own collegiate experience, the New England schoolmen naturally tried to offer in their
schools what their students sought in colleges, professional schools, and universities. They introduced a gospel of professional education that would join
an academic with a practical approach in the preparation of teachers for high
schools and special subjects. Eventually, they would add to it the professional
training of school administrators and normal school instructors.

It was this trend away from training teachers for rural elementary
schools toward creating more attractive opportunities for both normal school
teachers and their students that had prompted President Tillinghast of
Bridgewater to raise the alarm. He had no objections to enlarging the normal
schools' competencies in the direction of high school teaching and administration and of supplying the needs of city schools. But he was entirely opposed to
the suggestion that the normal schools give up on the training of elementary
school teachers. It was thus that he aroused others to speak of "the treason of
the normal schools" and that he asked for the then-utopian notion of a four-
year course for the teachers of rural as well as urban elementary schools.
Tillinghast recognized and admitted clearly that the problem in American
education lay with the rural common schools. He was to find receptive imi-
tators in the Midwest who sought to combine in their schools the training of
classroom teachers and professional educators.

The cities, meanwhile, had sought to solve their teacher shortage by lur-
ing into their schools the normal school–trained new teachers from the coun-

try and by developing their own city normal and training schools. In Boston, Worcester, Philadelphia, Baltimore, and other urban centers these city normals usually operated in or in conjunction with a high school and sought to hold the most promising high school graduates for an additional year of normal training. They then offered their normal graduates as teachers and administrators for grade and high schools. By and large city public schoolmen were pleased with the results. To train teachers and administrators for reasonably well-paid positions in city schools was not an impossible task.

During the century's second half, a division of labor occurred between the city and county normal and training schools on the one hand and the state normals on the other. The former supplied teachers for the classrooms while the latter strove to become scientific centers for preparing public education professionals for high school and administrative offices. In the Midwest they also offered summer institutes for teachers already at work, answered their neighborhoods' calls for high schools, served as community colleges, and provided training in modern and practical subjects for the sons and daughters of farmers and mechanics. Midwestern settlers who distrusted both the ability and the willingness of the private colleges and the land-grant universities to supply this demand embraced the normal school as a preferable alternative. These midwestern state normal schools then came to see the education of teachers as but one of their functions.

When they expanded their activities to include educational research and the training of educational leaders, normal schools competed and came in conflict with the universities and state colleges. In several states like Iowa and Kansas, the result was a desperate struggle for appropriations. Forced by circumstances to curtail their programs, the normal schools invariably shortchanged their training of elementary rural teachers and poured their energies into the training of teachers for high schools and special subjects, and sought to attain collegiate status as teachers colleges.

Their conflict and competition with colleges and universities and the appearance of schools of education in state and private universities in turn spurred on teacher educators to move into the graduate study of education and educational research. Those in normal schools and teachers colleges felt they had to offer similar opportunities to their instructors if they were not to lose them to the more attractive and prestigious positions in the larger universities. Those in the graduate departments or schools of large universities like Harvard, Columbia, and Chicago banished teacher training from their professional concerns.

The end result was that by 1900 the "treason" of the normal educators became a dominant trend. Normal pedagogues and professional educators, by and large, had given up on America's largely female elementary school teachers. They relegated the education of these teachers, such as it was, to high school normal classes, to county or city training schools, and to the undergraduate departments of teachers colleges and state universities, and, in doing so, spoke glibly of an "all-institutional responsibility" for teacher training.[2] Their own favored concern, however, became the graduate education of schoolmen like themselves. And this took place in the graduate departments of state colleges and universities.

Schoolmen vs. Teachers

The American classroom teacher had become the victim of the schoolmen's ambitious drive for professional respectability. In the 1980s any number of national reports and scholarly books have complained about the sorrowful state of America's public schools.[3] But with the exception of a few critical studies and dissertations little has been written on what we might expect to be the pacesetters for American teacher training, the graduate schools of education. America's professional leaders in their citadels of educational research and career development have, for the most part, escaped critical scrutiny.[4] Most institutional histories celebrate accomplishments rather than examine liabilities. Were it not that many of the critics of our public schools have asked why the education of American teachers has left so much to be desired, the centers of the academic study of education would not be held responsible for their retreat from the training of teachers. But that retreat surely accounts for part of the deficiencies of America's schools.

The developments that transformed the normal schools into teachers colleges and thence into liberal arts colleges and that stimulated the professional study of education in the universities not only discouraged the training of classroom teachers by the professional educators but also suggested to other parts of the academic enterprise that they ought to shoulder that training in part. Statistics tracing the numerical waxing and waning of various types of academic institutions engaged in teacher training from the 1870s to the 1950s show very clearly the precipitous decline of normal schools and teachers colleges and the rapid rise of liberal arts and multipurpose colleges and universities.[5] The 1920s brought the big change. The result has been that in the language of the educators, teacher education has become an "all-institutional responsibility."

It can indeed be argued that the transition from teachers college to state college brought a change of name only and that, without a corresponding substitution of a liberal arts faculty for an education faculty, no real change took place. It can also be conceded that the assumption of a responsibility for teacher education by a liberal arts college or the undergraduate college of a large university did not fundamentally alter their general education programs either. The changes that took place did, however, relieve the education faculty of its sole responsibility for teacher education and place the burden—and the onus, one might add—on many more shoulders. In his 1963 report, *The Education of American Teachers,* James Bryant Conant recommended just such sharing of responsibility:

> Each college or university should be permitted to develop in detail whatever program of teacher education it considers most desirable, subject only to two conditions: first, the president of the institution in behalf of the entire faculty involved—academic as well as professional—certifies that the candidate is adequately prepared to teach on a specific level or in specific fields, and second, the institution establishes in conjunction with a public school system a state-approved practice-teaching arrangement.[6]

Teacher educators, in the main, accepted such proposals only too gladly. It gave them the opportunity to share blame and responsibility for the defects the critics of American teachers and teacher education kept pointing out. It allowed them to turn with easy conscience and good grace to their "professional" tasks in their graduate schools of education. How well the shared responsibility for teacher education suited them may be surmised from Lindley Stiles's thoughts on teacher education as "an all-institutional responsibility." Stiles, then dean of the school of education at the University of Wisconsin, wrote in 1960:

> The education of teachers is too important to the nation to be left to the sole jurisdiction of any single group—whether it be composed of professors of education whose central concern has always been devoted to teacher education, or of liberal arts professors who recently have begun to recognize a long-ignored obligation to help make the policy for teacher education. Teacher education is properly the responsibility of the entire institution.[7]

The preceding chapters should have cast some doubt on Stiles's assertion that the central concern of education professors had *always* been teacher education, though no one need question the sincerity of Dean Stiles and his fellow educators' desire to share that concern with other colleagues in the university. Aware that the university was concerned for its reputation, Stiles reminded scholars in other fields that, whether they wanted this or not, they were held responsible by the public for the work of any of their colleagues. "Out of self-protection," he wrote, "if for no other reason, institutions must take steps to provide the type of organization and control that will guarantee maximum faculty cooperation to develop and maintain high-quality programs of teacher education."[8] What speaks through these lines is less a concern for the education of the classroom teacher than anxiety over the damaged reputation of the institution that provided that education.

If it had not already, it should now have become clear to America's teachers that the education professionals were going to dispose of teacher training and careers as it suited them, and that if teachers and their concerns were to be heard, teachers had to speak out for themselves. For most of the nineteenth century, America's common school teachers remained silent. They accepted as given and unalterable the unwillingness of local school boards to invest more heavily in the children's future and to provide more attractive wages and career opportunities for elementary school teachers. By their acquiescence they had strengthened prevailing attitudes toward women teachers as temporary employees. Whether teachers for the common schools were educated in normal or high schools or had never gone to any other grade of school than they were to teach in was of little or no account to the citizens who hired them. Male and female citizen-teachers were expected to perform a public service for a limited period in their lives. They were not expected to demand recognition as professionals, and, by and large, they accepted their status as hired public servants.

Professionalization, Unionization, and Professionalism

The forgotten person, then, in the onward march of professionalization in American public education has been the American elementary school teacher. Though in the past, administrators and teacher educators purported to speak for her, she came to realize through bitter experience that if she were ever to be recognized as more than a temporary employee in a large bureaucratic system, she would have to rely on her own resources to assert her professional competence. By the turn of the century she came to conclude that for her the way to professional recognition led through unionization.

The teacher union movement was the logical rallying point of those excluded from recognition and consideration by the gatekeepers of the profession. It was no accident that teacher unions were organized first by women elementary teachers in large cities like Chicago, San Antonio, Atlanta, and New York.[9] There, women teachers began to refuse to accept their assigned role as temporary workers. They insisted on being heard, if not as trusted advisers and esteemed colleagues, then as determined opponents and respected professionals. If they had played no role in the battles of the past, they would assume one in the struggles of the future. If their concerns had been of little interest to the spokesmen of the common school party, they would make sure no one could overlook them again. Teacher unionism was the vehicle by which the largely female elementary school teachers were able to make their voices heard. It was the counterpoint to the educational male establishment's drive toward professionalization.

The preceding chapters have already shown the many forms in which this professionalization appeared. The disregard shown by teacher educators, educational researchers, and administrators for women elementary school teachers was not the only form it took. It showed also in the ill-concealed distrust of democracy in higher education that pervaded the Carnegie Foundation's report on Missouri. It lay behind the schoolmen's suspicions of midwestern normal schools as people's or community colleges. It had fuelled the desire of the normal pedagogues to exchange the toils of teacher education for the prestigious pleasures of in-service training and research. The list could easily be lengthened.

During the 50 years from 1875 to 1925 these and other manifestations of professionalization were part of what we have come to associate with the entire movement known as progressive education. It pervaded the university departments of the new sciences of educational psychology and administration, the schools of education and the teachers colleges, and the growing establishment of public education officials throughout the country.[10] All these aspects of professionalization claimed to be "scientific" and efficient. They were systematic, hierarchic, and profoundly male-oriented withall. They could not but provoke the anger and stir the ambitions of the unionizing teachers.

Women teachers resented the appeal of professionalization to ambitious male colleagues whom it drew out of the elementary or high school classroom into principalships and superintendencies, into positions as instructors in normal schools, teacher colleges, and university schools of education, into university professorships and editorial positions with professional journals. An academic degree usually provided men with the ticket for advancement, and by their departure from the classroom they then strengthened the widespread perception of school teaching as an activity of low prestige, suitable for anyone with a minimum of normal training, and thus taken up chiefly by women.[11]

Women teachers had ample reason to complain of being kept out of positions of power and responsibility. According to David Tyack and Elisabeth Hansot, in 1905 all district superintendencies in the United States and 94.3 percent of all senior high school principalships were occupied by men. By contrast, women dominated teaching in the elementary classrooms (98 percent) and high schools (64 percent), and they were also permitted to serve as principals of elementary schools (62 percent). But even this pattern was not to remain. With the arrival of consolidated, or union, school districts, by 1972/1973 men had also come to dominate the elementary school principalships (80 percent) and to hold the majority of high school teaching posts (54 percent). Women now taught in most of the country's elementary school classrooms (84 percent) and in 46 percent of the secondary school classrooms.[12] The male administrator became public education's professional par excellence; teachers, whether male or female, were hired hands.

In addition to the more intangible, but nonetheless real, factors of low popular prestige and condescending treatment by superiors, teachers had hard, "objective" reasons for their dissatisfactions with their working conditions. Low salaries and high turnover, related as they were to each other, numbered chief among them. From statistics based on average incomes in the period from 1920 to 1936, Willard S. Elsbree quoted studies that placed the estimated life earnings of public school teachers below not only those in the traditional professions but also those in engineering, architecture, college teaching, social work, journalism, and library work. When average annual earnings were compared, public school teachers were also ranked below the skilled trades, and fared better than only nurses, unskilled laborers, farmers, and farm laborers.[13]

Economic hardships and the relative absence of incentives for promotion—some elementary teachers might have hoped for advance to high school teaching, and some high school teachers felt rewarded when transferred from shop to academic class—then added to the appeal of unionization. For women, classroom teaching had always been a dead end. Unionization promised a change. When in 1904 Margaret Haley challenged Chicago teachers to unionize she referred to the economic obstacles women faced and to overwork and insecurity of employment as potent reasons to protest. But she also stressed the patronizing lack of respect shown by both the public and schoolmen and the disregard shown for women's educational and scholarly qualifications. As particularly galling she cited the

> lack of recognition of the teacher as an educator in the school system, due to the increased tendency toward "factoryizing education," making the teacher an automaton, a mere factory hand, whose duty it is to carry out mechanically and unquestionably the ideas and orders of those clothed with the authority of position, and who may or may not know the needs of the children and how to minister to them.[14]

Unionization, then, has been the classroom teachers' answer to the decades-old neglect they have suffered at the hands of teacher educators and administrators. Women saw no reason why opportunities for professional advancement should not be open to them as well. They formed their unions while they watched the National Education Association, with its departments of superintendence and normal schools, serve as the national platform for administrators and teacher educators, who at their meetings discussed and promoted the cause of professionalization. For many decades this male network represented the profession to the outside world.[15] For these women teachers unionization has not been a rebellion against the idea of professionalism in teaching, but a demand that they be accorded the same professional recognition and opportunities that their instructors and superintendents have withheld from them. Women teachers organized, Wayne Urban wrote, "to pursue material improvements, salaries, pensions, tenure, and other benefits and policies which helped raise teaching in the cities to the status of a career for the women who practiced it."[16] For women, unionization has been the path to the professionalism of the American classroom teacher. America's women classroom teachers organized to gain the respect and the rewards they have been forced to do without for so long.

Postscript

I wrote this book in the conviction that historical scholarship, besides contributing to our knowledge of the past and our quest for meaning, also illuminates and speaks to the issues of its day. The history that deals with past events is always written in an ever-fleeting present and, through its author's mind, speaks to the needs, hopes, and aspirations of future readers. Though the subject of my book is the education of teachers in the past, the concerns that prompted me to choose this topic are nurtured in the present and pertain to the future.

In many ways, writing this book has been a *cri de cœur* for me. I have watched enough teachers teach, have taught enough future teachers myself, and have listened to enough conversations among students and teachers to know the enormous potential that is waiting to be released in the classrooms of this nation. I know of many gifted and inspiring teachers, and I have seen schools in which teachers and administrators were buoyed by the same cooperative spirit that made the classrooms hum with the excitement of learning. But I also know that we cherish such schools and teachers so much today precisely because we cannot take them for granted.

The challenge before us now is to bring about a renaissance of learning in our nation's public schools. I certainly know that—even if we were to succeed—a reform of teacher education and a dismantling of the rigid educational bureaucracies that have grown over the decades will not by themselves create the desired results. But I am also convinced that unless our educational establishments from the schools of education to the state, county, and city superintendencies free themselves from their fixation on the accouterments of scientific and administrative professionalization and put the focus on the center of education, that is, on teaching and learning and teachers and students, we shall wait in vain for that much-longed-for renaissance.

Writing this book I was struck by how very much to the point the old saying is that "as is the teacher, so is the school." It seems to me there is an abiding truth in it. All the money school districts lavish on computer work stations, athletic fields, and fancy auditoriums will accomplish little if the classroom teacher fails his or her students. Insofar as we as a people have the will and the power to influence the destinies of our children in our schools, we do it through our teachers. For ill or good, their defects or their strengths and, by implication, the defects and strengths of the education we provide for them, make the decisive difference.

My plea, therefore, is that we break the vicious cycle of low expectations, deficient performance, and tarnished prestige that has characterized the mutual relationships between society and its teachers. It is high time that we bury that unfortunate distinction between teachers as employees and administrators as professionals. Teachers can and should develop their own professionalism, not in imitation of the professionalism of doctors, lawyers, and school administrators, but through their own indigenous professional conduct in the classroom.

What, then, is teacher professionalism as contrasted with the professionalism of the administrator? Theodore Sizer, former headmaster of a private academy and ex-dean of the Harvard School of Education, once suggested that for teachers to be treated as professionals we need to grant them authority, stability, sensible working conditions, and appropriate compensation.[1] Teachers who are not free—at a moment's notice, if necessary—to adjust curricular or disciplinary measures without having to consult the office or having to fear a reprimand for unauthorized conduct, can not be expected to command respect and authority in their classrooms. Their students will know that these teachers enjoy neither the trust nor the respect of their superiors, and the students will act accordingly.

Teachers who, as the years go by, have come to expect to be shifted from class to class or school to school to satisfy some administrative convenience, cannot but look upon their assignments as temporary stopgap measures. They are not likely to give that last ounce of devotion to their work that students have a right to expect.

Teachers who must expect to have the recitation of a poem or a physics experiment or a class discussion on the death of Socrates interrupted at any moment by a public address system that, activated in the principal's office, spews out some inane message about tickets on sale for this or that event, cannot possibly be convinced that their teaching is regarded by principal or students as being of much importance.

Since in our society income is the measure of social worth, the budgets of our school boards and the relative pay of our teachers sum up well what, as a society, we think of schools and teaching—unavoidable institutions and a necessary occupation, both to be provided for with the least amount of expense. It is unrealistic to think that teachers who receive messages of this kind throughout their working years will be the paragons of virtue and devotion, of ability and mastery that we exhort them to be.

All of these circumstances—the lack of authority and stability, of sensible working conditions and adequate compensation—add up to one major defect: the denial of truly professional consideration for teachers. We can, if we want to, remedy this defect. Models and recommendations for what I am calling for are not lacking. I shall quote as one example one key paragraph of the Carnegie Forum's 1986 Report of the Task Force on Teaching as a Profession. It summarizes what is meant by a professional environment for teaching:

> One of the most attractive aspects of professional work is the way professionals are treated in the workplace. Professionals are presumed to know what they are doing, and are paid to exercise their judgment. Schools on the other hand operate as if consultants, school district experts, textbook authors, trainers, and distant officials possess more relevant expertise than the teachers in the schools. Bureaucratic management of schools proceeds from the view that teachers lack the talent or motivation to think for themselves. Properly staffed schools can only succeed if they operate on the principle that the essential resource is already inside the school: determined, intelligent and capable teachers. Such schools will be characterized by autonomy for the school as a whole and collegial relationships among its faculty.[2]

The key to this professional environment lies in the education, the competence, the autonomy, and the collegial authority of the classroom teachers. These men and women are the colleagues, not the subordinates, of their administrative fellow professionals.

What does the professionalism of the classroom teachers mean? It means that as far as the classroom, the curriculum, and the day-to-day pedagogical tasks are concerned, the classroom teachers are in charge. Their business is the primary business of the school. Administrators, by contrast, are colleagues, facilitators, and aids. They see to it that the daily routine of classroom assignments, bell schedules, bus routes, and all the myriad internal and external arrangements of the school are taken care of. They direct and supervise the school's daily activities in consultation with their teaching colleagues. Administrators are first among equals in their area of executive responsibility, just as the teachers are first among equals in all pedagogical matters concerning their classrooms.

Outstanding teachers, therefore, should be able to advance in their careers to positions of prestige and reward while remaining in the classroom. We should no longer tolerate what Dan Lortie once wrote as a commonplace observation of American public schools: "Teachers never did gain control of any area of practice where they were clearly in charge and most expert; day-to-day operations, pedagogical theory, and substantive expertise have been dominated by persons in other roles."[3] We need to hasten the day when class-room teachers can reach the places of highest prestige and remuneration in their profession without leaving the classroom for the superintendent's office. Then public school teaching will have become a profession.

If this history of teacher education with its strange highways and byways will help us to understand better why it has been such a hopeless task to expect change for the good to originate with our educational professionals, I shall be gratified. If it will suggest ways in which teachers might assert their claims to a professionalism of their own, I should be even happier. I am convinced that all of us—our children most of all—shall be happier when in our public schools teaching and learning rather than administration take the place of honor and authority and when we know that we can be proud again of our country's educational efforts. Then, too, will our teachers again be able to teach gladly.

Notes
Index

Notes

Preface

1. Chaucer's friar, of course, may be found in *The Canterbury Tales,* but it should also be noted that Bliss Perry wrote *And Gladly Teach* (Boston, 1935). Mortimer Smith called his book, *And Madly Teach* (Chicago, 1949). James D. Koerner is the author of *The Miseducation of American Teachers* (Cambridge: Houghton Mifflin Co., 1963).

2. Willard S. Elsbree's *The American Teacher* was published in New York by the American Book Company in 1939 and reprinted in 1970 by the Greenwood Press, Westport, Connecticut. Borrowman's two studies are *The Liberal and Technical in Teacher Education: A Historical Survey of American Thought* (New York: Teachers College, 1956), and *Teacher Education in America: A Documentary History* (New York: Teachers College, 1965). A less well-known but useful study is Walter S. Monroe, *Teaching–Learning Theory and Teacher Education 1890 to 1950* (Urbana: University of Illinois Press, 1952).

Introduction

1. See National Commission on Excellence in Education, *A Nation at Risk: The Imperative for Educational Reform,* A Report to the Nation and the Secretary of Education (Washington, D.C.: U.S. Department of Education, Superintendent of Documents, 1983); Mortimer Adler, *The Paideia Proposal: An Educational Manifesto* (New York: Macmillan, 1982); Ernest L. Boyer, *High School: A Report on Secondary Education in America,* The Carnegie Foundation for the Advancement of Teaching (New York: Harper & Row, 1983); John I. Goodlad, *A Place Called School: Prospects for the Future* (Hightstown, N.J.: McGraw–Hill, 1983).

2. A convenient survey of the standard criteria for professionalization is contained in Everett C. Hughes, "Professions," and Bernard Barber, "Some Problems in the Sociology of the Professions," in Kenneth S. Lynn, ed., *The Professions in America* (Boston: Houghton Mifflin, 1965), pp. 1–34.

3. See Wayne J. Urban, *Why Teachers Organized* (Detroit: Wayne State University Press, 1982).

4. The Holmes Group, *Tomorrow's Teachers: A Report of the Holmes Group* (East Lansing, Mich.: 501 Erickson Hall, 1986); and Task Force on Teaching as a Profession, *A Nation Prepared: Teachers for the 21st Century* (Hyattsville, Md.: Carnegie Forum on Education and the Economy, 1986).

5. See infra, Postscript, note 2.

6. For a similar critique of the Holmes report see William R. Johnson, "Empowering Practitioners: Holmes, Carnegie, and the Lessons of History," *History of Education Quarterly* 27 (Summer 1987): 221–240.

Chapter 1: Public Schools and Teacher Education: The Beginnings

1. The idea of public responsibility for schooling is embodied in the Massachusetts education laws of 1642, 1647, 1648, and 1789, which have been conveniently reprinted in Sol Cohen, ed., *Education in the United States: A Documentary History* (New York: Random House, 1974), Vol. 1, pp. 393–395, and Vol. 2, pp. 794–797.

2. Franklin's best-known writings on education consist of his *Proposals relating to the Education of Youth in Pennsylvania,* his *Paper on the Academy,* and his *Idea of the English School.* These essays can be found in Vol. 3, pp. 400–419, and Vol. 4, pp. 3–36 and 101–108, of *The Papers of Benjamin Franklin,* ed. Leonard W. Labaree and Whitfield J. Bell, Jr., with Helen C. Boatfield and Helene H. Fineman (New Haven: Yale University Press, 1959, etc.).

3. For the statement by the Philadelphia workingmen see John R. Commons et al., *A Documentary History of American Industrial Society* (Cleveland, Ohio: A.H. Clark Company, 1911), Vol. 5, pp. 94–107.

4. Massachusetts Board of Education, *Tenth Annual Report* (Boston, 1846), p. 110; also reprinted in Cohen, ed., *Education in the United States,* Vol. 2, p. 1097.

5. The phrase "the release of energy" is taken from James Willard Hurst, *Law and the Conditions of Freedom in the Nineteenth-Century United States* (Madison, Wis.: University of Wisconsin Press, 1956), pp. 3–32.

6. Stephen Simpson is cited in Joseph L. Blau, ed., *Social Theories of Jacksonian Democracy* (Indianapolis: Bobs-Merrill Company, 1954), p. 145.

7. Emerson's essay on the New England reformers is excerpted in Edwin C. Rozwenc, ed., *Ideology and Power in the Age of Jackson* (Garden City, N.Y.: Doubleday and Company, 1964), p. 170.

8. From among several good books available on the history of schooling in the city of New York see especially Carl F. Kaestle, *The Evolution of an Urban School System: New York City, 1750–1850* (Cambridge, Mass.: Harvard University Press, 1973); and Diane Ravitch, *The Great School Wars: New York City, 1805–1973* (New York: Basic books, 1974).

9. Thaddeus Stevens' speech can be found in Cohen, ed., *Education in the United States,* Vol. 2, p. 1064.

10. Mann's remarks on private schools appear in Massachusetts Board of Education, *First Annual Report* (Boston, 1838), pp. 56–57.

11. In Henry Barnard, *Report on the Condition and Improvement of the Public Schools of Rhode Island* (Providence, R.I., 1845), pp. 33–50; reprinted in John S. Brubacher, ed., *Henry Barnard on Education* (New York: 1931), p. 276.

12. Henry Steele Commager reprints the 1829 constitution of a lyceum in his *The Era of Reform, 1830–1860* (Princeton: Van Nostrand Company, 1960), p. 138.

13. The 1830 statement of the New York workingmen can be found in John R. Commons et al., *History of Labour in the United States* (New York, 1918), Vol. 1, p. 283.

14. In Blau, ed., *Social Theories,* p. 212.

15. Mann in Massachusetts Board of Education, *Second Annual Report* (Boston, 1839), pp. 40 and 43.

16. In Massachusetts Board of Education, *Twelfth Annual Report* (Boston, 1848), pp. 116–117.

17. The will of Stephen Girard can be found in Henry W. Arey, *The Girard College and Its Founder,* new and revised ed. (Philadelphia, 1876), p. 75.

18. Editorial in *The Massachusetts Teacher* (1851), 4, pp. 289–291; reprinted in Cohen, ed., *Education in the United States,* Vol. 2, p. 997.

19. On how the fear of anarchy affected classroom teaching see Barbara J. Finkelstein, "The Moral Dimensions of Pedagogy: Teaching Behavior in Popular Primary Schools in Nineteenth Century America," *American Studies* 15 (Fall 1974): 78–89.

20. Barnard, *Report on the Condition and Improvement of the Public Schools of Rhode Island,* p. 50.

21. The three statements of Brooks within quotation marks are taken from his *School Reform or Teachers' Seminaries* (Boston, 1837), pp. 2 and 15, and from his *Two Lectures* (Boston: John Wilson and Son, 1864), p. 5. On Brooks see Henry Barnard, "Proceedings of an Educational Convention in Plymouth County in 1838," *Normal Schools* (Hartford, Conn.: Case, Tiffany and Company, 1850), pp. 151–157, esp. note on p. 157, and John Albree, *Charles Brooks and His Work for Normal Schools* (Medford, Mass.: Press of J. C. Miller, 1907).

22. *American Journal of Education* 5 (September 18, 1858): 386–387.

23. See Barnard's *American Journal of Education* 16 (March 1866): 92.

24. See the text and appendixes of Elizabeth Porter Gould, *Ezekiel Cheever: Schoolmaster* (Boston: Palmer Company, 1904).

25. See Wilson Smith, "The Teacher in Puritan Culture," *Harvard Educational Review* 36 (Fall 1966): 394–411.

26. David F. Allmendinger, Jr., *Paupers and Scholars: The Transformation of Student Life in Nineteenth-Century New England* (New York: St. Martin's Press, 1975), pp. 91–93.

27. As quoted in Stanley K. Schultz, *The Culture Factory: Boston Public Schools, 1789–1860* (New York: Oxford University Press, 1973), p. 76.

28. In Washington Irving, *The Sketch-Book of Geoffrey Crayon, Gent.* (New York: Putnam's Sons, 1894), p. 253.

29. A good summary description of a teacher's situation in antebellum America can be found in Nancy Hoffman, ed., *Woman's 'True' Profession: Voices from the History of Teaching* (Old Westbury, N.Y.: Feminist Press, 1981), pp. 2–15.

30. From James G. Carter, *Essays on Popular Education* (Boston: Bowles and Dearborn, 1826), as excerpted in Cohen, ed., *Education in the United States,* Vol. 3, pp. 1288–1299.

31. From Board of Commissioners of Common Schools in Connecticut, *First Annual Report* (Hartford, 1839), as excerpted in Cohen, ed., *Education in the United States,* Vol. 3, pp. 1291–1292.

32. Maris A. Vinovskis and Richard M. Bernard, "Women in Education in Ante-Bellum America," Working Paper 73–7, Center for Demography and Ecology (University of Wisconsin–Madison, June 1973), p. 12 and Tables A5 and A6; see also their "The Female School Teacher in Ante-Bellum Massachusetts," *Journal of Social History* 10 (Spring 1977): 322–345. Their data have also been used in Carl F. Kaestle and

Maris A. Vinovskis, *Education and Social Change in Nineteenth-Century Massachusetts* (Cambridge, England: Cambridge University Press, 1980).

33. The figures in this paragraph have been derived from Table A7.11 in Kaestle and Vinovskis, *Education and Social Change*, p. 284.

34. See Table A7.11 in Kaestle and Vinovskis, *Education and Social Change*, p. 284, and Table 2 in W. Randolph Burgess, *Trends of School Costs* (New York: Russell Sage Foundation, 1920), p. 32.

35. Cited from the *New York Evangelist* in 1846 in *Minnesota History* 28 (June 1947): 134.

36. In Massachusetts Board of Education, *Eighth Annual Report* (Boston, 1845), p. 60; reprinted also in Cohen, ed., *Education in the United States*, Vol. 3, p. 1316.

37. On "the cult of womanhood" see Phillida Bunkle, "Sentimental Womanhood and Domestic Education, 1830–1870," *History of Education Quarterly* 14 (Spring 1974): 13–31.

38. On the alliance of school reformers and Protestant ministers see David Tyack, "The Kingdom of God and the Common School: Protestant Ministers and the Educational Awakening in the West," *Harvard Educational Review* 36 (Fall 1966): 447–469, and Timothy L. Smith, "Protestant Schooling and American Nationality, 1800–1850," *Journal of American History* 53 (March 1967): 679–695.

39. The collaboration of women and clergymen is discussed in considerable depth in Ann Douglas, *The Feminization of American Culture* (New York: Alfred A. Knopf, 1977).

40. My calculations are based on the weekly wages listed by Vinovskis and Bernard in their 1973 working paper, "Women in Education in Ante-Bellum America," Table A12.

41. For a generalized statement on teachers in Connecticut during the 1850s see F. C. Zakolski, "Social Psychology of the Nineteenth Century Teacher," *Teacher Education Quarterly* 6 (Spring 1949): 158–167.

42. See discussion of school enrollments and attendance in Kaestle and Vinovskis, *Education and Social Change*, pp. 9–26.

43. On the negative aspects of the district system as seen by the reformers, see Arthur O. Norton, ed., *The First State Normal School in America: The Journals of Cyrus Peirce and Mary Swift* (Cambridge, Mass.: Harvard University Press, 1926), pp. xxxii–xxxiv.

44. James G. Carter, "Outline of an Institution for the Education of Teachers," *Boston Patriot* (February 1825), reprinted in Norton, ed., *The First State Normal School*, pp. 227–245. The quotations in this and the following paragraph are from pp. 231, 233, and 237.

45. Rev. Thomas H. Gallaudet, "Remarks on Seminaries for Teachers," *Connecticut Observer* (January 5, 1825), reprinted in Henry Barnard, *Normal Schools and Other Institutions, Agencies, and Means Designed for the Professional Education of Teachers* (Hartford, Conn.: Case, Tiffany and Company, 1851), pp. 39–46. The quoted passage is on p. 41.

Chapter 2: The Atlantic Community of Whigs

1. Henry E. Dwight, *Travels in the North of Germany in the Years 1825 and 1826* (New York: G. & C. & H. Carvill, 1829), p. 244.

2. Ibid., pp. 247, 253.

3. In *American Annals of Education and Instruction* 1, part II (June 1831): 279.

4. William C. Woodbridge, "Seminaries for Teachers in Prussia," *American Annals* 1, part II (June 1831): 253–257.

5. "Seminary for Female Teachers," *American Annals* 1, part II (August 1831): 341–346; the quoted passage is from p. 342.

6. Ibid., p. 342.

7. Ibid., p. 344.

8. Ibid., p. 345.

9. Ibid., p. 341.

10. The report appeared in an English translation by Sarah Austin in London in 1834, was reprinted in New York the next year and in a second London edition in 1836. I refer in this book to the New York edition, Victor Cousin, *Report on the State of Public Instruction in Prussia* (New York: Wiley & Long, 1835). Selections from the report can be found also in Edgar W. Knight, ed., *Reports on European Education by John Griscom, Victor Cousin, Calvin E. Stowe* (New York: McGraw-Hill, 1930), pp. 113–240.

11. See Hermann Joseph Ody, *Victor Cousin: Ein Lebensbild im deutsch-französischen Kulturraum* (Saarbrücken: West-Ost Verlag, 1953), pp. 93–100.

12. See Cousin, *Report,* pp. 1–2. German files report that Cousin's contacts in Prussia extended only to a boarding school in Pforta, the charitable foundations for orphans at the University of Halle, and, besides his talks with officials, professors, and educators in Berlin and Potsdam, to school visits in Bonn and Cologne. See Altenstein to Friedrich Wilhelm III, July 30, 1831, MS in Geheimes Staats Archiv Berlin-Dahlem (hereafter abbreviated GSA Berlin-Dahlem), Rep. 89, H. Generalia, Abt. X, Nr. 2c, Vol. 1, pp. 187–195.

13. Cousin, *Report,* pp. 62–64, passim.

14. Ibid., p. 67.

15. Ibid., p. 141.

16. Ibid., p. 222.

17. Ibid., p. 237.

18. Ibid., pp. 253–254.

19. Ibid., p. 196.

20. Ibid., p. 193.

21. Ibid., p. 259.

22. Ibid., pp. 205–206.

23. Ibid., pp. 169–170.

24. Ibid., p. 171.

25. Ibid., pp. 172, 175.

26. Ibid., p. 292.

27. Thomas Nipperdey, "Volksschule und Revolution im Vormärz," in *Politische Ideologien und Nationalstaatliche Ordnung, Festschrift für Theodor Schieder,* ed. Kurt Kluxen and Wolfgang J. Mommsen (München and Wien: Oldenbourg, 1968), p. 133.

28. Altenstein to Friedrich Wilhelm III, July 30, 1831, MS in GSA Berlin-Dahlem, Rep. 92, # 27, pp. 187–195.

29. See the Königsberger and Litauischer Schulplan in Wilhelm von Humboldt, *Bildung und Sprache: Eine Auswahl aus seinen Schriften,* ed. Clemens Menze (Paderborn: Ferdinand Schoeningh, 1959), pp. 101–117.

30. Cf. Karl Bungardt, *Die Odyssee der Lehrerschaft: Sozialgeschichte eines Standes* (Hannover: Hermann Schroedel, 1965), pp. 29–30.

31. Süvern in Lothar Schweim, ed., *Schulreform in Preussen 1809–1819: Entwürfe und Gutachten* (Weinheim: Julius Beltz, 1966), pp. 128–131.

32. Altenstein to F. Wilhelm III, January 10, 1829, MS in GSA Berlin-Dahlem, Rep. 92, # 25, pp. 79–87.

33. Süvern to theological faculty, Berlin, December 15, 1823, MS in Zentrales Staatsarchiv Merseburg (hereafter abbreviated ZSA Merseburg), Rep. 76, VII, neue Sektion 1C, Gen., Teil 1, Nr. 1, Bd. 1.

34. Süvern's bill of 1819 can be found in Schweim, ed., *Schulreform*, pp. 123–221. The cited passages and quotation are from pp. 123–128.

35. Beckedorff's memorandum on the Süvern bill is reprinted in Schweim, ed., *Schulreform*, pp. 222–244. The quotation is from p. 228.

36. Friedrich Wilhelm III to the Abbott Steinmetz, December 5, 1736, in K. Schneider and E. v. Bremen, *Das Volksschulwesen im Preussischen Staat,* Vol. 1 (Berlin, 1886), p. 362; and Friedrich Wilhelm III, Circular Order of August 31, 1799, in Ludwig von Rönne, *Das Volksschulwesen des Preussischen Staates: Allgemeiner Teil* (Berlin: Veit und Companie, 1855), pp. 89–92.

37. Beckedorff in Schweim, ed., *Schulreform*, pp. 233–234.

38. Humboldt, *Bildung and Sprache,* p. 102.

39. Beckedorff, Fragment concerning Teacher Seminaries, c. 1820, MS in GSA Berlin-Dahlem, Rep. 92, # 25, pp. 61–64.

40. Quoted in Wilhelm Zimmermann, *Der Aufbau des Lehrerbildungs- und Volksschulwesens unter der Preussischen Verwaltung 1814–1840* (Köln, 1963), p. 52.

41. Friedrich Wilhelm III to Altenstein, June 15, 1822, MS in ZSA Merseburg, Rep. 76, VII, neue Sektion 1C, Gen., Teil 1, Nr. 1, Bd. 1; and Memorandum of Richter, February 10, 1822, ZSA Merseburg, Rep. 76, VII, neue sektion 1C, Gen., Teil 1, Nr. 1, Bd. 1.

42. Altenstein to all consistories and provincial governments, July 24, 1822, MS in GSA Berlin-Dahlem, Rep. 92, # 25, pp. 311–314.

43. Altenstein to F. Wilhelm III, September 9, 1822, MS in ZSA Merseburg, Rep. 76, VII, neue Sektion 1C, Gen., Teil 1, Nr. 1, Bd. 1.

44. Regulations of the protestant teacher seminary at Neuwied, 1826, paragraph 3a, MS in Landeshauptarchiv Koblenz (hereafter abbreviated LHA Koblenz), Bestand 405, # 2685, p. 6.

45. Kaweran to ministry, December 27, 1827, excerpt, MS in GSA Berlin-Dahlem, Rep. 92, # 27, p. 89.

46. Diesterweg to Provincial School Collegium, Koblenz, August 29, 1829, MS in LHA Koblenz, Bestand 405, # 3682, p. 45.

47. Cf. Andreas Flitner, *Die Politische Erziehung in Deutschland: Geschichte und Probleme 1750–1880* (Tübingen: Max Niemeyer, 1957), pp. 141–142.

48. Nicolovius to Cologne Consistory, July 26, 1816, MS in *Hauptstaatsarchiv Düsseldorf, Schloss Kalkum* (hereafter abbreviated HSA Kalkum), Akte Reg. Aachen 2136; and Church and School Commission Aachen to Koblenz Consistory, September 12, 1816, HSA Kalkum, Akte Reg. Aachen 2136.

49. Hardenberg to Altenstein, May 15, 1820, MS in GSA Berlin-Dahlem, Rep. 92, # 25, pp. 97–103.

50. Altenstein to Provincial School Collegium, Koblenz, February 26, 1827, MS in LHA Koblenz, Bestand 405, # 3682, unpaginated.

51. Royal School Collegium, Münster, to Rothert, December 26, 1830, MS in Nordrhein-Westfälisches Staatsarchiv Münster (hereafter abbreviated NWSA Münster), Provinzialschulkollegium # 1096, pp. 3–4, 13.

52. See Doris S. Goldstein, " 'Official Philosophies' in Modern France: The Example of Victor Cousin," *Journal of Social History* 1 (1967–1968): 260.

53. Douglas Johnson, *Guizot: Aspects of French History, 1787–1874* (London: Routledge & Kegan Paul, 1963), p. 128.

54. See R. R. Bolgar, "Victor Cousin and Nineteenth Century Education," *The Cambridge Journal* 2 (1949): 365.

55. For the unintended effects of this feature of the Guizot law, see C. R. Day, "Social Advancement and the Primary School Teacher: the Making of Normal School Directors in France, 1815–1880," *Histoire Sociale—Social History* 7, (1974), 87–102.

56. The basic text for Jefferson's fame as educational statesman is "A Bill for the More General Diffusion of Knowledge," reprinted with notes in *The Papers of Thomas Jefferson,* Julian P. Boyd, ed., Vol. 2 (Princeton: Princeton University Press, 1950), pp. 526–535.

57. I have relied primarily on "Der Königsberger und der Litauische Schulplan," in Wilhelm von Humboldt, *Werke in Fünf Bänden,* Vol. 4 (Stuttgart: Cotta, 1964), pp. 168–195.

58. Daniel Walker Howe, *The Unitarian Conscience: Harvard Moral Philosophy, 1805–1861* (Cambridge, Mass.: Harvard University Press, 1970), p. 261.

59. For Jefferson see entry in the *Concise Dictionary of American Biography* (New York: Charles Scribner's Sons, 1964), pp. 492–496; for Humboldt consult Paul R. Sweet, *Wilhelm von Humboldt: A Biography* (Columbus: Ohio State University Press, 1980), 2 vols., and Herbert Scurla, *Wilhelm von Humboldt: Werden und Wirken* (Berlin: Verlag der Nation, 1970).

60. In the "Notes on the State of Virginia," 1781–1785; excerpted in James B. Conant, *Thomas Jefferson and the Development of American Public Education* (Berkeley: University of California Press, 1962), pp. 95–96.

61. See Jefferson's letter of November 1785 to Philip Mazzei in Boyd, ed., *The Papers of Thomas Jefferson,* Vol. 9, p. 71.

62. In "Notes on the State of Virginia," in Conant, *Thomas Jefferson,* p. 94.

63. See "Ideen zu einem Versuch, die Grenzen der Wirksamkeit des Staats zu bestimmen (1792)," in Humboldt, *Werke,* Vol. 1, pp. 56–233.

64. "Königsberger Schulplan," in Humboldt, *Werke,* Vol. 4, p. 175.

65. See "Notes on the State of Virginia," the bill of October 24, 1817, and letter to Peter Carr, August 10, 1787, in Conant, *Thomas Jefferson,* pp. 95, 100–102, 123.

66. See "Litauischer Schulplan," in Humboldt, *Werke,* Vol. 4, p. 189.

67. Jefferson, Letter to Peter Carr, September 7, 1814, in Conant, *Thomas Jefferson,* p. 113; and "Litauischer Schulplan," in Humboldt, *Werke,* Vol. 4, p. 191.

68. In Conant, *Thomas Jefferson,* p. 110.

69. In "Ideen zu einem Versuch," Humboldt, *Werke,* Vol. 1, pp. 103–109.
70. Cousin, *Report,* p. 293.

Chapter 3: The Massachusetts Normal School

1. Samuel R. Hall, *Lectures on Schoolkeeping* (Boston: Richardson, Lord and Holbrook, 1829).
2. See note in *American Journal of Education* 5 (September 18, 1858): 386.
3. Charles Brooks, *Two Lectures* (Boston: John Wilson and Son, 1864), p. 5.
4. Quoted in Robert Ulich, *A Sequence of Educational Influences* (Cambridge, Mass.: Harvard University Press, 1935), pp. 53–54.
5. See Mason S. Stone, "The First Normal School in America," *Teachers College Record* 24 (1923): 263–271.
6. See Paul H. Mattingly, *The Classless Profession: American Schoolmen in the Nineteenth Century* (New York: New York University Press, 1975), pp. 84–112.
7. In *American Journal of Education* 16 (March 1866): 93–96.
8. See Arthur O. Norton, ed., *The First State Normal School in America: The Journals of Cyrus Peirce and Mary Swift* (Cambridge, MA: Harvard University Press, 1926), p. xliii.
9. In *American Journal of Education* 16 (March 1866): 96.
10. See David Asher Gould, "Policy and Pedagogues: School Reform and Teacher Professionalization in Massachusetts, 1840–1920," Ph.D. dissertation, Brandeis University, 1977, pp. 29–30.
11. For a discussion surrounding the selection of school sites, principals, and curriculum, see Raymond B. Culver, *Horace Mann and Religion in the Massachusetts Public Schools* (New Haven: Yale University Press, 1929), pp. 111–126.
12. See Carl F. Kaestle and Maris A. Vinovskis, *Education and Social Change in Nineteenth-Century Massachusetts* (Cambridge: Cambridge University Press, 1980), pp. 120–122.
13. See *The Common School Journal* 1 (February 1, 1839): 33–38.
14. Ibid., p. 96.
15. In *American Journal of Education* 16 (March 1866): 96.
16. See Arthur O. Norton, ed., *The First State Normal School,* p. xliii.
17. *The Common School Journal* 6 (September 2, 1844): 267.
18. See *The Common School Journal* 2 (August 1, 1840): 225–229.
19. Ibid.
20. Ibid.
21. See *The Common School Journal* 2 (March 15, 1840): 96.
22. See Culver, *Horace Mann,* pp. 127–148.
23. Carl F. Kaestle and Maris A. Vinovskis, *Education and Social Change,* p. 232.
24. For the sake of simplicity I shall refer to the school as the Framingham school, unless my reference is specifically to its period in Lexington or West Newton.
25. Massachusetts Board of Education, *First Annual Report of the Secretary* (Boston: Dutton and Wentworth, 1838), p. xx. For the high schools see Emit Duncan Grizzell, *Origin and Development of the High School in New England before 1865* (New York: Macmillan, 1923), pp. 123–126.
26. Michael Durnin, "New England's Eighteenth Century Academies: Their Ori-

gin and Development to 1850," Ed.D. dissertation, University of Pennsylvania, 1968, app. H; and Kaestle and Vinovskis, *Education and Social Change*, p. 27.

27. See Arthur O. Norton, ed., *The First State Normal School*, pp. xxv–xxx.

28. As David Gould has already pointed out in his dissertation, "Policy and Pedagogues," appendix I, pp. 463–476, information on the occupations of the parents of normal school students had been collected by the Massachusetts Board of Education. The classification scheme, however, changed over time, and thus Gould, who based his findings on the board's data, was forced to develop a system of his own, which distinguished among white collar, skilled and semiskilled, unskilled, and agricultural workers. Relying for my data on records kept in the Framingham and Westfield archives, I have also developed my own scheme. I recognize the following classifications: blue collar, composed of farm and nonfarm; white collar, composed of professional and nonprofessional; and unidentified (i.e., either missing or listed as unknown). The inferences drawn from tables based on these classifications are to be taken with some caution. While it may be reasonable to assign a shoe manufacturer to the white-collar and a shoemaker to the blue-collar categories, it is very hard to determine whether, for example, a shipbuilder should be classified under blue- or white-collar. I have restricted the label "professionals" to the traditional clergymen, physicians, and lawyers, but have included teachers. On the other hand, I have counted the occasional architect and surveyor among the white-collar occupations.

29. Norton, ed., *The First State Normal School*, pp. 41, 44.

30. Ibid., passim and pp. 45, 7.

31. Ibid., p. 41.

32. Ibid., p. 68.

33. See letters by George E. Emerson and Samuel G. Howe in *Common School Journal* 2 (August 1, 1840): 236–239.

34. Peirce to Mann, September 18, 1840, Mann Papers, cited in Willis Rudy, "America's First Normal School: The Formative Years," *Journal of Teacher Education* 5 (December 1954): 254; see also Electa N. L. Walton, "Historical Sketch of the First State Normal School in America," in *Historical Sketches of the Framingham State Normal School* (Framingham, Mass.: Alumnae Association, 1914), pp. 26–56.

35. Massachusetts Board of Education, *Fourth Annual Report of the Secretary* (Boston: Dutton and Wentworth, 1841), p. 46.

36. The figures for college students are taken from Colin Burke, *American Collegiate Populations: A Test of the Traditional View* (New York: New York University Press, 1982), p. 102.

37. Grizzell, *Origin and Development*, pp. 73–76.

38. Thomas J. Abernethy, "Education in Westfield 1669–1969," in Edward C. Janes and Roscoe S. Scott, eds., *Westfield Massachusetts 1669–1969: The First Three Hundred Years* (Westfield, Mass.: Westfield Tri-Centennial Association, 1968), pp. 145–156.

39. James Caruthers Greenough, "The State Normal School, Westfield," in Alfred Minot Copeland, ed., *A History of Hampden County Massachusetts*, Vol. 1 (New York: Century Memorial Publishing Company, 1902), pp. 279–280.

40. In Massachusetts Board of Education, *Sixth Annual Report of the Secretary* (Boston, 1843), pp. 28 and 29.

41. Grace F. Shepard, "Female Education at Wheaton College," *The New England Quarterly* 6 (December 1933), 803; and Paul C. Helmreich, *Wheaton College 1834–1912: The Seminary Years* (Norton, Mass.: Wheaton College, 1985), pp. 23, 99.

42. Sarah D. Stowe, *History of Mount Holyoke Seminary, 1837–1887* (South Hadley, Mass.: The Seminary, 1887), p. 72; and Elizabeth Alden Green, *Mary Lyon and Mount Holyoke: Opening the Gates* (Hanover, N.H.: University Press of New England, 1979), p. 182.

43. Helmreich, *Wheaton College*, p. 27.

44. Ibid., pp. 14, 103.

45. Kathryn Kish Sklar, "The Founding of Mount Holyoke College," in Carol Ruth Berkin and Mary Beth Norton, eds., *Women of America: A History* (Boston: Houghton Mifflin, 1979), p. 183.

46. David F. Allmendinger, Jr., "Mount Holyoke Students Encounter the Need for Life Planning, 1837–1850," *History of Education Quarterly* 19 (Spring 1979): 30; see also Tiziana Rota, "Between 'True Women' and 'New Women': Mount Holyoke Students 1837 to 1908," Ph.D. dissertation, University of Massachusetts, 1983, pp. 62–72.

47. Kaestle and Vinovskis, *Education and Social Change,* pp. 115–116.

48. *Common School Journal* 11 (August 1, 1849): 225.

49. Ibid.

50. Massachusetts Board of Education, *Sixth Annual Report of the Secretary.*

51. *Common School Journal* 12 (April 15, 1850): 116–117.

52. Ibid.

53. *Common School Journal* 11 (August 1, 1849): 225.

54. *Common School Journal* 12 (April 15, 1850): 116–117.

55. Gould, "Policy and Pedagogues," pp. 32, 70.

56. Quoted by Gould, ibid., p. 80.

Chapter 4: Massachusetts and Beyond: Varieties of Teacher Education

1. Thomas J. Abernethy, "Education in Westfield 1669–1969," in Edward C. Janes and Roscoe S. Scott, eds., *Westfield Massachusetts 1669–1969: The First Three Hundred Years* (Westfield, Mass.: Westfield Tri-Centennial Association, 1968), pp. 144–145; and see Alfred Minot Copeland, ed., *A History of Hampden County,* Vol. 2 (n.p.: The Century Memorial Publishing Company, 1902), 425–426.

2. Quoted in James Ralph Fiorello, "General Education in the Preparation of Teachers at Westfield State College, 1839–1960," Ph.D. dissertation, University of Connecticut, 1969, pp. 84, 88.

3. See Writers' Project, Massachusetts Work Projects Administration, *The State Teachers College at Westfield* (Westfield, Mass.: State Teachers College, 1941), p. 27; and *Common School Journal* 12 (April 15, 1850): 116–117.

4. Fiorello, "General Education," pp. 91–92.

5. Ibid., pp. 114–115.

6. Writers' Project, *The State Teachers College at Westfield,* p. 28.

7. Ibid., pp. 30–31.

8. Fiorello, "General Education," p. 93.

9. Quoted, ibid., p. 98.

10. Ibid., p. 116.

11. Ibid., p. 102.

12. *The American Journal of Education* 17 (1867-1868): 657.

13. Fiorello, "General Education," pp. 95-96.

14. Ibid., p. 103.

15. *Common School Journal* 11 (May 15, 1849): 145-147.

16. Albert G. Boyden, *History and Alumni Record of the State Normal School at Bridgewater* (Boston, 1876), p. 125.

17. *The American Journal of Education* 17 (1867-1868): 657.

18. Boyden, *History and Alumni Record,* pp. 127-128.

19. Quoted in *American Journal of Education* 17 (1867-1868): 699.

20. See David Asher Gould, "Policy and Pedagogues: Teacher Professionalization in Massachusetts, 1840-1920," Ph.D. dissertation, Brandeis University, 1977, p. 70.

21. See Elizabeth Flynn, "What's Past Is Prologue," a typescript history of Boston State College, Boston State College Archives.

22. "Report of Dr. Larkin Dunton on the Boston Normal School," *15th Annual Report of the Superintendent of Public Schools of the City of Boston, March 15, 1895* (Boston: Rockwell and Churchill, 1895), p. 297.

23. Ibid.

24. Ibid., p. 298.

25. Ibid., p. 332.

26. See Gould, "Policy and Pedagogues," p. 85.

27. Robert McGraw, "A Century of Service," in *The First 100 Years: Worcester State College* (Worcester, Mass.: WSC Office of Community Services, 1974), unpaginated.

28. Egbert R. Isbell, *A History of Eastern Michigan University, 1849-1965* (Ypsilanti: Eastern Michigan University, 1971), pp. 1-29.

29. Charles A. Harper, *Development of the Teachers College in the United States with Special Reference to the Illinois State Normal University* (Bloomington, Ill.: McKnight & McKnight, 1935), pp. ii. 78, 48-50.

30. Quoted in *American Journal of Education* 16 (September 1866): 451.

31. Charles Edward Hovey, in *Proceedings,* First Annual Convention, American Normal School Association, Trenton, N.J., 1859 (New York: A. S. Barnes & Burr, 1860), p. 49.

32. In "Principal's Report," *Illinois Normal University* (Springfield: Bailhache & Baker, 1859), p. 37.

33. Richard Edwards, "Normal Schools in the United States," *Proceedings,* National Teachers Association, 6th Annual Meeting, Harrisburg, 1865 (Hartford, 1865), p. 277.

34. E. C. Hewett, "More About Normal Schools," *Illinois Teacher* 17 (March 1871): 93.

35. First Annual Convention, American Normal School Association, Trenton, N.J., 1859 (New York: A.S. Barnes & Burr, 1860), pp. 18-19.

36. Alpheus Crosby, ibid., pp. 32, 34n.

37. Ibid., p. 106.

38. William Franklin Phelps, "Report on a Course of Study for Normal Schools," *Addresses and Journal of Proceedings,* American Normal School and the National Teachers' Association (Washington, D.C.: James H. Holmes, 1871), p. 13.

39. Ibid., p. 12.

40. Ibid.

41. Ibid., p. 17.

42. Samuel W. White, "The Means of Providing the Mass of Teachers with Professional Instruction," in *Addresses and Journal of Proceedings*, American Normal School and the National Teachers' Association (Washington, D.C.: James H. Holmes, 1871), p. 24.

43. Ibid., pp. 30, 31.

44. W. E. Crosby in *Addresses and Journal of Proceedings*, American Normal School and the National Teachers' Association (Washington, D.C.: James H. Holmes, 1871), p. 25.

45. Delia A. Lathrop, "Training Schools: Their Place in Normal-School Work," *Addresses and Journal of Proceedings*, National Education Association . . . 1873 at Elmira, New York (Peoria, Ill.: N.C. Nason, 1873), pp. 183–184.

46. See James A. Smart, *Teachers Institutes*, U.S. Bureau of Education, Circular of Information # 2 (Washington, D.C.: Government Printing Office, 1885).

47. Lathrop, "Training Schools," p. 184.

48. On Oswego see Ned Harland Dearborn, *The Oswego Movement in American Education* (New York: Teachers College Columbia University, 1925, and Arno Press, 1969), and Dorothy Rogers, *Oswego: Fountainhead of Teacher Education: A Century in the Sheldon Tradition* (New York: Appleton-Century-Crofts, 1961).

49. Lathrop, "Training Schools," pp. 185–186.

50. Phelps, "Report," p. 38.

51. Ibid., p. 39.

52. Ibid., p. 40.

53. William Franklin Phelps, "Report of Committee on Normal Training Schools," *Addresses and Journal of Proceedings*, National Education Association, Boston, 1872 (Peoria, Ill.: N.C. Nason, 1873), p. 37.

54. Ibid., p. 37.

55. Ibid., p. 40.

56. Avery Dwight Mayo, "The Assault on the Normal Schools," *Lectures and Proceedings*, American Institute of Instruction, 48 (1877): p. 35.

57. Avery Dwight Mayo, "The Normal School in the United States," *Education* 8 (December 1887): 229.

58. Ibid., p. 226.

59. Mayo, "The Assault," p. 39.

60. Mayo, "The Normal School," p. 231.

61. Ibid., p. 232.

62. George E. Gay, "Massachusetts Normal Schools," *Education* 17 (May 1897): 515–517.

63. Albert G. Boyden, "Massachusetts Normal Schools," *Education* 17 (June 1897): 612.

64. Ibid., p. 615.

65. See Gould, "Policy and Pedagogues," p. 29.

66. For more on this see William R. Johnson's forthcoming work on teacher education in Maryland.

67. See the 1877 statistical tables of the U.S. commissioner of education reprinted in the *American Journal of Education* 29 (1879): 356–365.

Chapter 5: Teacher Education in the Midwest

1. Charles A. Harper, *Development of the Teachers College in the United States with Special Reference to the Illinois State Normal University* (Bloomington, Ill.: McKnight & McKnight, 1935), pp. ii, 78, 48–50.

2. See Henry C. Johnson, Jr., and Erwin V. Johanningmeier, *Teachers for the Prairie: The University of Illinois and the Schools 1868–1945* (Urbana: University of Illinois Press, 1972), p. 13.

3. *The Illinois Teacher* 1 (1855), 16.

4. *Public Laws of the State of Illinois* (1857), pp. 298–299.

5. In *The Illinois Teacher* 3 (November 1857): 380; and *Second Biennial Report of the Superintendent of Public Instruction of the State of Illinois, 1857–1858* (Springfield, 1859), p. 54.

6. In "Secretary's Report," *Illinois Normal University* (Springfield: Bailhache & Baker, 1859), pp. 18–19.

7. Harper, *Development*, p. 52.

8. In *Proceedings of the Board of Education of the State of Illinois, 1857 and 1858* (Bloomington, Ill.: Wm. E. Foote, 1858), p. 10.

9. In *Proceedings,* First Annual Convention of the American Normal School Association, Trenton, N.J., August 19–20, 1859 (New York: A. S. Barnes & Burr, 1860).

10. In "Principal's Report," *Illinois Normal University* (Springfield: Bailhache & Baker, 1859), p. 39.

11. Helen E. Marshall, *Grandest of Enterprises: Illinois State Normal University 1857–1957* (Normal: Illinois State Normal University, 1956), p. 95.

12. Based on figures given in *Semi-Centennial History of the Illinois State Normal University, 1857–1907* (Normal: Faculty Committee, 1907), pp. 40, 47, 50, 52.

13. The percentages are based on numbers supplied by Edwards in *Tenth Biennial Report of the Superintendent of Public Instruction of the State of Illinois* (Springfield, 1874), p. 128.

14. Harper, *Development*, p. 102.

15. See John A.H. Keith, "The Development of the Model School," in *Semi-Centennial History,* pp. 77–83, and Marshall, *Grandest of Enterprises,* p. 93.

16. See *Proceedings of the Board of Education of the State of Illinois . . . 1874* (Peoria: N. C. Nason, 1875), p. 10.

17. Marshall, *Grandest of Enterprises,* p. 107.

18. Richard Edwards, *Decennial Address . . . 1872* (Peoria: N.C. Nason, 1872), p. 26.

19. R. G. Roots in *Proceedings of the Board of Education of the State of Illinois, 1868* (Peoria: N. C. Nason, 1869), p. 5.

20. In *American Journal of Education* 17 (1867–1868): 750.

21. See remarks of C. B. Denio in House of Representatives, as cited in *The Illinois Teacher* 3 (April 1857): 127.

22. Quoted in Superintendent of Public Instruction of the State of Kansas, *Annual Report, 1867* (Topeka, 1868), p. 67.

23. Edwards in *Proceedings of the Board of Education of the State of Illinois, 1870* (Peoria: N. C. Nason, 1871), p. 15.

24. See *Proceedings of the Board of Education of the State of Illinois . . . 1874* (Peoria: N. C. Nason, 1875), pp. 13–15.

25. See *Proceedings of the Board of Education of the State of Illinois . . . 1874* (Peoria: N. C. Nason, 1875), p. 14.

26. E. C. Hewett, "More About Normal Schools," *Illinois Teacher* 17(March 1871): 92.

27. Robert Allyn, "President Allyn's Report," in *10th Biennial Report of the Superintendent of Public Instruction of the State of Illinois, 1873–1874* (Springfield, 1874), p. 184.

28. Quoted in Eli G. Lentz, *Seventy-five Years in Retrospect: From Normal School to Teachers College to University: Southern Illinois University 1874–1949* (Carbondale: University Editorial Board, 1955), p. 37.

29. Robert Allyn, "President Allyn's Report," in *11th Biennial Report of the Superintendent of Public Instruction of the State of Illinois, 1875–1876* (Springfield, 1876), p. 212.

30. Lentz, *Seventy-five Years in Retrospect,* p. 33.

31. W. F. M. Arny to John W. Geary, in National Archives and Records Service, General Records of the Department of Agriculture, Letters, Reports, Essays, etc., Vol. 12, p. 857.

32. Territory of Kansas Session Laws, *Private Laws, 1858,* pp. 84–85, 90–91.

33. State of Kansas, *Laws of the State, 1863,* pp. 93–95.

34. Superintendent of Public Instruction of the State of Kansas, *Annual Report, 1863* (Topeka, 1864), p. 30; and *Annual Report, 1864* (Topeka, 1865), pp. 19–20. The salary data come from the superintendent's annual reports, 1870–1877.

35. Lyman B. Kellog, "The Founding of the State Normal School," *Collections of the Kansas State Historical Society* 12 (1911–1912): 88.

36. In Frank W. Blackmar, ed., *Kansas: A Cyclopedia of State History,* Vol. 2 (Chicago, 1912), p. 759.

37. Lyman B. Kellog, "Normal Education in Kansas," *Proceedings and Lectures of the National Teachers' Association . . . 1866* (Albany: New York Teacher, 1867), p. 122.

38. Kellog, "The Founding," p. 96.

39. *Report of the Principal of the Kansas State Normal School . . . 1865* (Emporia, 1865), p. 4.

40. See Harper, *Development,* pp. 163–166.

41. Lyman B. Kellog, *Official Reports of the State Normal School . . . 1870* (Topeka, 1870), pp. 12–13.

42. Superintendent of Public Instruction of the State of Kansas, *Annual Report, 1869* (Topeka, 1870), p. 88.

43. Clifford S. Griffin, *The University of Kansas: A History* (Lawrence: University Press of Kansas, 1974), p. 131.

44. Albert R. Taylor, "History of Normal-School Work in Kansas," *Kansas State Historical Society Quarterly* 6 (1900): 117–118; and Griffin, *The University of Kansas,* p. 132.

45. Kansas State Board of Administration, *First Biennial Report to the Governor and State Legislature of Kansas, 1914–1916* (Topeka, 1916), p. 15.

46. C. O. Wright, *100 Years in Kansas Education,* Vol. 1 (Topeka: Kansas State Teachers Association, 1963), p. 78.

47. George F. Zook, Lotus D. Coffman, and A. R. Mann, *Report of a Survey of the State Institutions of Higher Learning in Kansas,* Department of the Interior, Bureau of Education Bulletin, 1923, # 40 (Washington, D.C.: Government Printing Office, 1923), p. 66.

48. Quoted in Merle Curti and Vernon Carstensen, *The University of Wisconsin: A History,* Vol. 1 (Madison: University of Wisconsin Press, 1949), pp. 47, 74–75.

49. Curti and Carstensen, *The University of Wisconsin,* Vol. 1, p. 22.

50. In *General Acts Passed by the Legislature of Wisconsin, 1857* (Madison, 1857), pp. 93–98. An amended version of May 17, 1858, included "union or high schools" in the institutions to be benefitted.

51. J. B. Pradt, "Essays on Normal Schools," *Wisconsin Journal of Education* 3 (November 1858): 141.

52. Editorial, *Wisconsin Journal of Education* 6 (August 1861): 59–60.

53. Curti and Carstensen, *The University of Wisconsin,* Vol. 1, pp. 108–113, 168; and Albert Salisbury, *Historical Sketch of Normal Instruction in Wisconsin, 1846–1876* (Madison, 1876), pp. 23–25.

54. Curti and Carstensen, *The University of Wisconsin,* Vol. 1, p. 118–119.

55. In the *Fifteenth Annual Report of the Superintendent of Public Instruction of the State of Wisconsin for the Year Ending August 31, 1863* (Madison, 1863), p. 27.

56. In the *Sixteenth Annual Report of the Superintendent of Public Instruction of the State of Wisconsin, . . . 1864* (Madison, 1865), p. 11.

57. In the *Seventeenth Annual Report of the Superintendent of Public Instruction of the State of Wisconsin, . . . 1865* (Madison, 1866), p. 99.

58. Salisbury, *Historical Sketch,* pp. 30, 32.

59. Ibid., p. 26.

60. *General Laws Passed by the Legislature of Wisconsin in the Year 1866* (Madison, 1866), pp. 160–165.

61. Curti and Carstensen, *The University of Wisconsin,* Vol. 1, p. 230.

62. Editorial in *Wisconsin Journal of Education* 6 (August 1861): 60.

63. Curti and Carstensen, *The University of Wisconsin,* Vol. 1, pp. 445, 446.

64. See *Private and Local Laws of the State of Wisconsin, 1866,* pp.151–152, 463–465, 476–478, 484–485, 723–724, 965–966, 971, and passim.

65. Editorial in *Wisconsin Journal of Education* 9 (April 1865): 268.

66. Jeff Wasserman, "Wisconsin Normal Schools and the Educational Hierarchy, 1860–1890," *Journal of the Midwest History of Education Society* 7 (1979): 3.

67. *Report of the Board of Visitors of the State Normal School at Platteville* (Platteville, 1867).

68. The information on the graduates of Platteville State Normal School in this and the following paragraphs has been culled from the school's annual catalogues.

69. Irving H. Hart, *The First 75 Years* (Cedar Falls: Iowa State Teachers College, 1951), p. ix.

70. Ibid., p. 81.

71. Ibid., p. 14.

72. William C. Lang and Daryl Pendergraft, "A Century of Service and Lead-

ership: 1876–1976," MS history of the Iowa State Normal School, Special Collections, University Library, University of Northern Iowa, Ch. 3, p. 147.

73. Hart, *The First 75 Years,* p. 107.

74. Ibid., p. 84.

75. Ibid., p. 15.

76. Ibid., p. 117.

77. Lang and Pendergraft, "A Century of Service," Ch. 5, p. 15.

78. Ibid., Ch. 5, p. 17.

79. Ibid., Ch. 4, p. 250.

80. Hart, *The First 75 Years,* p. 81.

81. Ibid., p. 16.

82. Lang and Pendergraft, "A Century of Service," Ch. 5, p. 9.

83. Hart, *The First 75 Years,* p. 88.

84. Lang and Pendergraft, "A Century of Service," Ch. 6, p. 6.

85. "Report of the President to the State Board of Education, August 1, 1910," p. 362, quoted, ibid., Ch. 6, p. 7.

86. Hart, *The First 75 Years,* p. 91.

Chapter 6: The Professionalization of Teacher Education

1. In the *Annual Report of the Superintendent of Public Instruction for the State of Wisconsin for the Year Ending August 31, 1867* (Madison, 1867), p. 35.

2. "Proceedings of the Wisconsin State Teachers Association," *Report of the Department of Public Instruction, 1871.*

3. "Normal Schools," *Wisconsin Journal of Education* 9 (March 1879): 108.

4. Jeff Wasserman, "Wisconsin Normal Schools and the Educational Hierarchy," *Journal of the Midwest History of Education Society* 7 (1979): 2.

5. In *Annual Report of the Superintendent of Public Instruction of the State of Wisconsin for the Year Ending August 31, 1874,* (Madison, 1874), p. 149.

6. Wasserman, "Wisconsin Normal Schools and the Educational Hierarchy," pp. 3–4.

7. See Jurgen Herbst, "Nineteenth-Century Normal Schools in the United States: A Fresh Look," *History of Education* 9 (1980): 227.

8. James P. Wickersham in "Proceedings," Department of Superintendence of the National Education Association, February 14–16, 1888, *U.S. Bureau of Education, Circular of Information # 6,* 1888 (Washington, D.C., 1888), p. 73.

9. J. W. Dickinson, ibid., p. 75.

10. Jerome Allen, ibid., p. 79.

11. A. W. Edson, "Legitimate Work of a State Normal School," *Education* 16 (January 1896):274–277.

12. See supra, Ch. 4, "The Westfield Approach" section.

13. George E. Gay, "Massachusetts Normal Schools," *Education* 17 (May 1897): 516, 517.

14. Albert G. Boyden, "Massachusetts Normal Schools," *Education* 17 (June 1897): 611–616.

15. In the *Bienniel Report of the State Superintendent of the State of Wisconsin for the Two Years Ending June 30, 1888,* (Madison, 1888), p. 191.

16. In the *Bienniel Report of the State Superintendent of the State of Wisconsin for the Two Years Ending June 30, 1884,* (Madison, 1885), p. 75.

17. *Annual Report of the Board of Regents of Normal Schools of Wisconsin, 1880–81* (Madison); and *Bienniel Report of the State Superintendent of the State of Wisconsin for the Two Years Ending June 30, 1900* (Madison, 1901), p. 92. See also Kenneth M. Zeichner, "The Role of the Teacher's Institute in Nineteenth Century Wisconsin," unpublished paper presented at the annual meeting of the American Educational Research Association, Boston, April 1980.

18. *Wisconsin Journal of Education* 28 (February 1898); and *Annual Report of Superintendent of Public Instruction, 1900,* p. 26.

19. *Wisconsin Journal of Education* 37 (March 1905); pp. 58–59.

20. *Bienniel Report of the State Superintendent of the State of Wisconsin for the Two Years Ending June 30, 1898* (Madison, 1898), p. 71.

21. *Annual Report of the State Superintendent of the State of Wisconsin for the Year Ending 1881* (Madison, 1882), p. 245.

22. *Wisconsin Journal of Education* 21 (September 1891), and 22 (March-June 1892).

23. *Wisconsin Journal of Education* 31 (March 1901); 67–70.

24. *Wisconsin Journal of Education* 23 (June 1893): 123–124.

25. Merle Curti and Vernon Carstensen, *The University of Wisconsin: A History,* Vol. 2 (Madison: University of Wisconsin Press, 1949), pp. 260–261.

26. Helen E. Marshall, *Grandest of Enterprises: Illinois State Normal University, 1857–1957* (Normal: Illinois State Normal University, 1956), pp. 174–175, 215.

27. Charles A. Harper, *Development of the Teachers College in the United States with Special Reference to the Illinois State Normal University* (Bloomington, Ill.: McKnight & McKnight, 1935), pp. 201–210.

28. Harper, *Development,* p. 223. On American Herbartianism see Harold B. Dunkel, *Herbart and Education* (New York: Random House, 1969), pp. 119–126, and Dunkel's *Herbart and Herbartianism: An Educational Ghost Story* (Chicago: University of Chicago Press, 1970), pp. 241–283.

29. Marshall, *Grandest of Enterprises,* pp. 194–197, 220.

30. David Felmley, "The New Normal School Movement," *Educational Review* 44 (April 1913): 409–410.

31. Ibid., p. 412.

32. See Table V in Jurgen Herbst, "Professionalization in Public Education, 1890–1920: The American High School Teacher," in Werner Conze und Jürgen Kocka, eds., *Industrielle Welt: Bildungsbürgertum im 19. Jahrhundert,* part I, *Bildungssystem und Professionalisierung in internationalen Vergleichen* (Stuttgart: Klett-Cotta, 1985), p. 525.

33. C. W. Bardeen, "Why Teaching Repels Men," *Educational Review* 35 (April 1908): 351–358.

34. Felmley, "The New Normal School Movement," p. 414.

35. See Earl W. Hayter, *Education in Transition: The History of Northern Illinois University* (DeKalb: Northern Illinois University Press, 1974), p. 146. Normal granted its first two bachelor of education degrees in 1908; Northern, by contrast, granted one in 1911 and waited until 1921 for the second.

36. Felmley, "The New Normal School Movement," p. 410.

37. Marshall, *Grandest of Enterprises,* p. 309.

38. Felmley, "The New Normal School Movement," p. 412.

39. As quoted in Marshall, *Grandest of Enterprises,* p. 249.

40. Felmley, "The New Normal School Movement," pp. 412–413.

41. Julian W. Abernethy, "The Passing of the Normal School," *Education* 23 (February 1903): 325–330.

42. Will Grant Chambers, "The Passing of the Normal School: A Reply," *Education* 23 (April 1903): 484, 485.

43. Ibid., p. 486.

44. See Felmley, "The New Normal School Movement," pp. 409–415.

45. Henry C. Johnson, Jr., and Erwin V. Johanningmeier, *Teachers for the Prairie: The University of Illinois and the Schools, 1868–1945* (Urbana: University of Illinois Press, 1972), pp. 29, 34.

46. Ibid., p. 50.

47. Ibid., p. 58.

48. Ibid., p. 63.

49. Ibid., p. 70.

50. Ibid., p. 101.

51. Ibid., p. 121.

52. Ibid., p. 143.

53. Ibid., p. 160.

54. Ibid., p. 179.

55. Ibid., pp. 180–181.

56. Ibid., p. 150.

57. Ibid., p. 204.

58. See Marshall, *Grandest of Enterprises,* p. 252, and Johnson, Jr., and Johanningmeier, *Teachers for the Prairie,* pp. 138–139, 176–177.

59. Clifford S. Griffin, *The University of Kansas: A History* (Lawrence: University Press of Kansas, 1974), pp. 273–277.

60. Irving H. Hart, *The First 75 Years* (Cedar Falls: Iowa State Teachers College, 1951), p. 13.

61. Ibid., p. 18.

62. William C. Lang and Daryl Pendergraft, "A Century of Service and Leadership: 1876–1976," MS history of the Iowa State Normal School, Special Collections, University Library, University of Northern Iowa, Ch. 6, p. 19.

63. Ibid., Ch. 6, p. 18.

64. Ibid., Ch. 6, p. 43; see "Report of the President to the State Board of Education," August 1, 1912, in *Report of the Iowa State Board of Education,* September 25, 1912, pp. 431–432.

65. John W. Cook to Homer H. Seerley, November 26, 1912, in Lang and Pendergraft, "A Century of Service," Ch. 6, p. 61.

66. Hart, *The First 75 Years,* p. 21.

67. Curti and Carstensen, *The University of Wisconsin: A History,* Vol. 1, p. 732.

68. Ibid., Vol. 2, p. 252, and Vol. 1, pp. 335, 446.

69. Ibid., Vol. 1, pp. 732–737.

70. Ibid., Vol. 2, p. 254.

71. Ibid., Vol. 2, pp. 255–257.

72. Ibid., Vol. 2, p. 262.

73. Ibid., Vol. 2, pp. 264–266.

74. *Wisconsin Journal of Education* 47 (May 1915): 121–125, and 48 (February 1916): 31–32.

75. *Wisconsin Journal of Education* 50 (May 1918): 126–131.

76. *Proceedings of the Board of Regents of Normal Schools,* Madison, July 18, 1918, and July 27, 1922.

77. "Why College Courses in the Normal Schools?" *The Wisconsin News,* Milwaukee (December 6, 1922).

78. See *The Capital Times* (Madison, March 8, 1923), p.2.

79. Governor's Message, *Assembly Journal* (July 6, 1923), pp. 1883–1884.

80. *Wisconsin Session Laws . . . 1925* (Madison, 1925), Ch. 101.

81. *Wisconsin Session Laws . . . 1929* (Madison, 1929), Ch. 240.

82. "Report of the Wisconsin Interim Legislative Committee on Education," *Journal of the Senate* (February 26, 1931) (Madison, 1931), pp. 357–564, passim.

Chapter 7: Professionalization: The Betrayal of the Teacher

1. Albert R. Taylor, "History of Normal School Work in Kansas," *Kansas State Historical Society Quarterly* 6 (1900): 119–120.

2. Webster Paul Rees, "History and Development of the Kansas Program for Training High School Teachers in Public Institutions," typescript, Kansas State Historical Society, Topeka, 1932, p. 81.

3. Taylor, "History of Normal School Work in Kansas," pp. 119–120.

4. Leavenworth Public Schools, *6th Annual Report of the Superintendent for the Year Ending 6-30-1870,* p. 119.

5. George F. Zook, *Report of a Survey of the State Institutions of Higher Learning in Kansas,* U.S. Bureau of Education, Bulletin # 40 (Washington, D.C.: Government Printing Office, 1923), p. 68.

6. Ibid., pp. 66, 72.

7. William S. Learned et al., *The Professional Preparation of Teachers for American Public Schools: A Study Based upon an Examination of Tax-Supported Normal Schools in the State of Missouri* (New York: Carnegie Foundation, 1920), p. xv.

8. Ibid., p. xvi.

9. See supra, Ch. 6.

10. Learned et al., *The Professional Preparation of Teachers,* pp. 82–83.

11. Ibid. The quotations in this paragraph are from pp. 83, 91, and 170.

12. Ibid., p. 83.

13. Ibid., pp. 70–73.

14. Ibid., pp. 74–75.

15. Ibid., pp. 77–79.

16. Ibid., p. 91.

17. Ibid., p. 97.

18. Ibid., p. 80.

19. Ibid., p. 76.

20. Ibid., p. 12.

21. Ibid., p. xvii.

22. See supra, Ch. 6, "Normal Schools vs. Universities: Kansas and Iowa."

23. Learned et al., *The Professional Preparation of Teachers,* p. 13.

24. Ibid., p. 428.

25. Ibid., p. xvii.

26. Ibid., pp. xv–xix.

27. See Jurgen Herbst, "Professionalization in Public Education, 1890–1920: The American High School Teacher," in Werner Conze and Jürgen Kocka, eds., *Bildungsbürgertum im 19. Jahrhundert,* part I, *Bildungssystem und Professionalisierung in internationalen Vergleichen* (Stuttgart: Klett-Cotta, 1985), pp. 495–528.

28. On Cheever see Elizabeth Porter Gould, *Ezekiel Cheever: Schoolmaster* (Boston: Palmer Company, 1904); on the New England schoolmaster see Wilson Smith, "The Teacher in Puritan Culture," *Harvard Educational Review* 36 (Fall 1966): 394–411.

29. In *Remarks on the Seventh Annual Report of the Hon. Horace Mann, Secretary, Massachusetts Board of Education* (Boston: Charles C. Little and James Brown, 1844), pp. 11 and 24.

30. See Robert D. Bole and Laurence B. Johnson, *The New Jersey High School: A History* (Princeton, N.J.: D. van Nostrand, 1964), pp. 51, 81.

31. Theodore R. Sizer, *Secondary Schools at the Turn of the Century* (New Haven and London: Yale University Press, 1964), p. 44.

32. Reported in Fred Washington Atkinson, *The Professional Preparation of Secondary Teachers in the United States* (Leipzig: Breitkopf and Haertel, 1893), p. 10.

33. Edward A. Krug, *The Shaping of the American High School, 1920–1941* (Madison: University of Wisconsin Press, 1972), p. 187.

34. Edwin Dexter, "The Present Status and Personnel of the Secondary Teaching Force in the United States," *4th Yearbook,* National Society for the Scientific Study of Education (Chicago: University of Chicago Press, 1905), pp. 51 and 52.

35. On the Committee of Ten see supra, Ch. 6.

36. James H. Baker, *Of Himself and Other Things* (Denver: privately printed, 1922), pp. 23, 44.

37. In *The Academy: A Journal of Secondary Education* 5 (March 1890): 85.

38. In Leslie A. Butler, *The Michigan Schoolmasters' Club: A Story of the First Seven Decades 1886–1957* (Ann Arbor: University of Michigan Press, 1958), pp. 14, 18.

39. Reprinted in Sizer, *Secondary Schools at the Turn of the Century,* pp. 260–262.

40. "Address of President Angell," *The School Review* 4 (May 1896): 261.

41. For an example of this attitude see Avery D. Mayo, "The New Teacher in America," *Addresses and Journal of Proceedings,* National Education Association, 1879 (Salem, Ohio: Allan K. Tatem, 1879), p. 62; see also supra, Ch. 4.

42. Arthur G. Powell, *The Uncertain Profession: Harvard and the Search for Educational Authority* (Cambridge, Mass.: Harvard University Press, 1980), pp. 30, 31.

43. Edgar B. Wesley, *NEA: The Building of the Teaching Profession* (New York: Harper & Brothers, 1957), pp. 67–68.

44. On Eliot and the schools see Hugh Hawkins, *Between Harvard and America: The Educational Leadership of Charles W. Eliot* (New York: Oxford University Press, 1972), and Edward A. Krug, ed., *Charles W. Eliot and Popular Education* (New York: Teachers College Bureau of Publications, 1961).

45. On the Committee of Ten, see Sizer, *Secondary Schools at the Turn of the Century.*

46. Powell, *The Uncertain Profession,* p. 65.

47. Quoted in David Tyack and Elisabeth Hansot, *Managers of Virtue: Public School Leadership in America, 1820–1980* (New York: Basic Books, 1982), p. 97.

48. Quoted in Powell, *The Uncertain Profession,* pp. 52–53.

49. Ibid., pp. 78, 79.

50. Powell, *The Uncertain Profession,* pp. 108, 109.

51. Ibid., p. 159.

52. Ibid., p. 179.

53. Ibid., p. 195.

54. Ibid., p. 269.

55. Ibid., p. 281.

56. As quoted in Lawrence A. Cremin, David A. Shannon, and Mary E. Townsend, *A History of Teachers College, Columbia University* (New York: Columbia University Press, 1954), p. 22.

57. Ibid., p. 36.

58. Ibid., p. 66.

59. Ibid., p. 140.

60. Ibid., pp. 80, 81.

61. Michael B. Katz, "From Theory to Survey in Graduate Schools of Education," *Journal of Higher Education* 37 (June 1966): 325–334.

62. Ibid., p. 327.

63. Ibid., pp. 327, 328.

64. Woodie White, Jr., "The Decline of the Classroom and the Chicago Study of Education," *American Journal of Education* (February 1982): 147, 148.

65. Ibid., p. 156.

66. Ibid., p. 153.

67. John F. Bobbitt, *The Supervision of City Schools: Some General Principles of Management Applied to the Problems of City School Systems,* the 12th Yearbook of the National Society for the Study of Education (Chicago: University of Chicago Press, 1913), p. 55.

68. Charles Judd, "Educational News and Editorial Comment," *Elementary School Journal* 15 (September 1914): 2.

69. Charles Judd to Harry Pratt Judson, n.d., quoted in White, Jr., "The Decline of the Classroom," p. 160.

70. Floyd W. Reeves and John Dale Russell, *The University of Chicago Survey,* Vol. 5, *Admission and Retention of University Students* (Chicago: University of Chicago Press, 1933), pp. 183, 208.

71. White, Jr., "The Decline of the Classroom," p. 171.

Chapter 8: What of the Teacher?

1. George B. Emerson, in *Proceedings,* First Annual Convention of the American Normal School Association, Trenton, N.J., August 19–20, 1859 (New York: A. S. Barnes & Buhr, 1860), p. 37.

2. On this see infra, note 7.

3. Titles that appeared in 1983 were, National Commission on Excellence in Edu-

cation, *A Nation at Risk: The Imperative for Educational Reform,* A Report to the Nation and the Secretary of Education (Washington, D.C.: U.S. Department of Education, Superintendent of Documents); Ernest L. Boyer, *High School: A Report on Secondary Education in America,* The Carnegie Foundation for the Advancement of Teaching (New York: Harper & Row); James S. Coleman, Thomas Hoffer, and Sally Kilgore, *High School Achievement: Public, Catholic, and Private Schools Compared* (New York: Basic Books); John I. Goodlad, *A Place Called School: Prospects for the Future* (New York: McGraw-Hill); and Theodore R. Sizer, *Horace's Compromise: The Dilemma of the American High School* (Boston: Houghton Mifflin).

4. A notable exception is Arthur G. Powell, *The Uncertain Profession.* For other, less critical, studies see David M. Florell, "Origin and History of the School of Education, University of California, Los Angeles," Ph.D. dissertation, University of California at Berkeley, 1946; Claude Eggertsen, ed., *Studies in the History of the School of Education, University of Michigan, 1868–1954* (Ann Arbor: University of Michigan Press, 1955); John S. Brubacher, *The Development of the Department of Education at Yale University, 1891–1958* (New Haven: Yale University Press, 1960); H. G. Good, *The Rise of the College of Education of the Ohio State University* (Columbus: College of Education, Ohio State University, 1960); Lloyd W. Colvin, "A History of the School of Education at the University of Oregon," Ed.D. dissertation, University of Oregon, 1964; and Leon Levitt, "A History to 1953 of the School of Education of the University of Southern California," Ed.D. dissertation, University of Southern California, 1970. The new volume by Geraldine Joncich Clifford and James W. Guthrie, *Ed School: A Brief for Professional Education* (Chicago: University of Chicago Press, 1988), appeared too late for me to consider in this volume.

5. See Lindley J. Stiles et al., *Teacher Education in the United States* (New York: Ronald Press Company, 1960), pp. 95–101.

6. James Bryant Conant, *The Education of American Teachers* (New York: McGraw-Hill, 1963), pp. 213–214.

7. Stiles et al., *Teacher Education in the United States,* p. 470.

8. Ibid., p. 471.

9. See Robert L. Reid, ed., *Battleground: The Autobiography of Margaret A. Haley* (Urbana: University of Illinois Press, 1982), and Joan K. Smith, *Ella Flagg Young: Portrait of a Leader* (Ames, Iowa: Educational Studies Press, 1979).

10. For an analysis of educational progressivism see Lawrence A. Cremin, *The Transformation of the School: Progressivism in American Education, 1867–1957* (New York: Random House, 1961), and Raymond E. Callahan, *Education and the Cult of Efficiency: A Study of Social Forces That Have Shaped the Administration of the Public Schools* (Chicago: University of Chicago Press, 1961).

11. See my "Professionalization in Public Education, 1890–1920: The American High School Teacher," in Werner Conze and Jürgen Kocka, eds., *Bildungsbürgertum im 19. Jahrhundert,* Part I, *Bildungssystem und Professionalisierung in internationalen Vergleichen* (Stuttgart: Klett-Cotta, 1985), p. 496.

12. David Tyack and Elisabeth Hansot, *Managers of Virtue: Public School Leadership in America, 1820–1980* (New York: Basic Books, 1982), p. 183. On the historical relationship of women as teachers and men as administrators, see Myra H. Strober and

David Tyack, "Why Do Women Teach and Men Manage? A Report on Research on Schools," *Signs* 5 (Spring 1980): 494–503.

13. See the adaptation of statistics given by Harold F. Clark, *Life Earnings in Selected Occupations in the United States* (New York: Harper, 1937), p. 5, in Willard S. Elsbree, *The American Teacher: Evolution of a Profession in a Democracy* (New York: American Book Company, 1929), p. 437.

14. Reprinted in Marvin Lazerson, ed., *American Education in the Twentieth Century: A Documentary History,* Classics in Education (New York: Teachers College Press, 1987), pp. 66–69.

15. See Wayne J. Urban, *Why Teachers Organized* (Detroit: Wayne State University Press, 1982), pp. 111–133, and Tyack and Hansot, *Managers of Virtue,* pp. 140–144.

16. Urban, *Why Teachers Organized,* p. 22; see also the studies of teacher unionization in Chicago by Marjorie Murphy, "From Artisan to Semi-Professional: White Collar Unionism among Chicago Public School teachers, 1870–1930," Ph.D. dissertation, University of California, 1981; and Robert L. Reid, "The Professionalization of Public School Teachers: The Chicago Experience, 1895–1920," Ph.D. dissertation, Northwestern University, 1968.

Postscript

1. Theodore R. Sizer, "The Secret Ingredient: People," *The New York Times Education Spring Survey* (April 15, 1984), 35; see also his *Horace's Compromise: The Dilemma of the American High School* (Boston: Houghton Mifflin, 1983).

2. Report of the Task Force on Teaching as a Profession, *A Nation Prepared: Teachers for the 21st Century* (Hyattsville, Md.: Carnegie Forum, 1986), pp. 57–58.

3. Dan C. Lortie, *Schoolteacher: A Sociological Study* (Chicago: University of Chicago Press, 1973), p. 12.

Index

Academies, teacher education in, 57–58, 66, 94, 123, 124, 126, 128
Adams, Charles Francis, 176
Administrators, 87, 91, 157, 176, 197
Agassiz, Louis, 88
Agricultural education, 94, 95, 118, 124, 127, 154
Allmendinger, David, 22–23, 81
Allyn, Robert, 117
Altenstein, Baron Karl von, 35, 40, 42, 44–45, 46, 49, 54
American Association of Colleges for Teacher Education, 149
American Association of Teachers Colleges, 148
American Education Society, 23
American Home Missionary Society, 119
American Institute of Instruction, 22, 58–60, 62, 74
American Lyceum, 17, 33
American Normal School Association, 98–104 *passim,* 111, 119, 144
American Psychological Association, 183
Andover Theological Seminary, Massachusetts, 119
Angell, James Burrill, 174
Apperception, 146, 172
Arny, W. F. M., 118

Bagley, William Chandler, 153
Baker, James H., 172, 173
Baltimore, Maryland, normal school in, 108, 187
Barnard, Henry, 12, 16, 18, 20, 24, 55, 89, 124, 144

Barre, Massachusetts, normal school in, 62
Bateman, Newton, 114
Beckedorff, Ludolf von, 43, 44, 47
Bernard, Richard, 24–25
Blaine, John J., 159
Bobbitt, John Franklin, 183–84
Borrowman, Merle, xii
Boston, Massachusetts, normal school in, 92, 93, 97, 108, 187
Boston English High School for Boys, 92
Boston Girls' High and Normal School, 92, 93
Boston School Committee, 93
Boston schoolmasters, 171, 172, 173
Boston State College, 93
Boston State Teachers College, 93, 97
Bowdoin College, Maine, 67, 70, 71, 87, 88
Bowman, John G., 155
Boyden, Albert G., 106–7
Bridgewater, Massachusetts, normal school in, 60, 97, 106, 143, 186
Bridgewater tradition: in Midwest, 94–98; defined, 97, 102; in Illinois, 98, 110, 112, 113; in Kansas, 118, 119; in Iowa, 138, 139; mentioned, 5
Brooks, Charles, 21, 26, 27, 29, 32, 39, 58, 62, 119
Brunson Institute, Wisconsin, 126
Burrill, Thomas, 152
Butler, Nicholas Murray, 180

Cape Girardeau, Missouri, normal school in, 167, 168
Carlsbad decrees, 42
Carnegie Forum, Task Force on Teaching, 3, 9, 188, 197

225

Carnegie Foundation for the Advancement of
Teaching: report on Iowa State Normal
School, 155; report on state normal schools
in Missouri, 166–69, 191
Carter, James G., 22, 23–24, 30–31
Cary, Charles P., 157
Cedar Falls, Iowa, normal school in, 94, 95,
135–39, 154–56; mentioned, 149, 166
Chadbourne, Paul Ansel, 127
Chambers, Will Grant, 150, 151
Channing, William Ellery, 18
Charleston, Illinois, normal school in, 148
Chaucer, Geoffrey, xi
Cheever, Ezekiel, 22, 171
Chicago, normal school in, 146, 150
Child-study movement, 146
Cincinnati, Ohio, normal school in, 108
Citizen-teachers, 59–60, 74, 91, 140, 153,
185
City training schools, 4, 100 102
Clark University, Worcester, Massachusetts,
93
Clay, Henry, 13
Cleveland, Ohio, normal school in, 108
College party, 174–75
Columbia University, 180–81, 184, 187
Committee of Ten, 172, 173, 176
Common school party, 174–75
Common schools. See Public schools
Common-core protestantism. See Religion in
education
Conant, James Bryant, 178–79, 189
Cook, John Williston, 145, 146
Cooper, James Fennimore, 18
Cornell College, Iowa, 138
Correlation of studies, 146
Crosby, Alpheus, 98
Crosby, W. E., 100
County normal schools, 100–102, 140, 144,
145, 158, 159, 160
County training schools. See County normal
schools
Cousin, Victor: report on public instruction
in Prussia, 22, 35–39, 47; travels in
Europe, 35; analysis of report, 39, 40,
47–50; sympathetic to Altenstein, 47–48;
advocates advanced primary schools,
49–50; mentioned, 4, 21, 54, 55, 56, 58,
64, 186
Culture epochs, 146, 172

Dartmouth College, New Hampshire, 110,
119
Davis, Emerson, 71, 87, 88
DeGarmo, Charles, 146, 151–52
Degrees, academic, 148, 157–59 passim,
164–65, 178–81 passim, 184, 191
DeKalb, Illinois, normal school in, 148
Dewey, John, 182–83
Dexter, Edwin Grant, 152–53
Dickinson, John Woodbridge, 74, 89–90, 91,
93, 143, 175
Diesterweg, Adolph, 45, 92
Dunton, Larkin, 92, 93
Dwight, Edmund, 60
Dwight, Henry Edwin, 32

Eastern Illinois State Normal School. See Nor-
mal schools, in Illinois, at Charleston
Eastern Illinois Teachers Association, 153
Educational administration, 183, 184, 191
Educational psychology, 183, 191
Educational science, 145–47, 177, 179,
182–84
Edwards, Ninian W., 109–10
Edwards, Richard, 62, 97, 98, 112–16 pas-
sim, 119, 120
Eliot, Charles William, 173, 176–77
Elsbree, Willard, xii, 192
Emerson, George B., 186
Emerson, Ralph Waldo, 15, 18
Emporia, Kansas, normal school in, 94,
118–23, 161–65

Father Peirce. See Peirce, Cyrus
Felmley, David, 145–51 passim, 153–55 pas-
sim, 174, 175, 184
Feminization, 26, 86, 147–49
Fichte, Johann Gottlieb, 40
Fiorello, James Ralph, 88, 89
Five steps of instruction, 146
Ford Foundation, 179
Fort Hays, Kansas, normal school in. See
Normal schools, in Kansas, at Fort Hays
Fowle, William B., 84–86, 90
Framingham, Massachusetts, normal school
in, 65
Franklin, Benjamin, 13, 17
Free School Society of New York, 15
Friedrich Wilhelm III, 40, 43, 44
Frommichen, Sophia, 33–35